SO-AFU-428

Don't Call It Frisco

By Herb Caen Don't Call It Frisco · Baghdad: 1951
Baghdad-by-the-Bay · The San Francisco Book

To Col. Douglas B.
MacMullen, who
loves The City by the
Golden Gate, and Never
called it "Frisco."
    Al G. Waddell
July 7, 1976, with all
golden memories.

Herb Caen

Don't Call It Frisco

DOUBLEDAY & COMPANY, INC., GARDEN CITY, NEW YORK, 1953

Library of Congress Catalog Card Number 53-9990

Copyright, 1953, by Herb Caen
All Rights Reserved
Printed in the United States
At the Country Life Press, Garden City, N.Y.
First Edition

Designed by Diana Klemin

Chapters

Don't Call It Frisco 11

San Franciscana 15

Nothing Ever Happens 19

Confessions of a Columnist 23

Only Yesterday 38

Once a Newsboy 42

Speaking of the Weather 45

Punch Lines 52

The Lost Week 60

The Silver Fox 65

Color of the City 73

Well, I Liked 'Em 86

Joe 99

Pop (Lucien Caen, June 25, 1877–
June 6, 1950) 102

Down the Old Skid Road 106

Off the Beaten Path 113

Papa Pierre 120

Holiday at Half-Mast 126

7

CONTENTS

Footnote to a Police Action 130

They Called It Frisco 131

Vacation Blues 135

Minnie 172

The Sunshine Spreader 174

Call Me Al 181

For Future Reference 185

Dearie, Do You Remember? 190

It's Hard to Be Good 194

On a Pearl Harbor Anniversary 204

Just Foolin' Around 208

Kaleidoscope 228

Barney & Tiny's Circus 232

Gloomy Sunday 241

Our Own Zoological Garden 245

Mickey 247

That Was San Francisco 255

You Can't Do That 259

Gesundheit 263

These Foolish Things 267

Mr. San Francisco 275

Index 279

Don't Call It Frisco

Don't Call It Frisco

Don't call it Frisco—it's SAN Francisco, because it was named after St. Francis of Assisi. And because "Frisco" is a nickname that reminds the city uncomfortably of the early, brawling, boisterous days of the Barbary Coast and the cribs and sailors who were shanghaied. And because "Frisco" shows disrespect for a city that is now big and proper and respectable. And because only tourists call it "Frisco," anyway, and you don't want to be taken for a tourist, do you?

So don't call it Frisco—even though there's a big bar on Sixth Street that is called The Frisco in neon letters ten feet high. That's just one of those things that sneak by now and then when a city doesn't pay attention. One of these days, a Vigilance Committee will come along and tear down that sign, letter by letter, and string up the offending proprietor from the nearest lamppost.

Because you don't call it Frisco. Not right out loud, anyway.

It's San Francisco. More than half of it is under water (of its 93.1 square miles, only 44.82 are land). The City Hall, its tower taller than the Nation's Capitol, is geographically located at 37° 47′ North latitude and 122° 25′ West longitude, in case you'd like to set sail for it. Its attitudes range from cordial to lofty, and its altitudes range from sea level to 933 feet. Three islands—one of them man-made—lie within its boundaries. More than half of its entire area is washed daily by the ocean's tidal currents. And its streets are always dirty.

It's San Francisco. It has skyscrapers that rest on filled-in land, rows of streets (named and mapped) that are under water, old hill-top mansions with tiny windows that shut out the view, new houses built expensively on stilts to command a view, Italian restaurants run by Chinese, Chinese restaurants run by Negroes, run-down cable cars that still run up the hills, poor people who own sailboats, rich people who live in the shadow of yesterday with all shades drawn, bridges and Bridges, crooked streets, crooked tunnels, and honest cops who wear old-fashioned seven-point stars. The other kind wear seven-point stars, too.

It's San Francisco. The daily mean maximum temperature, what-ever that "mean" means, is 62.6 degrees. The daily mean minimum temperature is 50.4 degrees. The weather is seldom mean, even on maximeanimum days. There is less fog, statistically, than there seems to be, actually. The U. S. Lighthouse Service, which has no visible connection with the Chamber of Commerce, reports only 153 hours of fog over the Bay annually. The number of foggy days over the city is never reported, reportedly. But take it from me—there's enough to satisfy everyone, and dissatisfy somebody.

It's San Francisco. The 790,000 residents of the Nation's eleventh largest city call each other on 470,000 telephones, some of which have not fallen into the hands of bookmakers. They live at 266,000 addresses, most of them invisible to postmen and callers, and they try to park their 250,000 automobiles in 225 public garages and

14,000 legal downtown parking spaces. There is a parking problem.

It's San Francisco, and it has all kinds of people—25,000 Chinese, 44,000 Negroes, 166,000 single people who are envied or pitied by the 380,000 married people, 100,000 who are widowed or divorced, 130,000 who were born in foreign countries (including certain parts of Oakland), and almost 500,000 who commute daily from and to the East Bay, the Peninsula, and Marin County—and each of whom insists he gets home in 20 minutes, but never has and never will. The average San Franciscan is 37.1 years old. As I write this, I am an average San Franciscan. As you read this, you can believe it.

It's San Francisco. Its people are always doing something. Looking for a place to park (and getting tagged for parking in it). Hunting for a room with a view (and never looking at it). Searching for a bar (San Franciscans drink more, per capita, than the citizens of any other city that makes the same statement). Being born (18,000 a year). Dying (10,000 a year). Getting married (8000), divorced (4500), murdered (42), self-destroyed (181), and into auto accidents (18,000). The cool gray city of love, unquote, is a white-collar city (of its 460,000 employed residents, only 26,000 are laborers and 106,000 are clerical workers; the rest are foremen, executives, and labor organizers). The San Franciscan's per capita income is the highest in the nation; so is the cost of living, but it's worth it. You get more for your money in San Francisco. More view, more water, more hills, more bills, more thrills, and more arguments from visitors who don't think it's the greatest city in the world.

It's San Francisco. It has one Mayor (and the present one, Elmer E. Robinson, is ample), 11 Supervisors who think they should be Mayor, 353 churches, 1379 saloons, 7, 14, or 21 hills, 90 theaters that show the "best movie in town" simultaneously, 8 radio stations, 3 television stations that bring you the latest commercials, 521 hotels with 45,000 guest rooms (and several hundred house detectives to check the guests), and 207 schools that do the best they can with the material at hand. Over 100,000 planes, carrying 1,500,000 passengers, fly in and out of its airport each year. Its two great bridges have carried more than 400,000,000 vehicles since they were opened. And, according to official statistics, 4430 ships enter the harbor each year, and 4497 depart. Anybody seen or heard of those other 67 ships?

It's San Francisco. Fortunately, it's made up of much more than statistics. Perhaps, in the ensuing pages, the cold figures cited above will come to life. For San Francisco—the ever-changing, never-changing city I like to call Baghdad-by-the-Bay—can never be summed up in a column of figures, or even in a column of type. I know, because I've tried. The results, such as they are, follow.

Oh—and one more thing.

Don't call it Frisco. Don't ask me why. Just don't.

San Franciscana   The tourist, looking at the city for the first time, shakes his head in a puzzled way and sighs: "This San Francisco—it sort of gets you. There's something about it. I don't know quite what it is, but it's something" . . .

And the San Franciscan smiles and nods, for he thinks he knows what it is . . . It's the gay fluttering of the flags and pennants on the downtown minarets, outlined against a blue sky flecked with fast-rolling fog . . . It's the never-cloying thrill of standing at the bow of a proud old ferryboat as it churns its white way in an arc across the Bay and then eases, like a practiced firehorse, into its slip under the Ferry Building's ageless tower . . . It's the pride, reborn again and again, that comes when you stand on a Marin mountaintop and gaze over the water at your magic city, gleaming like an endless mosaic that covers each hill with castles and fills each valley with romantic lights and shadows . . . It's the metropolitan stage setting that unfolds before your eyes from Twin Peaks—the solid, stolid Mission, where each house is a time-touched landmark; Market Street, cutting its steamroller swath across a field of concrete and leaving a trail of neon; and, in the far distance, the Bay Bridge hunching its thin shoulders and reaching out to clutch the Oakland shore with fingers of steel.

The expatriate, lonely in a faraway place, feels the clutching pang of homesickness and says to himself: "I can't seem to get it out of my system. What is it about that place that won't let go of you?" . . .

But even as he wonders, he knows some of the answers . . . It's the pearly-gray breakers off Ocean Beach, glittering dully under a filter of cold sunshine and beating themselves to death on the steaming rocks . . . It's the tiny white sailboats floating across the peaceful surface of Spreckels Lake in Golden Gate Park—a fleet carrying no cargo except the idle dreams of the children who watch wide-eyed from the shores, and the memories of the oldsters who sit on the nearby benches and watch their years sailing gently away . . . It's a jumbled, kaleidoscopic picture that no artist can ever capture, for only the mind's eye can see it: the golfer in Lincoln Park, silhouetted against the Golden Gate Bridge; the girl with flowing blond hair, standing at Land's End to watch the setting sun; the sudden Sunday roar from Kezar Stadium during football season; the silken rustle and the wisp of perfume that always seem to decorate the air on Post, and Stockton, and Grant; the ivory clatter of a chopstick in Chinatown, the vagrant, upstairs strain of an accordion in North Beach, the creak of an old fishing boat at the Wharf—these are some of the secret treasures that a San Franciscan hides in his heart.

The seasoned world-traveler looks about with practiced eye, and he thinks of Naples and Marseilles, of Johannesburg and Hong

Kong, and then he shrugs and smiles thinly: "It's all of these and none of these. It's got something I can't put my finger on" . . .

The elusive charm that you can never quite pin down; sometimes you feel it where you least expect it . . . In the grim, warehouse-studded wastes beyond Third Street, where the railroad tracks wander in aimless patterns and the backwash of the Bay lifts a stale smell along the rotting shoreline . . . On a street of rickety stairs clinging to the bony ridges of Telegraph Hill, leading to wooden shacks that seem to be hiding from those who would tear them down in the name of progress and improvement . . . In a tinny tenderloin saloon, where only the B-girls are brassier than the jukebox—and the gray ghosts of the Barbary Coast cackle in the corners at such a pale copy of the wickedness they invented for a city . . . On the lower step of a Powell cable on a rainy night, with the water splashing in your face and the headlight gleaming dimly on the rutted streets, and the old homes on Jackson parading slowly past in a pageant that hasn't changed for half a century.

The native, talking of the various delights of other places, suddenly stares into the distance and murmurs: "But I could never really leave San Francisco. I don't know why it is, exactly, but I couldn't" . . .

And even as he gropes unsuccessfully for the words, he knows some of the answers to his "whys" . . . The excitement of a first night on Geary Street, with the limousines inching up to the lighted marquees and the lobby buzzing with brittle small talk . . . The expectant hush in the Opera House as the lights go down and the golden curtains arise silently to disclose An Event . . . The tingling fun of following Montgomery Street's trail through skyscrapers and

high finance, past the little bistros where today's bohemianism lives
its imitation of a life that died long ago, and into the big heart of
Little Italy . . . The politicians and the lawyers and the socialites
filing into the Palace's Garden Court at noon, to feed on fine food
and the satisfaction of knowing they are part of a great ritual in a
city that savors its traditions as richly as its equally rich diet . . .
The bustle in the St. Francis lobby, the flutter of pigeons rising
around the Dewey Monument, the click-clang of the traffic signals,
the peace (at any price) along shop-studded Maiden Lane, the
deep rumble of a bus in the Stockton Tunnel—these are the odds
without end that sing out, in their various voices, to the heart of a
San Franciscan.

They all say the same thing—"It's got something, I don't know
what"—and there is no answer, really; even the love of a city is a
personal thing . . . For some, it's the crisp new efficiency of Stonestown, and for others, it's the decaying glamour of a gingerbread
mansion on Franklin Street. There is the San Franciscan who is
strangely moved by the far-off note of a foghorn, and another who
thrills to a soaring skyscraper, and still another who finds his city
in the shaded, winding ways of St. Francis Wood . . . For the
city has something, somewhere, for everyone. Find it, and you've
found that indefinable "something"—your San Francisco.

Nothing Ever Happens   The city stirs restlessly under its cold blanket of fog. All around you can hear the flick-flacking of the windshield wipers, and hear the whine of tires scrambling up the slippery slopes of Nob Hill and Russian Hill. Almost lost in the misty half-light, shadowy figures dart in and out of the alleyways in North Beach and Chinatown, and the cops walk two-by-two along old Kearny and drab Third Street, their eyes as alert as their saunter is casual. Each street lamp, every auto head-light wears its own halo, shining out over 1001 unwritten dramas that are enacted endlessly in this storybook city . . . But to the newspaperman, facing his deadline and his empty stretches of white paper, it's the same old question and the same old answer: "What's new?" "Nothing's new, nothing's going on."

But even as he says it, he knows that's not true. Something is always happening among the metropolitan million—if only he could put his finger on it, if only the pulse weren't so elusive. He can close his eyes and see the stories that will never be printed: the "happy young couple" in their wedding-cake house in the Sunset, staring across the room at each other with icy hate that always stops just

short of hot rage, violence, headlines; the seventeen-year-old un-
married mother on Telegraph Hill who makes marijuana cigarettes
that are peddled by an overdressed young paisano from Fisherman's
Wharf; the prominent Montgomery Streeter who was photographed
with his fashionable wife at the opera—while his girl friend stormed
alone in a Taylor Street apartment where he keeps her, and not too
secretly . . . But the deadline draws closer and the newspaperman
looks out the window and sighs: "Nothing ever happens, there's no
news today."

It's so easy to say, and they all say it . . . "I don't know nothin',"
shrugs the cabdriver, shoving his cap to the back of his head. He
has just delivered an attractive blond "model" to the hotel suite of
a visiting politician, but he don't know nothin'—nothin' you can
print . . . "Quiet, don't know when I seen it so quiet," muses the
bartender, carefully blowing on a glass and polishing it. He has just
given a worried young girl the address of a neighboring butcher
who calls himself a doctor and performs expensive abortions, but
it's quiet, it has to be quiet . . . "Town's dead, all right," agrees
the stony-eyed cop on the busy downtown street corner. "Ain't seen
any life around this corner for months." He has just come down
from the bookie joint up those nearby stairs, and he knows what
goes on in that little hotel across the street, but the town is dead
because it's safer for everybody to think it is . . . And so the newspaperman runs his fingers through his hair, and the chanted ritual
drums loudly in his brain: "Nothing to report, nothing's happening
today."

But it's going on all around him, all the time . . . At any hour,
in any section of the great city, the news is breaking and dying

unseen, the news that isn't news because it's too true, too real, too everyday . . . Out in the Mission, the tired cocktail waitress looks at the guy with the big diamond ring and all she can think is that her feet hurt and all of a sudden his proposition doesn't sound so bad. A few days from now, her Mission friends will wonder what became of her . . . In a smoky hideaway in the Fillmore, the thrill-seeking daughter of a wealthy Pacific Heights family looks a long time at the white powder being shoved her way, and pretty soon the word *heroin* will lose its dread sound, and she'll be lost, too, in a cloudy dream that always ends with a sudden, brutal awakening . . . Out at Ocean Beach, the young girl keeps moaning, "No, no, no," and then her boy friend's fingers tighten around her throat, tighter, tighter, tighter—but he stops just in time, just short of the sirens and the front pages and the autopsy . . . And so the clock races toward the deadline, and the phone is silent, and even the mighty presses seem ready to roar: "No News Today!"

Where is all the news that's fit to print, and who is fit to print it . . . The cocktail party in a lavish Telegraph Hill apartment is urbane and alive with meaningless talk that nobody ever listens to —but the news is there, and the news that is never reported. It's in the guilty eyes of that handsome couple (married to other people) as they stare daringly at each other over the upraised highball glasses, it's in the guarded touch of their finger tips as they pass in the crowd. And all around them, everybody makes a great show of not noticing . . . High in a skyscraper office in the financial district, a man looks at his books for the twentieth time and looks again at his bills and looks once more at the coldly negative letter from his banker—and then he wanders over to his twentieth-story

window and looks down into the dark, deserted street. But he shakes
his head and walks quickly away. People don't jump out of windows
anymore. They go into bankruptcy. Even if it means dropping out
of the Pacific-Union Club, even if it means his wife will leave him.
As long as it doesn't get into the papers (that could ruin a ruined
man) . . . Backstage at the Opera House they talk about more than
music. They talk about this star and that (and this one who's
romancing with that one) and especially they like to gossip about
the famous singer and the Noted Patron of the Arts who seems
interested in more than her voice. It's loose talk, possibly true talk,
but why pay attention to it—what can you prove? . . . And so the
stories live and die, never quite resolving themselves into news—the
news that is fit to print.

Now the deadline is upon him, and the newspaperman looks at
the cable cars crawling up California Street, and the great rusty
freighters slithering past each other in the fogbound Bay, and the
cars honking their irritable way along Market . . . He thinks of
the whispering intrigues going on—perhaps at that very moment—
behind the bolted doors of old Chinatown, and the silent violence
behind the drawn shades of North Beach, and the gilded lies being
bandied about among the silks and satins of a Russian Hill apartment . . . And then, like a thousand newspapermen before him,
he turns back to his empty paper in his mute typewriter and sighs:
"There's no news today."

Confessions of a Columnist

July 5, 1938, might have been just another day to you and the world at large, but to me it was memorable indeed. A career that had been marked by unswerving mediocrity and dogged devotion to Benny Goodman records suddenly took a turn for the worse.

On that day, I became a daily newspaper columnist in San Francisco, a job I have clung to ever since through storm and strife, a World War, and a succession of managing editors who have never failed to greet my copy with a doleful shake of the head and a fistful of black pencils with which, to my everlasting gratitude, they have removed the more inane and offensive portions.

At the outset of this dull recital, I should like to say that after fifteen-odd years at the odd job—"Well, it's better than digging ditches," a columnist always says, eying the nearest ditchdigger enviously—as I was saying before I interrupted myself, after fifteen years on the job, I still know as little about it as I did on that July day in 1938.

On the mornings after I have written what I consider a particularly nauseous effort, I slink around with my overcoat collar turned up and my beanie pulled down over my ears, avoiding everyone

—only to be greeted with fairly loud cries of "Good job, boy!" and "You really did it this morning!" and just plain "Well, now!"

And after I have batted out a rare gem that was difficult to type, what with patting myself on the back, I have walked the streets expectantly, eyes bright and ears pointed, and have been rewarded with a succession of black looks and such warm remarks as "For this he gets paid?" and "Save your money, kid, you'll need it."

All I can say is, it's hard, friend, hard. I do the best I can, but most of the time it's not enough. It's the readers' fault. I'm afraid they know what they want, and know when they're not getting it— which is most of the time.

All seriousness aside, it's no minor responsibility to be handed a column of white space in a metropolitan newspaper. In fact, there was a definite sensation of being hit in the stomach when my editor hit me in the stomach and said, "It's all yours. Write a thousand or so words every day about San Francisco, and make them sing, sing, sing!"

True to my instructions, I have whistled, hummed, and even yodeled at the typewriter, but so far I haven't written a column that sings. Some of them groan a little, and others are strained to the point where they emit a high whine clearly audible to the readers. But as for a column that sings, it is still to be born, and not at my hands, I'm afraid.

Anyway, it has long been my contention, in speeches before journalism students and others eager to be misled, that it's impossible to write a good column every day, year in and year out, about any city, even San Francisco.

It's a point I prove, beyond the shudder of a doubt, each morning in *The Examiner,* the journal that is currently stuck with me.

The first decision that faces a fledgling columnist is the necessity of deciding which type of column to write.

He has three choices, roughly. He can write a so-called "think" column, in which he takes one subject each day and proceeds to beat it to death by expressing a variety of opinions about it, all the opinions being his own. This kind of column calls for a writing device known as "padding." Obviously, no columnist can "think" his way through one subject every day, so he fills the gap with hope-fully humorous asides and strings of clichés that accomplish their purpose; they fill the space.

I discarded the "think" column without a second thought—for without second thoughts, how can you make it to the bottom of the page?

Then there is the "folksy" column. The conductor of this par-ticular line really has it pretty soft. He takes a phone call from a subscriber ("customer," he usually calls him) about a parking prob-lem; a letter from a veteran who needs an old piano; adds some cornball opinions and observations of his own on women who take a long time to dress and dentists who talk to you when you can't answer back—and presto-no-change-o, he's got a column.

I had no trouble avoiding the "folksy" column. I'm no humani-tarian, but the "customers" are entitled to a fairer shake than that.

This brings us to the third type—the "scattershot" column, crammed with short items on a variety of subjects. This kind of column is, obviously, a lot more work, but it attracts a wider audi-ence, at least theoretically. As that great practitioner of the art,

Walter Winchell, once expressed it: "People don't get bored if you change the subject often enough."

And so, each day, you shoot about twenty arrows into the air—some of them sharp, some of them not so sharp—and hope that at least one will hit the reader as he skims through it, sniffing anxiously for a name he recognizes, a place he knows about, or a situation he is mildly interested in.

Not wishing to appear as much of a bore as I am, I decided on the "scattershot" column. So far, I haven't regretted the choice. There is almost nothing that can't be said between . . . those three dots . . . that have become the punctuation-and-trademark of the columnist.

I suppose you think that the life of a columnist is an easy one.

The opinion is current that he is overpaid, overfed by restaurateurs anxious for a plug, overliquored by saloonkeepers eager to win his favor, overhandshaked by politicians who like to see their names in print, and overindulged by beautiful dancers and singers who need only one little plug in his little old column in order to achieve fame and success.

True, all true.

But to the columnist with some kind of conscience—any kind will do—all these things (except for the overpaid part) can be a trial.

He can't conscientiously plug a restaurant if he knows he's being served fancier fare than the regular customers. Unless he is so naïve that he shouldn't be let out alone at night, he can't be taken in by fawning saloonkeepers. The tactics of the average politician are so obvious that neither he nor the politician takes them seriously. And as for the beautiful singers and dancers—well, one little plug in that little old column probably wouldn't do them any good anyway. And besides, they aren't THAT beautiful.

And so the wary columnist—and you've got to be wary to last longer than a year or two—tries to steer a middle course. In the process of getting older and wiser, he begins to praise with caution, criticize only sparingly and with qualifications, and obligate himself as rarely as possible to people and things he doesn't wholeheartedly believe in.

In short, the first lesson a columnist must learn is that he isn't omnipotent, all-wise, and all-seeing, with the editor-given right to fire at random. At his best, he should be as "average" as his most average reader. Then, and only then, will he have his greatest audience.

We come now to the Department of Self-Pity, a crowded little bide-a-wee populated almost exclusively with item-and-dot columnists.

The main problem facing the guy who tries to cram twenty "newsy" notes into his daily space is the old one of accuracy. He tries to check and double-check as many as he can, but unfortunately, the paper comes out several times every day, and there are only a few hours between editions. And unless he is writing a so-called "timeless" column, filled with such nuggets as "The average American has a tooth filled every three years," he can't prepare his copy days in advance. In other words, he is up against the deadline every minute, and therefore, he must trust his "usually reliable sources" on a lot of stories.

And sad to relate, it's not too unusual for a "usually reliable source" to be wrong.

For example, I heard one day that Roy Buell, division manager of the Telephone company, was being considered for the job of Superintendent of the United States Mint. The tip came from a well-connected politician with a .999 record for accuracy.

I phoned an even better-connected Republican insider and asked: "Roy Buell being considered for the Mint job?" He confirmed it. Then I called Buell himself, and he answered with what I considered charmingly feigned surprise: "Gee, I hadn't heard, but it's certainly flattering." As a final check, I contacted the chairman of the Republican County Central Committee, asked about Roy Buell, and got an affirmative answer.

I had received the tip from a good source. I had triple-checked it. The name of Roy Buell had been mentioned a dozen times in the conversations. And yet, Roy Buell wasn't the man being considered for the job at all. It was Ross Buell, an executive of the Wells-Fargo Bank.

Each of the persons checked—except Roy Buell himself, of course —had assumed that I was calling Ross Buell "Roy" for some reason of my own, and hadn't bothered to correct me.

More amusing, perhaps, is the Case of the Non-Moving Car.

One morning, I got a phone call from an anonymous woman who said:

"I live on Seventeenth Street in the Mission, and I just had to tell you about this. For the last five years, a car has been parked across the street, and it's never been moved. Just stands there, day in and day out. But that's not the funny part. Every year, whoever owns the car gets new license plates for it. Did you ever hear the beat of it?"

No, I'd never heard the beat of it. I was intrigued with the whimsy of it all. A car, never driven, with new plates every year.

I got the reverse directory—the one that lists phone numbers by addresses—and called the house in front of which the non-moving car was parked. No answer. I phoned the neighbors to the right and to the left, and both gave approximately the same answer:

"Come to think of it, I never have seen that car driven. I guess that's right. It's just been standing there for years. We can't even figure out who keeps the tires from going flat."

So, satisfied, I ran a squib about the strange car on Seventeenth Street. That same morning, I got a rather angry, but mainly puzzled, call from the man who owns the car. He couldn't decipher the item at all, and understandably.

He had a job nightly from 11 P.M. to 7 A.M. and always drove to work. He slept all day. It was simply that the three neighbors I had checked had never talked to him, and had never seen him drive the car.

Then there is the problem of the columnist's manners. I will now proceed to demonstrate that if he observes the rules of behavior, he is wrong, and if he doesn't, he is wrong, too.

One night, my editor invited me to a party where the guest list included Elsa Maxwell, Gertrude Lawrence, Noel Coward, and an assortment of almost equally distinguished names.

"Quelle bonanza!" I murmured to myself. I spent the evening drifting from group to group, listening to the various brilliant conversations, and then rushed back to the office to write about the gay, gay goings-on, quoting all the guests liberally and adding a few gems of my own.

Next day, the editor summoned me to his office. His red hair was bristling with Lucky Tiger and well-controlled fury.

"Young man," he said, making that term sound like an epithet, "it's time you learned something about manners. When you're invited to a social event, you're there as a guest, not a reporter. And polite guests don't tell the world about the parties they attend."

Although flattered by his all-inclusive estimate of my audience, I never forgot his reproof.

A few weeks later—my social calendar is not exactly crowded, as you can see—I was invited to an affair at a Peninsula estate, where ever so many fascinating people were fluttering about. Mrs. Lawrence Tibbett, for one. And ever so many amusing things happened, right before my very eyes. But true to the code as outlined by my editor, I refrained from writing a word about it.

I saw Mrs. Tibbett a few days later. She looked me up and down contemptuously and snapped: "And you call yourself a reporter. Why, even *I* could have written ten columns about the things that happened at that party. Good Heavens!" And she swept away.

I am seldom invited to parties any more. Half the hosts are afraid I'll write about them. And the other half are afraid that I won't.

At a football game, you can't tell the players without a scorecard —and, while reading a column, you aren't getting full measure unless you know some of the tricks of the trade. At the risk of being expelled from The Society for the Prevention of Letting the Public In on Things, I should like to outline a few of the more accepted chicaneries.

When you run across an item that reads "The Jonathan Shackletons III say it isn't so," you can be pretty sure that a couple of days earlier, the columnist has written: "Too bad about the Jonathan Shackletons III. After numerous beefs in public places, they have decided to wash up their six-year marriage—and about time. Jonathan has been seen often enough in the company of that beautiful blond showgirl, and Mrs. Shackleton is rumored to be interested in more than the driving ability of her handsome Latin-American chauffeur."

Now you might think that "The Jonathan Shackletons III say it isn't so" isn't much of a retraction—assuming the original item was untrue—but a lot of columnists (include me out) get away with it.

Then we have the item that reads something like this: "It isn't generally known, but Joe Mayflower is quitting the National Doughnut Hole Corporation and will go into business for himself." "It isn't generally known"—except to Joe Mayflower, his friends, the Corporation and everybody connected with it. It isn't generally known—because the columnist generally knows that the readers don't give a damn. But by saying "It isn't generally known," he hopes to fool his followers into thinking he's cutting them in on something terribly insidey.

Another fascinating device is the "Don't be surprised" approach. The item reads like this: "Don't be surprised if the Mayor names Ronald Rigolo to the Police Commission. City Hall guessips say it's in the wind."

It's in the wind, all right. In fact, the Mayor told the columnist the night before, in an off-guard moment at a night club, that he was going to do just that. But by printing it as gossip, the columnist hopefully assumes that his readers will sigh admiringly: "Some boy, he's sure in the know on what's cookin', huh?"

An offshoot of the "Don't be surprised" gimmick is the "prediction" racket. The columnist reports from his Olympian height: "Prediction: Attorney Albert Wimberdroop will be appointed to the

State Supreme Court." This is a very big deal. The Governor knows he's about to appoint Wimberdroop, an old campaign supporter. All the papers know it. Wimberdroop and his friends and enemies know it.

However, by making a "prediction" out of it, the columnist feels he is entitled to crow, in a later column: "As predicted here, Albert Wimberdroop yesterday was named to the State Supreme Court. This dept.'s predictions are 99.8 per cent accurate, an amazing record." If he does say so himself, and invariably he does.

Of course, these are rather legitimate angles in the illegitimate journalistic business of columning. Far beyond the pale of decency, it seems to me, is the more recent development—the oblique, or impossible to deny successfully, type of gossip item.

This one is likely to read: "Their friends are hoping that it isn't true about the Andrew Tackhammers." The implication is clear, but what are the Tackhammers going to do about it? And as far as the readers are concerned, what is it that the friends are hoping is untrue, and why are they hoping, and how come they're expressing their hopes about their friends to a columnist? If the Tackhammers complain to the columnist that they can't imagine what he's writing about, the best they can hope for is an item reading: "The Andrew Tackhammers holding hands at the Snowbird Club, debunking the fears of their best false friends."

After that one, the poor Tackhammers, who weren't having any troubles in the first place, wind up without friends. This puts them so on edge that they eventually have a terrible quarrel and get a divorce.

Their miseries are complete when the columnist then blithely prints: "They denied it when we told you the first time, but the

Andrew Tackhammers are washing up. The sillies. Why the elaborate cover-up when Everybody Knew?"

But there are other pitfalls awaiting the columnist who tries to stay on respectable middle ground.

A principal one is monotony—the use of the same names over and over. In a way, this is only natural, for in any city, only a comparatively few people are widely known, and hence "news" (if, indeed, the journalistic axiom that "names make news" has any validity, which I sometimes doubt). Nevertheless, the deadline-ridden columnist is likely to hammer certain names to death, because he knows they are easy to contact, easy to write about, and easy to work an item out of because they are aware of what makes an item.

After receiving a few dozen complaints from readers about "the same old names," I started an annual column called "New Faces of 1951," or whatever the year, and filled it with stories about people whose names had never before appeared in print. It was an almost instantaneous failure. In place of a few dozen original complaints, I got a few hundred beefs from readers who pouted: "Fevvinsakes, who wants to read about a buncha nobodies like ourselves?"

Another occupational hazard is the typical topical item, the kind you always feel you've read somewhere before—the not-so-amazing coincidence, the hopefully bright saying, the all-too-predictable surprise ending. These stories read O.K., are simple to write, and probably contain even an element of truth. However, I suspect that if any or all of them could be checked thoroughly, they would turn out to have happened more like the following:

SMALL WORLD DEPT.   The soldier and the sailor sat quietly at opposite ends of the bar in Joan's Club, a favorite rendezvous for servicemen. Now and then the sailor would stare with more than passing interest at the G.I. Finally he walked over to the soldier, laid a friendly hand on his shoulder, and said:

"Say, aren't you Joe Slabodky, who went to Mission High in '26 and was all-City center on the football team?"

"No," answered the soldier. "I'm Mike Krsnch, and I went to Balboa High in '32 and was captain of the chess team."

"Oh, sorry," said the sailor, returning to his end of the bar.

"Sokay," said the soldier, who paid for his drink and left.

Joan on phone to columnist: "So these two brothers—a soldier and a sailor—they haven't seen each other for twenty years and tonight they meet in my bar. I tellya, I just stood there and cried . . ."

OF HUMAN INTEREST   Tessie Plumcake, a widow with four small towheaded children, drew her life savings of $2319 out of the bank to make a down payment on the home she had dreamed of for seven long years. Worried about pickpockets on streetcars, she decided to take a cab home—and when she got out, she left the money on the back seat in a paper bag. The cab driver, Willie Strinkle, discovered the money later, and took it home gleefully to his wife, who said: "Willie, we oughta keep this dough and blow town, but let's face it. The cops'd catch up with us sooner or later."

"Shucks," sighed Willie, "I guess you're right. It kills me, but I'll take it back."

Cab press agent to columnist: "So this poor widow leaves her money on the back seat. Well, you know how honest our drivers are . . ."

SAFETY LAST   Mrs. Lillian Pfeffernuss, prominent Lower Marina matron, had a bad week. On Monday, she fell off her husband's yacht and was almost drowned. On Tuesday, she was hit by a falling safe. On Wednesday, her favorite horse, Clydebottom, threw her in Golden Gate Park, and then, to show he wasn't kidding, rolled on her. On Thursday, she fell asleep under a sun lamp and was burned to a crisp. So on Friday, when friends asked her to go skiing, she said: "Not me. If I go, I'll probably break a leg. I'll stay home where it's safe."

So she stayed home, spent a quiet evening reading, and went to bed.

Neighbor to columnist: "Poor Lillian. So she stayed home, took a bath, slipped, and sprained her ankle. Isn't that a kick?"

PETS UNLIMITED   Every Sunday for the past five years, Dr. Samuel Milksop of Ingleside Terrace has taken his dog, Hoover, to Ocean Beach for a romp in the sand and the waves. Last Sunday, while the Doctor turned his back to buy himself a Goofieburger, Hoover disappeared. After searching in vain, Dr. Milksop sadly returned home—where he found Hoover on the doorstep waiting for him? Don't be silly. Hoover was picked up by some people on Russian Hill, and is living very happily with his new masters.

Dog to columnist: "I ever tell you about the doctor I used to belong to? Bright man, very bright. Could always find his way home without me."

MEET THE PEOPLE   Philander T. Phogg, a mousy little clerk who lives in a guest house on Gough Street, hasn't smoked, gambled, had a drink, or taken out a girl in all his sixty years. Last Thursday night, as he was celebrating his birthday all alone in his tiny room, his neighbor from across the hall burst in and said:

"Come, come, Philander, this is no way to celebrate your sixtieth birthday. Let's get a couple of dames and go to a night club and live it up a little."

"Now you're talking," said Philander, grabbing his coat. "I've been waiting sixty years to make Ripley's column, and I guess I ain't never gonna. Let us be off."

Item in Herb Corn's column two days ago: "Philander T. Phogg of Gough Street hasn't smoked, gambled, had a drink, or taken a girl out in all his sixty years." End of item.

ONCE A SAN FRANCISCAN, ALWAYS ETC. Tim Haversack was born in San Francisco forty years ago, and was fond of saying, "Honest, there's no place like San Francisco," even though he'd never been anywhere else. "I was born here," he'd say, "and I'll die here if it kills me." Two months ago, Tim's company transferred him without warning to Bangor, Maine, and he cried real, honest tears before he boarded the Eastbound plane. As his friends poured him aboard, he was too choked up for words. "I'll write," he finally squeezed out.

Tim's friends last week got their first letter from him.

"You can have Frisco and those silly cable cars and that crazy fog," he wrote. "Give me Maine every time, it's wonderful!"

Postcard from Haversack to columnist: "Oh, how I miss dear old San Francisco! You can put in your column that I'd give anything for just one little whiff of that good old fog!"

KIDDIE CORNER The students in Miss Slocum's first-grade class were asked to describe the taste of various objects, and little Frankie

Sholom, six-year-old of the prominent Al Sholoms, arose and said: "Ginger ale tastes like my foot's asleep."

"Very good, Frankie," said the teacher, reaching for a phone to call a columnist. "That's very clever indeed."

"I'll say it is," answered Frankie. "I read it last month in *Reader's Digest*."

Only Yesterday   The years go scudding past, gray and gold like the fog-tinged sunset, and the restless city changes its moods and its modes—and now we of the "younger" generation, no longer young, have our memories, too. The people and the places that seemed so bright, so indestructible, so impervious to time— where are they now? Vanished (quite suddenly, you tell yourself in surprise) into the yesterdays that flicker but refuse to die.

Gone, the young, unthinking years when everything was as it should be and nothing would ever change—when you smiled indulgently at talk about bridges across the Bay and busses instead of streetcars and traffic jams in peaceful Golden Gate Park. When you sipped your two-bit cocktail and ate your de luxe one-dollar dinner and waited all of ten minutes (cursing every second) for the auto ferry to take you to the football game in Berkeley.

You rode the train to Mill Valley and you climbed Mount Tamalpais aboard "the crookedest railroad in the world" and Harry Bridges was nobody to take seriously yet and Bill Saroyan was merely a crazy young writer who lived on Carl Street and would undoubtedly starve to death if it weren't for his kindly friends.

That was our San Francisco and we took it for granted. We didn't know, then, that we were living our own legend—storing up memories for future reference.

The lumbering old Geary streetcars, so big, so gray, so rattly—now they seem like one of the few remaining links with a past that we hardly grasped as we lived it.

But only yesterday the streetcars were everywhere. They trooped in imperial fours along Market, and their impatient clanging could be heard all over the city. For only a nickel you could ride from the Ferry Building to the Beach—the biggest nickel's worth in the world, the Muni boasted—and the city clanged along in tempo with its streetcars' bells.

There was no gray, then, in Jake Ehrlich's black hair, and the young lawyer lunched every day at Fred Solari's, surrounded by his sycophants. The waterfront's labor leaders, still fighting for a toehold, ate and plotted in a place near the Embarcadero called, oddly enough, the Canary Den, and the rising young tycoons strove mightily for an invitation to the Palace Hotel's "Cabinet Table," where decisions affecting the whole city were made to the clink of wine glasses and the delicate burps induced by rich foods.

The town's most illustrious madam reigned supreme in a hilltop mansion overlooking (at close range, sometimes) our best people, and she was so accepted as a sinstitution that even the sightseeing busses paused in their rounds to let the tourists in on the open secret. On a Kearny Street corner, "The Fountainhead of Corruption" ruled discreetly in his bail bond palace, and all was right with whatever was wrong in this most worldly of all possible cities.

The older generation was already lost in its memories—and to us everything was new and exciting, and we suspected we were living in the only true San Francisco.

Anson Weeks was the sensation supreme at the Mark Hopkins, and he featured a rather pitiable young singer named Bob Crosby, who couldn't sing, and who, when he wasn't trying, sat uncomfortably at a piano which he couldn't play. Radio Station KFRC was in the City of Paris, and its initials meant, according to a sign facing Union Square, "Keep Freely Radiating Cheer." The Fairmont was full of red plush chairs filled with white plush ladies, both of which emitted a musty, dusty cloud when patted on the back.

It was considered great fun of a Saturday afternoon to slide down the marble slide at Lurline Baths, and the only complaint about the ten-cent hamburgers at the Beach was that they were a little too filling—which was also true of the fifteen-cent milk shakes at Blum's.

A short man named Joe Merello, who wore a white hat and bet lavishly on the races, was firmly entrenched in a Sutter Street night club called the Moderne, and showed little concern for such rising upstarts as Bimbo Giuntoli and Charlie Low; in fact, he was even heard to speak lightly of the mighty Frank Martinelli and Tom Gerum, who ran the Bal Tabarin and would undoubtedly continue to do so for the next fifty years.

But the places to be seen, really, were the Persian Room at the Drake, where fabulous hot hors d'oeuvres were passed out free during the cocktail hour, or, after hours, in the Blue Room at the Music Box, where Sally Rand and her houris graciously allowed the town's gay blades to buy them drinks until dawn.

There was even discreet gambling, in the best possible taste, in two adjoining white houses on Bay Street. The drinks and the clubhouse sandwiches were always free, and yet, oddly enough, the place seemed to make money—until the neighbors summoned the police. Because the customers' cars were blocking their driveways.

The city was a delightful confusion to us then—and yet, it was really very well ordered.

The wealthy people seemed to be those who deserved it by right of birth and heritage, and they lived, snugly and smugly secure, in the neighborhoods that everybody agreed were theirs. Nobody got suddenly and mysteriously rich overnight—even the cops, who had a good and sophisticated idea of what was going on in every part of the city. San Francisco dreamed along, each group in its pre-ordained niche, and everybody knew everybody else since the time they were in Lowell High together.

That was our city, the city of stage shows on Market and parking spaces on Post and fifty-cent Italian dinners in North Beach and—oh yes—the best streetcar service in the country.

If we thought about it at all, we thought it would last forever. But although it was only yesterday, an era has vanished already. And only when the thick fog blankets the city and the horns cry their hearts out in the Bay can we fool ourselves into thinking that we are young again in the San Francisco of our dreams.

Once a Newsboy ...

This Louis Lurie, I guess you've heard of him.

In San Francisco, he's not just another millionaire, see. He's a rich millionaire. A rich millionaire with money, even. And all kinds of real estate and used skyscrapers and shiny limousines on which the sun never sets, they're that shiny.

But things weren't always so kopasetic with this Lurie. He starts out in life the hard way, peddling newspapers for Hearst in Chicago. I mean standing on those windy street corners night after night, shivering and freezing.

He has a buddy selling newspapers on the same corner, another kid named Louis. Only this is Louis Macloon. And when things are quiet, Louis and Louis kill time by lagging pennies against a wall.

You know the game. You try to toss your penny as close to the wall as you can, and so does the other guy, and if your penny is closer to the wall, you're the winner.

Well anyway, time marches on, and both these Louis kids manage to do pretty good for themselves. Lurie winds up in San Francisco, making a mint in real estate, and Macloon becomes a theatrical producer in Chicago, doing all right. Not as good as Lurie, mind you, but not starving either.

So one day Macloon is thinking about presenting a new play in Chicago, starring Nancy Carroll or somebody like that, and he's a little strapped for dough. In fact, what he needs the worst way is $30,000, or the whole deal is off.

So who does Macloon think of, right off? Right off he thinks of his old newsboy buddy-chum, Louis Lurie. And so he quick sends him a telegram in which he apologizes for asking for such a paltry sum—but please rush it. By certified cashier's check.

Lurie, it seems, remembers his old friend Macloon very well indeed. He sends him a warm telegram right back, containing one word.

"No," it says.

Macloon fires a reply in short order. "Once a newsboy, always a newsboy," he wires.

All in all, a great day for Western Union, but a bad one for Louis Macloon.

But a short time later, who shows up in Lurie's palatial office on Montgomery Street but Brother Macloon himself. Breezy as you please, he swaggers past the receptionists and secretaries and enters The Great Man's sanctum.

The office staff, which has heard about the exchange of telegrams, gathers around Lurie's door with ears flapping, expecting brash Mr. Macloon to get thrown out on his macloon any minute.

But all is quiet except for some mysterious clicking noises.

Well, a few minutes pass by, and Macloon comes walking out of Lurie's office, whistling a merry tune. He holds up a check for $30,000, waves it before the goggled eyes of the staff, and then stuffs it into his pocket.

"Once a newsboy, always a newsboy," he chuckles, flipping a coin high in the air, "and they all like to lag pennies."

Then he hands his penny to Miss Flanagan, Lurie's redoubtable secretary.

"Give this to your boss after I leave," he grins. "Tell him that I used to beat him back in Chicago—when we were newsboys—with this same weighted penny!"

Speaking of the Weather   LOVELIEST DAY OF
THE YEAR   Sunday's Bay, a polished mirror of blue glass
smudged here and there by the sailboats whose wings barely flutter
in the baby breeze . . . Ugly Alcatraz squatting sullenly in the sun,
its imperfections reflected perfectly on the still waters below . . .
The steaming, gravel roofs of the Skid Road hotels, splotched with
the dead-white skins of those who seldom venture out of their dark
holes in the quest of that mark of distinction and affluence—a sunburn . . . The tiny kids running naked over the rolling greens of
Golden Gate Park, while their parents snore under the trees, their
faces covered with the Sunday snoozepapers . . . The tiny stoops
on the narrow old houses on North Beach, suddenly overcrowded
to the danger point as the old folks drag out the dining-room chairs
to sit in the warm waves of funshine; but, traditionalists to the end,
the men keep their hats on—for it is Sunday, and they are gentlemen
of the old country . . . At the Beach, seven daring swimmers
pounding their way out to Seal Rocks, climbing to the topmost
point—and then, one by one, diving spectacularly back into the sea
as the tourists gape, gawk-eyed, from the Cliff House windows . . .
In the dead light of the half-moon, long strips of fog appearing on

the horizon beyond the Golden Gate, signaling, in frosted silence, the end of a September day to remember.

The weather, not sex, is Topic A in San Francisco.

Everybody talks about it, from morning till night, and, despite Mark Twain's sniffish observation, nobody wants to do anything about it. The people like it just the way it is—so completely unpredictable that a weatherman seems superfluous. He does his best, but he finds it unpredictable, too.

In San Francisco, you can swelter in January and freeze in July. You can shiver in the sun and get a sunburn in the fog. You can be dressed correctly, climatically speaking, at 10 A.M., and be overdressed (or underdressed) by noon.

The weather is even different on opposite sides of the street. A typical San Francisco sight is that of men sunbathing in bare-chested splendor on the grassy slopes of Union Square—while, directly across Post Street, the town's traditionally well-dressed women hurry to lunch at El Prado, smothered in minks and not at all uncomfortable.

Of course, you might interject at this point that no woman is uncomfortable in mink, but that's another story.

THE RAINS CAME   And they come in a thin gray drizzle, knifed by a spectacular dawnrise that splashes the Golden Gate Bridge with a nickel's worth of sunbeams and draws a cut-rate rainbow across the brooding skies . . . By noon, the great city smells warm and damp, like a schoolroom packed with children wearing rubbers, and the umbrellas are crowding thick along Post Street (with the women, as usual, walking under the awnings, their umbrellas tilted forward at an angle designed to do the most damage) . . . The cops—was it only yesterday that they directed traffic in their blue shirtsleeves?—move like gloomy reflections across the crowded intersections, almost invisible in a sea of bumpers, and the taxis take a deep breath and try in vain to keep a grip on the slippery red bricks of California Street . . . In Golden Gate Park, the rain drips teardrops from a million leaves, and the bright flowers at the base of Uncle John McLaren's statue turn their faces to the ground in sorrow . . . Night falls fast to kill the day that didn't smile once— and soon the neon glows bright yet cold along Third Street and Howard, where the thin-shouldered men whose shoes and souls are worn through shuffle slowly along in the red reflections on the wet pavement . . . The September song, sweet with its dying memories of summer, ends, and October comes coldly to Baghdad-by-the-Bay.

San Franciscans love any and all observations on their weather, especially their own. Mrs. Matt Dooley once said: "Our weather is like a wayward child—when it's bad, we make excuses for it." A local poet rhapsodized: "Blessed are they who live by the Bay; one day they are hot, the next they are not." The Chamber of Commerce used to embellish the streetcars with streamers reading, "It's Cool in San Francisco," but they finally had to stop. Too many wags kept adding a *d* to the second word.

VERY WARM FOR OCTOBER   The city is a little strange, a little unlike San Francisco. A heat haze muffles the glowing lights of the Shell and PG & E buildings, making them misty and unreal. Steam rises from the tepid Bay, and a dank smell of fish and stale water cloaks North Beach, drowning out even the heavy-hanging garlic. Along the Marina, windows are wide open, framing a hundred little domestic scenes enacted unashamedly before the eyes of passers-by; a passion for privacy is merely an added burden when the weather gets too close for comfort. In the tenderloin, the suffocating saloons are empty, for the patrons buy their drinks and then crowd onto the sidewalk to down them. And the tenement dwellers between Van Ness and Fillmore sit by their open windows and drink their beer until well after midnight . . . There is no metropolitan pace in the city on a night like this. The signals click to green, and the cars move sluggishly ahead. Busses drone along in a dream. The great warm blanket presses down and the city stirs slowly, restlessly —waiting to be roused by the alarm clock of the cool fog which is sure to come.

The radio announcers have fun with the weather, too. One, on Station KLX, tickled his listeners no end by reporting: "San Francisco, fair and warm. Except for night and morning fog lasting all day." Another announced one time: "There will be high fog in San Francisco. Dissipating in the afternoon."

One day, when the weatherman predicted fog and none appeared, Howard Young telephoned the weather bureau and asked for an explanation. "I dunno what happened," drawled the weatherman. "I guess it got lost in the fog."

The weather even has something to do with the death rate, a fact I learned when I happened to ask a mortuary operator one fine May day: "How's business?" He answered: "Terrible. But then, it's always quiet now. Nobody dies during the summer months in San Francisco." That's true, more or less. Whereas about 900 San Franciscans will die during a January, the toll drops to less than 700 in May, and even Dr. J. C. Geiger, the one-time City Health Director, is at a loss to explain it.

"Shucks," he said. "I can never tell January from May around here, and I don't see how Death can, either."

SO THIS IS MARCH   Cold rain falling from blue skies, the icy sun painting pale rainbows over the East Bay hills, Twin Peaks rising thinly green in an imitation of spring as the wind whistles to keep warm in the tall thickets of Sutro Forest . . . The first blossoms opening bravely in the Park, only to die miserably in the minor hurricanes that scatter them far and wild across the wet grass. The Bay an ugly gray, foaming and writhing against its shores as though looking for a place to hide. And the thin ribs of the Golden Gate Bridge, shivering so visibly that you wish you had a blanket to throw over them . . . The Skid Rowgues huddled in doorways, the Union Square pigeons pressing themselves against the Dewey monument, the cable car riders fighting to get off their favored bottom step and into the closed compartment, the men tearing their hair and losing their heads as they chase their hats along Mont-gomery Street—this is one moment in the March that comes gustily to Baghdad-by-the-Bay. And the next moment, who knows? It may be May!

San Franciscans have a peculiarly resentful attitude toward warm weather ("warm" being anything over 70). On the morning after a particularly hot Sunday, Dave Falk and his wife Marge drove to work from their home in the Anzavista sector. The fog was thick, the windshield wipers were flick-flacking, and Dave said happily to Marge:

"Now why couldn't it have been a nice day like this yesterday?"

I must confess, though, that I do feel sorry for the uninitiated tourists. After all, San Francisco is in California, and California to them is the land of sunshine and orange groves, and so they come to town completely unprepared, sartorially, for what they find.

One May morning I saw a convention delegate struggling through the rain at Powell and Post in an outfit consisting of a powder-blue sports jacket, yellow sweater, white panama hat, gray slacks, and black-and-white shoes. As he stood there miserably, waiting for the signal to change, I sidled up to him in my parka (we weren't in a no-parka zone) and asked: "Where you from, friend?"

Raising the brim of his wilted panama, he sighed: "I'm from Indiana—and back there, we always thought San Francisco was in California."

So I kicked him, but it couldn't have hurt very much.

I was wearing galoshes.

MIRACLE IN NOVEMBER   The ageless Bay, stirring sleepily under a soft blanket of haze that transforms freighters into ghost ships, fishing boats into fitful shadows, and harsh Alcatraz into a magic island, dimly seen . . . The men of the financial district, strolling along with their hats in their hands—instead of their hands on their hats . . . Along the shaded streets of Pacific Heights, kids lazily tossing a football back and forth; in the springlike atmosphere, a baseball would seem more appropriate . . . Sun-spangled waves splashing softly and indolently against the black rocks below the Cliff House, and raising their heads a little here and there as though in surprise at their own gentleness . . . Young lovers at Coit Tower, spooning under a moon that must have been held over from

June; spellbound tourists taking a ride on the cables and shaking their heads in the warm wonderment of it all; Post Street's clothes-horsey women limply fanning themselves with the tails of their mink stoles; the sidewalk flower stands exuding such clouds of heavy perfume that their owners should be arrested for fragrancy . . . This is a November day in the city where the weather is never just fair; it's always perfect, in the eyes and hearts of its people.

Punch Lines

They never happen in real life, they say—those stories with the surprise ending, the sudden snapper, the O. Henry punch line. The cynics insist they have to be contrived, with the facts shuffled around a little here and there to provide the proper build-up to the one-sentence payoff.

True enough, in a general sort of way. But in fifteen years of column-writing, I've run across a few stories that fit the punch line formula perfectly, without the poetic necessity of toying with a single sequence. They merely had to be told the way they happened —one, two, three, boom, punch line.

In April, 1952, I printed the short-short story of beautiful Providencia Rodriguez, the kind of woman who drove men wild—literally.

In a fit of jealousy, her first husband pumped four bullets into her body one night. Providencia lived. The husband went to jail for eight years.

Later, hot-blooded Providencia married James De Jesus, a San Francisco ship painter. James kept thinking about those four bullets in her body. They didn't worry her, but they bothered him. So he sent her to a doctor and had the bullets removed.

One April night, in the Mission District, James De Jesus, in a fit of jealousy, grabbed a pistol and killed Providencia.

With four bullets.

I picked up this story in December, 1951, and printed it this way:

OF HUMAN INTEREST   The most poignant story of the week, for my dough, concerns Norma Talmadge, who's now a San Franciscan with a home on Twin Peaks.

The great movie queen of two decades ago got a most flattering tribute the other day: the wounded veterans at a nearby Army hospital voted her the star they'd most like to see in person during the Christmas season.

Not Lana Turner. Not Betty Grable. But (how wonderful to be remembered!) Norma Talmadge. Why, who'd think that kids from Korea would even know her name?

And then came the heart-tugging explanation. These are wounded veterans who wanted to see her, all right (and they did). But—they are all veterans of the First World War.

A scene I'll never forget took place one somber December day in the St. Vincent de Paul Church. Father Thomas O'Kane, the church's noted pastor, preached the most eloquent sermon of his career—to the smallest group he has ever addressed.

Only six people were in the church. There was Elizabeth Cleary, who was dead, and there was Patrick Cleary, her husband, who sat in the front pew. With him were Al Sodini, manager of Bank of America's Polk–Van Ness branch, and his wife, Rose, who have been

Patrick's good friends (and the guardians of his meager funds) for years. And in the back-row sat two little old ladies, the only other friends to attend the funeral.

Father O'Kane spoke a long time. He told of the beauties of the church, and described the sun streaming through the stained glass windows. "Dearly beloved, in life we are all in darkness," he said in a voice that resounded through the almost empty edifice. "Through death we enter into everlasting life . . ."

As he spoke his words of hope and comfort, a smile came slowly to the face of Patrick Cleary. His voice remained steady, but when Father O'Kane saw that smile, he could not keep back the tears for Elizabeth, who was dead, and Patrick, who is blind.

Some of these so-called "natural" stories are a little on the silly side, I must admit.

Like this one—which begins with Greg Hobson, an aspiring artist who sells suits at Moore's (he aspires on the side), walking into Bernstein's Fish Grotto and asking for a whole crab. When it was brought to him, he studied it carefully and then decided: "It's the wrong color. Bring me another."

Well, they thought he was a little peculiar, to say the least, but they brought him another. This one was O.K.

"I'll take it," he said, putting the crab under his arm and walking out.

As you've guessed by now, Hobson wanted the crab for painting, not eating. And after he'd done the crab's portrait, his fellow workers at Moore's admired the canvas so much that it was hung in the suit department.

A few days later, a suit customer walked in, saw the painting of the crab, and said: "I'd like to buy that to hang in my office." Which he did. The purchaser: George Skaff, then manager of Bernstein's Fish Grotto.

Greg Hobson's crab was home again.

Then we have the tale of Rudy Samson, a San Francisco man-about-town who is really a man and actually about town. When he married beautiful blonde Sally Wickman, he gave her a baby-blue Cadillac convertible.

"To match your eyes, darling," he said. And it did.

Shortly after, she smashed the car head-on into another in Marin County, and wound up in the hospital. The car was a total wreck, but Rudy went right out and bought her a new one. This time it was a black Cadillac convertible.

"To match your eyes, darling," he said. And it did.

A San Francisco lawyer had an enjoyable time for himself during a trial in Judge Charles Snook's court in Oakland. A very attractive woman occupied a front row seat every day, and the lawyer managed to strike up a few conversations with her.

And then he invited her to have dinner with him as soon as the trial was over.

On the last day of the proceedings, Judge Snook called him into his chambers and smiled:

"Well, now that the trial is ending—don't forget that you have a date to take my wife to dinner!"

An Air Force Captain, name of Cooper, came to San Francisco from Tucson and went to court in an attempt to get his minor daughter away from the custody of his ex-wife.

"Why?" asked Superior Judge Eustace Cullinan.

"It's like this, Your Honor," explained Captain Cooper. "She's keeping the child in a very unwholesome environment. They're living on Telegraph Hill—the 300 block on Lombard—and everybody knows that Telegraph Hill is full of, uh, let us say, sissies."

"Case dismissed," ruled Judge Cullinan, who lives at 329 Lombard.

I never drive past the beautiful "Portals of the Past" in Golden Gate Park without remembering that somewhere in that area lies a dog—buried in a silver casket.

The story goes back to the mid-twenties, when Amadeus G. Langenberger, the wealthy art collector, had a pet poodle named "Boisie." One day, "Boisie" was run over by a car and killed. Heartbroken, Langenberger had a silver casket made for the poodle, and, one dark midnight, he drove out to the Park, and dug a grave near the "Portals," and buried his pet.

A police officer came along while Langenberger was in the middle of his strange chore, started to order him away, and then listened sympathetically to his story.

"Go ahead," the officer finally sighed. "And I'll keep your secret. Nobody'll ever know there's a dog buried here."

And he was as good as his word—although his fellow officers used to wonder why, once in a while, he'd stroll over near the "Portals of the Past" and drop a flower on the ground.

Now, twenty-five years later, they know. Because a relative of Langenberger's, deciding that the story—unlike the principals—should not die, gave me the details.

I called this vignette "Blue Blood and Red Silk"—a very social item about a very social San Francisco family.

A little-known member of the clan—a widower uncle—died recently. He was a simple man, a meatcutter by trade. By mutual, unspoken consent, he didn't bother much with his relatives, and they returned the quiet insult.

But his death notice appeared in the newspapers, and the fashionable friends of his fashionable family turned out for the funeral. Outside the chapel, the clan's chesty dowager—the late meatcutter's sister—gathered the flock around her and said in hushed tones:

"Considering the set we move in, it might be better to avoid mention of my brother's occupation."

Then she added condescendingly, "Not that it wasn't an honorable calling, of course."

The family filed silently into the flower-banked chapel and took their places in the front row. They had hardly seated themselves when the last and most elaborate floral piece was carried in—a mass of white gardenias, draped with a red silk brassard.

And lettered on it in gold were the words: "Rest In Peace—Local 508—Amalgamated Meat Cutters."

C. W. Taylor, Jr., of Palo Alto, who is totally blind, was standing at Fifth and Market streets one afternoon when an old woman stepped up to his left side (he carries his white cane on the right) and said:

"Please, sir, could you help me across the street?"

Safely on the other side, she noticed his white cane for the first time and gasped: "You're blind! Heavens, I might have been killed!"

I saw his gray-haired widow eating alone in a little Bush Street lunch counter one recent night—and that brought back memories of Tony. His story was one of those "it could only happen here" things, and it could only have happened when it did: during the Terrible Twenties.

Tony was a partner in a North Beach barbershop, but he had ambitions. There was a dedicated fierceness in the way he saved money, and when he'd amassed $9000, he spent more time on Montgomery Street than behind the chair in North Beach. Playing the stock market.

Tony's luck was fantastic. With an excitement bordering on hysteria, he watched his pile grow to $100,000, then to half a million. He gave his half of the barbershop to his partner, but he kept a key to the front door, explaining:

"I'm a rich man now, but there's one thing I want to keep on doing. Every morning I'm going to come in and shave myself. Then I'll remember I'm really just a little man."

But he wasn't the same Tony now. Although he still shaved himself in his old barbershop every morning, he spent the rest of the day in the ticker tape emporiums, speculating wildly. His luck held. Soon he was a millionaire—with trembling hands. Montgomery Streeters will never forget the sight of Tony staring at the incoming quotations on the big board, absent-mindedly tearing a $43,000 dividend check to bits.

Tony kept the key to the barbershop in his pocket, but he was beyond all that now. He never went there any more—he was too big a man. He built a vast home across the Bay and went to Europe for antique furniture and art treasures. Among other things, he built a chapel in the mansion and each Sunday he had a private service.

"Now that I'm rich," said Tony, "God can come to me."

But God didn't come to Tony. Disaster came instead, with the crash of the stock market. Tony, like all the other Tonys of his day, was wiped out.

One morning, he reached into his pocket and pulled out the key to the barbershop—where he used to shave himself every morning so he wouldn't forget that he was really just a little man. Then, slowly, he walked over to the North Beach address, opened the door, and got out his favorite razor.

And that's where they found him. In the first chair. With his throat cut.

The Lost Week   The city belongs to the ages during The Lost Week between the great holidays. In the soft glow of Christmas, the wild pace we know as Today dies down to a golden gray. A nostalgic haze spreads over the hills and the Yesterdays live again. As you look, with your eyes blinded by memories, even the mighty bridges seem to disappear, the Bay is once again alive with darting ferryboats, and the San Francisco that was—is.

In the sudden hush of The Lost Week, the Sunset with its wedding-cake houses vanishes into cold, thin air, and you can see the sand dunes rolling endlessly to the beach. There is no modern neon-studded Cliff House—only the soaring, white chunk of gingerbread perched precariously above Seal Rocks. In the swirling mists high overhead, Mayor Adolph Sutro roams his Heights, and waves down at an occasional clattering carriage. And yes, that's Ben Butler, the celebrated sea lion, sitting in front of the Cliff House, shaking flippers with thousands who stand in line to say "Hello, Ben," and get a lofty, detached bark in return.

There is a strange quiet during The Lost Week, even along Montgomery Street—the dark canyon that is lighted by dollar signs. The skyscrapers seem small and empty and you can see giants roaming the sidewalks—Abe Ruef, striding toward his silver-domed Sentinel Building; Ralston and Sharon, fighting their bitter fight for an empire; A. P. Giannini looking up at the magnificence of his Bank of America headquarters and shaking his head in disbelief as though to say: "What have I created?" You look up at the hulking buildings and remember the broken brokers who hurled themselves out of those upper windows in 1929—following the same line that their stocks took before them.

The old, dear city—how it refuses to die, how swiftly it leaps back to life when you have a moment to look beyond the Here and the Now. South Park, the "oval square" below Bryant between Second and Third—your eyes travel over its present meanness and you can see it as it was when George Gordon built it so many years ago (was it 75 or 85?). He was chic, he was British, and South Park was chic and British—a faubourg with touches of Kew Gardens and St. James Square, by far the most fashionable spot in San Francisco.

The park was rimmed with fine homes—Senator Gwin's there and Peter Donahue's, over there, and farther down, the Barton house where two hundred couples danced at a gala ball each year. And look, the Zeitska Academy for Young Females—twenty-four only, from the finest families, and they're coming out to take their daily stroll through the park, past the dandies dozing on benches, past the old duffers with their ivory canes and snuffboxes. This is South Park at the height of its glory, with Bishop Kip making his rounds, and eating the muffins made especially for him by fine cooks imported from Europe.

But nothing so delicate and tender as South Park could live long. Soon Rincon Hill became the center of elegance, and you could reach it from the Park by strolling down a long promenade. An interesting stroll, too, for you rubbed elbows with Bret Harte, and Charles Warren Stoddard, and sometimes on a fine day, Robert Louis Stevenson.

The Lost Week—time to rebuild the Lost City that is never quite beyond reach. The intersection of Polk and California, for instance. Today you look around and see Blum's and a bank and a bar and a drugstore. Look into yesterday, and you see Author Hugh Walpole, tramping from door to bore in search of lore about Frank Norris and his *McTeague*. At the corner, Joe Hoffman calls out from his cigar stand: "Hey, where's that friend of yours, that Norris. He promised me a book. Haven't seen him lately." And Walpole regards him sadly and answers: "Frank Norris, my friend, has been dead for seventeen years."

Chinatown, now such a jumble of neon and modern fronts and back-scratchers and more back-scratchers. But here and there you can still see how it was when Arnold Genthe prowled its back alleys with his concealed camera, taking pictures so alive that even today you can look at them and smell the faint pork in the air, the frying rice, perhaps even the opium. And then you stroll through Portsmouth Square and look past the drifters and grifters lounging on the benches. You see it in all its color of almost a century ago—with gorgeous Chinese mandarins airing their caged birds, tattooed Maoris roaming around in feathered robes, Russians lurking in heavy sables, even on the warmest days.

How far back do you want to go? Once you start, there is no turning back, and there is no era too distant to be clearly glimpsed, or too close to be out of perspective:

Jimmy Rolph in his blue suit and his cowboy boots, driving a streetcar down Market and waving at the cheering mobs as only he could wave . . . Mark Twain and Prentice Mulford, walking into Woodward's What Cheer House—but not for a drink. Oh no. There was something much more precious on the second floor: the only free library in town . . . John L. Sullivan, The Great Champion, playing the role of the blacksmith in *Honest Hearts and Willing Hands* at the old Bush Street theater—and mangling his lines so badly one night (perhaps he'd had a few too many?) that the audience booed him; whereupon he dropped his hammer, waddled up to the footlights, and ad libbed magnificently: "I hereby challenge any —— —— — —————— in the house to a fight, here and now." The curtain came down and The Champ was through. As an actor.

The roaring days of North Beach in the bootlegging era—when the most feared gang called itself, melodramatically enough, "The Forty Strong." And they proved their strength in various genteel ways. Like burying a suspected hijacker up to his nose in a cellar, demanding "Where didja hide the likker or we finish the job," and standing over him with a shovel. Or pouring gasoline over another victim, out at Ocean Beach, and casually flicking lighted matches at him until he talked. These were "The Forty Strong," a name that can still bring a glimmer of fear to the eyes of many in North Beach.

The spars of the sailing ships rising straight and thin along the Embarcadero, the Sunday hikers singing their echoing airs as they wait for a boat in the Ferry Building, the half-cable trolley climbing noisily up the Fillmore hill, the Tower of Jewels glowing like magic at the 1915 Fair, the bicycles and carriages rolling along the winding roads of Golden Gate Park, the "open houses" that were really open (come one, come all) on New Year's Day—these are the memories that come flooding back during The Lost Week, when the great city stands still and fat, and looks around at its many lives, and remembers how much it has to live for.

The Silver Fox   The first time I ran into Joe Bernstein, he was staring with elaborate concentration into the window of a sea food restaurant on Powell Street. Inside the window was a large chunk of ice, and inside the ice was a good-sized fish.

Well, you know how it is when somebody stands and stares at something in a loud and meaningful silence. Pretty soon a crowd of about a dozen people had gathered around Joe, and they were all staring open-mouthed at the open-mouthed fish in the chunk of ice.

At the precisely proper moment—just before the crowd was likely to melt away—Joe announced in a loud voice: "I tellya, that's the biggest Spanish mackerel I ever saw. No sir, never saw a Spanish mackerel that big. Some mackerel."

Most of the people nodded knowingly in agreement, and a few even said "Yeah" or "Sure is." But a little man near the other end of the window grunted "Sea bass," and went on staring at the fish.

Every nerve in Joe Bernstein's body snapped to attention. This was the moment he had been waiting for. His baby-blue eyes widened in an artful blend of innocence and ignorance.

"Pardon me, sir," he said, "Did I hear you call that Spanish mackerel a sea bass?"

"Yeah," said the little man without even looking around. "Sea bass."

"Well, sir," continued Joe, teetering back and forth on his heels, "I never thought I'd live to see the day when a man called a Spanish mackerel a sea bass."

The crowd pressed in closer, and Joe beamed at them in puppy-dog friendliness as he announced above the clang of a passing cable car: "Tellya what, friend. I'll bet you twenty dollars that that fish is a Spanish mackerel."

The little man glanced at Joe with just the suggestion of a sneer. "And I'll betcha twenty dollars that it's a sea bass," he snapped.

"Fine, fine," purred Joe. "Now leave us go inside and find out."

The crowd pressed its noses against the window and peered inside. They saw Joe and the little man talk to the manager. They saw the manager move his lips. And then they saw Joe, his face collapsing in consternation, reach into his pocket, pull out a greenback, and hand it to the little man.

"It beats me, I can't figure it out," said Joe slowly to nobody in particular as he returned to the Powell Street sidewalk. "Here I've got every fish in the sea running on my side except a sea bass—and I lose."

Joe Bernstein had good reason to feel morose. He had visited that restaurant the day before, and had found out that the fish in the block of ice was a Spanish mackerel. But even a sure-thing gambler —and Joe Bernstein is that—is bound to make a mistake once in a while.

How could he have known that the little man who took his

twenty-dollar bet worked in that restaurant? And that he himself had taken out the Spanish mackerel and put in the sea bass the night before?

But these are the little unexpected fillips that add spice to the life of a gambler—a life that Joe Bernstein, "The Silver Fox," lived to the hilt.

In flamboyant San Francisco, he was flamboyantly at home in an unexpectedly lavish apartment in the building above Tiny's Waffle Shop on Powell. The elevator that took you up to his floor was rattle-trappy, and the door to the apartment was a banality of glass panes, but once inside, you were almost suffocated in a heavy fog of expensive colognes, and blinded by acres of white walls and white furniture.

On the walls there were autographed pictures of show business luminaries, like Helen Morgan and Gertrude Niesen, for "The Silver Fox" enjoyed the thin, spurious atmosphere of the saloons when he wasn't engaged in his principal pursuit: the hard search for the easy buck.

Despite his dashing nickname of "The Silver Fox"—a title I hung on him years ago in a particularly uninspired moment—Joe wasn't an especially dashing figure. He did have silver-gray hair, however, framing a broad, heavy-lipped face. He dressed in expensive bad taste, was usually seen in the company of brittle redheads with bad teeth and good legs, and wasn't above betting so noisily at the baseball games that he sometimes came to the attention of the police, whose hearing, where gamblers are concerned, isn't notoriously acute.

However, "The Silver Fox" was in the San Francisco tradition—a guy who got around, who grabbed more than his share of checks and who was on a first-name basis with bank presidents and newsboys. The shirt he'd gladly give you off his back was likely to be silk and monogrammed; and whether he had a buck in his pocket or $10,000, his manner was always the same—smooth, smiling, friendly. He called everybody "pal." And he naïvely believed everybody was his pal.

One time, after he had won $150,000 in a marathon poker game, "The Silver Fox" was dining at Larry's in North Beach with Jake Ehrlich, the lawyer, who suggested: "Joe, it's time you put some money away for a change. Now gimme $100,000, I'll buy you an apartment house, and you'll have a steady income for the rest of your life."

Bernstein thought that over for a minute, and then shook his head.

"Why not?" demanded Ehrlich.

"Because," said Joe, "you can't shove an apartment house into the middle of a pot, that's why."

Like all gamblers, money, as such, didn't mean much to Joe. After he'd lost $90,000 in a three-day poker battle and friends would marvel at his seeming unconcern, Joe would explain: "Money is just my stock in trade—like ties to a necktie salesman or cans to a grocer. Right now, my stock is a little low, pal. But I've got a little left—and that's all I need to get a little more. If the cards are right, it'll roll in."

Joe was as honest as his nights were long—but he wasn't above enjoying the trick bets taught to him by Titanic Thompson, the fabulous bettor and sportsman. The Spanish mackerel incident was one trick bet that went awry, but they usually worked.

For instance, suppose you were standing at a bar, and an outstandingly well-dressed man walked by. With a little discreet prompting from Joe ("Some fancy dresser, huh?"), you'd be likely to say: "One of the best dressed men I've ever seen."

"True, true," Joe would agree with oily joviality, "but you can never tell about guys like that. Sometimes they look so fancy—and they aren't even wearing underwear."

"Well, now," you say, "I'll bet HE'S wearing underwear."

"And I'll bet you $100 he isn't wearing any underwear at all," counters Joe.

The well-dressed man, truly a splendid fellow, agrees to accompany you to the men's room, and sure enough—no underwear. And you would have to be a terrible cad to suspect that he and Joe had planned the whole thing beforehand: But that's the way things go sometimes.

Or suppose you're driving down to Bay Meadows race track with Joe and a group of people, and you pass a highway sign reading: "Bay Meadows—10 miles."

"Ten miles to the track, eh?" muses Joe, fondly stroking his double chin. "Good. We should be there in five minutes."

"Five minutes?" you say patronizingly. "For Heaven's sake, Joe, we aren't flying. We'll be lucky if we get there in fifteen minutes."

"Well, pally," shrugs Joe. "I think you're wrong. In fact, I'd be willing to wager a small sum—say, twenty-five dollars—that we're there in five minutes."

"If you wanna throw your money away, it's O.K. with me," you smile smugly. "It's a bet."

Five minutes later, you arrive at Bay Meadows. And certainly Joe Bernstein isn't the kind of guy who'd drive down the highway the night before and move a signpost up the road—just for a little joke and twenty-five dollars.

However, he did enjoy his little jokes.

Once upon a long time ago, according to his old friends, Joe married a girl who frowned loudly upon his gambling activities. In fact, she hated gambling as much as Joe loved her, and so his buddies were only mildly surprised when he gave up the cards and got a steady job, clerking in a store.

They lived in a tiny apartment, and she cooked for him, and at night they listened to the radio or took in a movie, and went to bed early. Joe's friends, of course, were busy making book on how long this blissful state would continue; it went on for quite a while, and as a matter of fact, the happy couple managed to save quite a bit of money.

Almost as much as Joe was in the habit of winning or losing on the turn of a card or a roll of the dice.

But the inevitable happened in its usual inevitable way. One morning, at work, Joe got wind of a particularly big poker game— the kind you were likely to walk away from broke or with $100,000. The gambler's blood ran hot in his veins. He went to the bank, drew out all the money they'd saved so painstakingly, and got into the game.

Within an hour, he was broke. He had no job to go back to. So he slowly walked home, his hands in his empty pockets. His wife took one look at his long face, and knew immediately what had happened.

"Joe!" she gasped, clutching at her throat. Then she dropped to the floor in a faint.

"The Silver Fox" stood over her for long seconds, his mind a fevered muddle, his instincts working wildly in all directions. But he knew what he had to do, what any born gambler would do in his predicament.

He reached down, snatched the diamond necklace he'd given her for a wedding present, pawned it—and went back to the game.

But lest you think that Joe had not acted the part of a complete gentleman, let me say that he threw a pitcher of water into her face before he left the apartment. She recovered nicely—her consciousness, her senses, and her perspective.

Joe was soon a bachelor again.

It was only recently, in San Francisco, that Joe had one of his really bad nights. The game was upstairs in a building on Powell Street, and Joe entered the fray with a fat bankroll and hopes that were soaring like Coit Tower on a fogswept night. "Pals, I'm ready tonight," he said gleefully, rubbing his chubby, well-manicured hands together.

But that night, the cards acted as though they hated him personally. The long, tense hours dragged past, each one dragging a few thousands dollars more out of his roll. At last, around 5 A.M., he admitted defeat. He had lost $27,000—but, at least, he had kept a ten-dollar bill. "For breakfast," he laughed hollowly, making his bleary-eyed way out into the dawn.

However, Joe wasn't quite ready for breakfast yet. He wandered along Turk Street, and found a two-bit poker game in operation in a dank, smoky room behind a cigar stand. He threw down his ten dollars and got into the game, and by 9 A.M., when he was ready for breakfast, he had won eighty dollars.

The other players in the little game looked at him with mingled awe and admiration as he got up painfully from the table at the end of twelve hours that had cost him $27,000—minus $80.

"Boy," sighed a player, watching Joe shuffle out the door. "There goes one lucky guy."

San Francisco, where "The Silver Fox" spent some of the best dollars of his life, doesn't see much of him any more. Times change. The cool gray city is getting cooler and cooler toward gamblers and gambling—and it's getting increasingly difficult for a guy to risk an honest buck in a legitimate poker game. When the Joe Bernsteins stroll along Powell Street these days, the cops no longer call them by their first names and clap them on the back. They're more likely to call the paddy-wagon and clap them into jail.

Joe feels more at home now in a place like Las Vegas, where gambling is a legalized industry and almost everybody is a gambler. "It's nice," says Joe in the manner of a refugee who has found his homeland at last. "It's nice to be part of the majority for a change."

San Francisco isn't quite the same without "The Silver Fox" and his ilk. It might be quite true that they never did anything for anybody except themselves—but they splotched the downtown scenery with their own peculiar brand of Runyonesque color, and their disappearance leaves a gap that no necktie salesman, no ribbon clerk, no bank teller will ever fill in the metropolitan picture.

Color of the City

Listen, My Children, and You Shall Hear: The miserable foghorn on Alcatraz, with its moan that seems to say, over and over, "Ohhhhhh Gawwwd" . . . The airy tinkle of the glass wind chimes in the doorway of Chinatown's trinket shops, luring the tourists with their tiny, unreal voices . . . The siren that blasts out thrice daily from the Ferry Building—at 8 A.M., noon, and 4:30 P.M.—as though to remind all San Francisco that there's still a sign of life in that old gray guardian of the Bayfront . . . The pre-6 A.M. rat race of trucks and jalopies down Market to the produce district—each driver trying to beat the rest to the day's fresh fruits and vegetables; and to the losers go the spoils . . . The inimitable click-clang of the fast-disappearing birdcage traffic signals—a sound that every San Franciscan can hear in his mind's ear, no matter where he happens to be . . . The toylike tolling of the bell on the State Belt Line's engine as it jerks along the Embarcadero in the postmidnight hollowness, just soft enough to lull the Telegraph Hill set to sleep . . . The solitary slap of the cable in the Powell Street slot on a wet, drippy night—so lonely that it seems to be talking to itself as it makes its endless rounds . . . These are some of the many voices

of Baghdad-by-the-Bay, blending into metropolitan music for ears
that never tire of its sound.

SAN FRANCISCANA   Smack in the heart of concrete-hard, neon-
bright Broadway in North Beach stands the gentle church known
as Our Lady of Guadelupe—the scene of one of the most colorful
ceremonies of the December season . . . It all starts at 4 A.M., on
the anniversary of the apparition of the virgin Guadelupe. Silence
has fallen over the long, dark street, and the bars and restaurants
have closed. Then, quietly, the musicians from the district's Mexican
night spots gather in the courtyard—and, led by Trumpeter Pedro
Noriega, blast out suddenly with the pulsing strains of "La Maca-
rena," the traditional entrance music of the bullfighters . . . The
sleepy Italian neighbors open their windows and lean on the sills
to watch and applaud. And the devout, who come from as far away
as Fresno and Stockton, walk slowly into the church, lighting the
night with flaming candles . . . Then, after the singing of many
hymns, the services begin, in this Mexican church in the heart of
North Beach, under the direction of—Father Charles Murphy.

OF HUMAN INTEREST   Most of the motorists who drive to work
through Golden Gate Park knew "Slow Motion." He was a cautious
old squirrel with a white spot on his nose, and he lived near the
Nineteenth Avenue–Lincoln Way entrance to the Park.

"Slow Motion" was well aware of the perils of the machine age.
That's why he lived so long, and that's how he got his nickname—
by the slow, wise way he crossed the busy Nineteenth Avenue road
through the Park, looking first to the right, then to the left, always
giving automobiles the right of way, and then darting across.

Most of the time you'd see "Slow Motion" sitting on a bench, alongside somebody with a bag of peanuts. He'd even let you pat him on the head, but first you had to feed him a peanut. It seemed to be his rule—no peanut, no pat. "Slow Motion" knew his way around.

But don't look for "Slow Motion" when you drive through the Lincoln Way portals these days. One awful night, a big wind whistled through the trees of Golden Gate Park. A branch crashed down—and when they picked it up, they found "Slow Motion" underneath, crushed to death. Nature had finally caught up with the wise old squirrel who had learned how to live in the world of men and machines.

BAGHDAD-BY-THE-BAY   The Southward-setting sun, lighting up the soaring towers of the Golden Great Bridge like twin strips of neon . . . The metropolitan magic of Third and Townsend at dusk, when a pall of drifting black smoke hangs over the busy, dizzy scene of scurrying commuters, zig-zaggravating taxis, lumbering busses—and, in the half-lighted background, the squat, hunch-backed bulk of the bridge across Channel Street . . . The shadowy figures that float at midnight through the back alleys of China-town—mysterious men with their hats pulled low, their coat collars turned up, their hands plunged deep in pockets; in the daylight you don't look twice at them, but in the quiet gloom they set fire to your imagination and your mind races back crazily to the nights of tong warfare in Old Chinatown, and the smell of death in musty doorways . . . The sparkling crown jewels of the Marina—the night lights of the ships riding at anchor, in quarantine, off Yacht Harbor, their great hulks barely silhouetted in the soft glow.

TINY TRADITIONS   Trying to flip your cigarette butt into a cable car slot . . . Borrowing your gal's lipstick and painting the toenails on Ralph Stackpole's huge statues in front of the Stock Exchange . . . Sucking in your breath as you drive along Pacific between Stockton and Kearny—so narrow that your fenders have to pull up their skirts to squeeze past the parked cars . . . Sitting outside on the Telegraph Hill steps while waiting for your table at The Shadows . . . Dropping in at India House for a drink—where, with Host David Brown behind the bar, and everybody knowing everybody else, the atmosphere is always cocktail-partyish . . . Rushing to meet someone under the famed clock in the St. Francis lobby, and asking foolishly: "Hope I'm not too late—what time is it, anyway?" . . . Listening to an old-timer report wisely: "Y'know, the old town isn't what it used to be," and countering triumphantly with the late Will Irwin's gambit: "No, and it never was" . . . Riding on the outside step of a Powell cable, because it's the manly thing to do; and because you might reach your destination before the conductor gets around to collect your fare.

BREATHLESS MOMENT   San Francisco, viewed under glass from Top o' the Mark one September night at 7:10 was at its spectacular best—so overwhelmingly beautiful that a hush fell over the crowded room and people crowded silently against the windows to drink in the glamorama . . . Exactly 7:10—and out in the Pacific, the fiery sun slipped with incredible swiftness behind a filmy curtain of far-off clouds—and out of the East Bay hills rose a white full moon, pale and wanderful . . . Not a ripple broke the ageless face of the Bay, and across its surface rode a tug pulling a barge, leaving a wake so long and straight that it seemed to be etched forever in stone . . . Behind the Ferry Building, dressed up in its holiday lights of red, white, and blue, rose a smoky plume from an idling ferryboat—and not a zephyr disturbed the still air to blow it away . . . As the golden day died slowly before your eyes, the lights came on in rhythmic twinkles that turned every street into a river of stop-and-glow lights; a white flood washed up over Coit Tower—and Telegraph Hill all at once loomed dark and lumpy, as though somebody had stood back and pelted it with houses . . . Then the moon was full up, throwing a million gallons of cream over the black waters under the Bay Bridge . . . It was now 7:15—five minutes had stretched into infinity—and slowly the people who had seen almost more than their eyes could bear walked away from the windows and back to their seats. All of a sudden, a drink seemed awfully flat.

LITTLE LANDMARKS   Old South Park, the restful rectangle tucked away neatly behind the sagging houses and blunt ware-houses of lower Third Street, an evergreen sentimemento of the era when that drab neighborhood was nobbier than Nob Hill . . . The "lost" International Settlement on Mission near Twentieth: Spanish, Italian, and Mexican beaneries and All-American hamburger jernts, clustered together in a powerful nosegay that holds you smellbound . . . The wonderful, natty characters who saunter into the Mont-gomery Street bond emporiums, lounge in the back of the room, and peer at the latest stock quotations through powerful binoculars; the old numbers racket, viewed at a respectable distance . . . The old-timers of Fisherman's Wharf (you can spot them by the birettas on their grizzled heads) who spread their nets on the sidewalk and run their hard fingers nimbly through a maze of knots and meshes, repairing a rip here, a snag there—all the while spouting an endless string of Sicilian dialect; perennially colorful characters—because they don't try to be . . . The garish, brightly lighted supermarkets of the "new" Chinatown, their outward brilliance masking the heart-break that goes on in the dark alleys behind them: bent old ladies from the nearby slums, puttering through the discarded crates in search of fruit, vegetables, anything that the rats haven't got to before them . . . The gay signal flags that flutter from Standard Oil's shiplike service station at Fisherman's Wharf—little pennants that say, in the language of the sea, "Gas" and "Oil" . . . The famed bronze fence around the Pacific-Union Club on Nob Hill ("The Bronze Curtain")—which cost $30,000 to build in the nineties, and would cost $75,000 to duplicate today; in other words, it's worth more than some of the members . . . The old gal who lives at Twenty-sixth and Mission, right above Ferd's News Stand; every morning, she dangles a rope out her window, whereupon Ferd ties her *Examiner* to it—and she yanks it up . . . The Bay Bridge, as glimpsed from the outer reaches of Bush Street, looking like nothing more than a runway between the gasoleaning towers of Shell and Standard . . . Spirit of San Francisco: The Plaza Florists on Sutter, with its daily vase of cornflowers out front on the sidewalk, free for the buttonholes of the passing boulevardiers . . . Hidden from the eyes of passers-by at Ninth and Market: a beautiful little garden behind a Chinese restaurant and a market—carefully tended every night by a little crippled man; flowers, a birdhouse, a birdbath, a pigeon roost, all flourishing in this garden that blooms secretly in the hard heart of a city.

DAY ON THE BAY   Sunday's "opening day" for Baghdad's fleet of yachts—a memorable mélange of white sails against blue skies,

pennants fluttering in a spanking breeze, masts and spars silhouetted against a backdrop of skyscrapered hills and checkerboard
streets . . . The preparade massing of the boats in the deep swells
beyond Golden Gate Bridge, with the tiny speedboats darting in
and out like carefree brats, the big cruisers snorting and cluck-
clucking like short-tempered parents, the sailing vessels making the
graceful, feminine sweeps of proper ladies out for a Sunday stroll
. . . The familiar craft in the long line-up: Jimmy Orr's pretty little
job called the *Ugly I;* Arvid Norman's *Extravagance,* flying its
amusing house flag (a dollar sign, with wings); George Olsen's
Why Walk, with its passengers dancing to an accordion; Dan
McLean's square, boxlike *Spoonbill,* built for comfort and laughs
(she even has a piano aboard); Paul Koss's *Pee Kay Too,* its big
twin screws churning up a wake for the others; Henry Doelger's
$250,000 *Westlake,* making some of the other mariners turn green—
and not from mal de mer; Russell Chatard's long, low, steam-driven
Colleen, once the property of the silent screen star, Colleen Moore;
and a hundred others, jammed with bright-eyed youngsters and
hung-over oldsters hoisting highball glasses in the glinting sunlight
. . . Typically San Francisco—this small town of great friends afloat
on their Bay, waving to each other as they pass, smiling in the warm
peace of a Sunday quite unlike any other Sunday in the world
today.

THE CROSS ON MOUNT DAVIDSON   In fitting majesty, it
towers 1038 feet above the Pacific, can be seen fifty miles at sea,
stands in glowing view of two million people, and measures 103 feet
from top to bottom (the original plans called for a cross exactly one
hundred feet high, but there was enough concrete on hand for an

extra three feet—so on it went) . . . This shining beacon of faith
and peace was first lighted in 1934 by President Roosevelt, who
pressed a golden key that shot an impulse all the way from the
White House (in 1936 his WPA workers put in $28,000 worth of
improvements around the cross, and the papers announced happily:
"Women need not be afraid to wear high-heeled shoes on this year's
Easter pilgrimage") . . . Holy peace and quiet haven't always
reigned on Mount Davidson. In 1925, the cross—it was wooden,
then—was destroyed by a fire set by a couple of teen-agers who
confessed: "We just wanted to do something exciting this evening."
In 1933, a temporary wooden cross toppled to the ground in a wind-
storm, after another pair of teen-agers had loosened the supporting
steel cables. And in 1936, five cops staged a shooting and drinking
orgy on the summit—firing twenty-five shots around the place without hitting anybody or anything . . . Through the war-darkened
years of 1941–44, the great cross, largest in the world, stood dark,
too—but in these years of crisis it stands bathed in light, a symbol
of hope in a world that is still struggling up a dark mountainside.

YOU'RE A SAN FRANCISCAN   If one of your secret, never-
ending ambitions is to find a tiny, wonderful restaurant tucked away
at the end of an alley nobody ever heard of—a secret place that
would be "your" restaurant; you never find it, but you never stop
searching . . . If you picture the "typical Montgomery Streeter" as
a tall, dapper, mustachioed gent who wears a Homburg with éclat
and a long overcoat with finesse—but can't find anybody to fit the
description (or the clothes) except Attorney Jerome Politzer, who
is hereby awarded the Politzer Prize . . . If you think nothing of
flipping a dollar tip to the hatcheck girl—but feel like you've hit the

jackpot whenever you park alongside a meter and find thirty free minutes still registered on it . . . If you have a recurrent nightmare that involves zooming down the one-way First Street ramp off the Bay Bridge and—omigosh—finding yourself nose-to-nose with a car coming up the ramp; back, you crazy son-of-a-gun, back . . . If your idea of a perfect day is to visit your braggart friends down the Peninsula ("where the sun always shines") and find that the weather is worse there than in San Francisco; whereupon you can feel nice and smug in your overgloat . . . If you never get stuck behind a Muniserable bus in the Stockton Tunnel without wondering whether it's possible to die, then and there, of gasphyxiation.

HOLIDAY AT HOME   The stark exclamation marks on the city's Fourth of July sky line—the hundreds of flagpoles, standing naked and ashamed on this most banner of week ends . . . The tourists waiting blankly on the Market Street corners for a parade that never came along; and the cops who told them "No July Fourth parade today" had no answer for the question that came hard and fast: "But why?" . . . The empty streetcars rattling through the empty streets of the empty city, getting nowhere in their clattery search for somebody going somewhere . . . Along Third Street, the service-men celebrating their Independence Day by lounging dispiritedly against the dusty windows of padlocked liquor stores or shuffling along with their hands in their pockets, their eyes on the ground, their minds a million years away on the July Fourths of their child-hood . . . Firecrackers exploding here and there in sporadic bursts —a feeble defiance of the statute that robs every small San Francisco boy of his inherent right as a citizen; here, the law can lay its hand on the punk with a punk in his hand . . . The thousands of cars streaming across the bridges—filled with people getting tangled up with each other in their frantic efforts to get away from each other; and coming home, bumper to bumper, nerve against jangled nerve, to the city that yawned and dozed for three days of a long, lost week end.

BAGHDAD-BY-THE-BAY   A tiny tug towing a tired old freighter across the glassy Bay—looking like a dog walking its master . . . Sun-splashed waves breaking gently on the cool sands of China Beach, favorite watering spot of the Frozen Few who know that the February sun is merely bright, not warm—but don't care . . . A helicopter, ungainly as a pelican, toying with the tall towers of the Golden Gate Bridge and then fluttering away in search of a more dangerous game . . . The roller coaster view from the corner of Hyde and Francisco, enough to make your stomach catch its breath . . . The whining sigh of the winches at work in the dead of the night along the Embarcadero—where the ships are lighted as dramatically as a stage set and the shadowy workers suddenly become heroic figures in a tableau that never loses its impact . . . Green bananas in huge bunches, inching along on a conveyor belt into the warehouses of the Produce District—while, in the adjoining alleys, down-and-outers root around among the discarded husks and leaves, their dignity dying in the face of their hunger . . . Colorful old Commercial Street, which has one thing in common with mighty Market; you can look down them both and see the Ferry Building at the end—and no other streets can make that statement . . . The Buddhist Mission on Washington, which was built, slowly and painfully, by a human chain gang of Chinese men and women, passing the bricks from hand to hand in the spirit of the old pioneers . . .

The last of the ferryboats, setting out across the Bay with a proud blast of gray and white smoke—a plume of honor that always inspires a silent salute from those who love Baghdad-by-the-Bay.

SAN FRANCISCANA The waterfront might be just a ghost of its former self, but it's still colorful. For example, Harry Bridges' longshore union had an election recently—and on the ballot, the candidates were listed by their full names, plus their Embarcadero nicknames. Thus we found "Baggy" Bertani, "Cigar" Barlow, "One Round" Hogan, "Sue the Bandit" Lopez, "Punchy" Tristano—and, by the far the best of all, "Rigger" Mordus.

There's no business like Joe business in a building at 1024 Pacific Avenue—where you'll find the offices of Dr. Lawrence Joe, Insurance Broker Martin Joe, and Public Accountant Walter Joe. These are all Chinese Joes. No relation to the Italian, or "Original" Joes.

Ever wonder why the Italian Market on Grant Avenue in Chinatown (operated by Chinese) is called the Italian Market? Wasn't named that in a whim of fitsy, or even a fim of witsy. Before North Beach blossomed out with its own big markets, Italian housewives shopped there regularly—and the Chinese owners tacked on the name in gratitude.

Dick Clark, a young advertising man, rented an apartment in "Little Italy," on the cliff behind New Joe's on Broadway. Anxious to make a good impression, he asked the Italian landlady first thing: "What are the rules of the house?" "Just one," she said sternly. "Sometimes we have parties here. And when we do, don't knock on the ceiling—come up and have a drink with us!" . . . That—is San Francisco.

A prominent New York couple, members of the Du Pont clan,

arrived in town one day, clutching an oldish guidebook that listed
"San Francisco's Leading French Restaurants." Being lovers of la
cuisine française, they started at the top of the list and worked
down. First they went to the St. Germaine, and found that it had
vanished. They went to Camille's and were greeted by an Italian.
They tried the Normandie and discovered that it's owned by an
Irishman. At La Favorite, they found two Spanish brothers in
charge. No Frenchmen were to be seen anywhere at La Buvette—
and they came to the end of the trail at the Paris Louvre, whose
bosses are two Italians and a Czech . . . They should've tried Mac's
Irish Grill. THAT'S owned by a Frenchman.

COLOR OF A CITY   A great gray mob of fog tiptoeing in under
the Golden Gate Bridge and then expanding happily—like kids
who've managed to sneak past the toll collector . . . The now-
classic silhouette of a California Cable, outlined dimly in a midnight
mist; a roller-ghoster whose every trip is a sentimental journey . . .
The impressively metropolitan intersection of Montgomery, Post,
and Market, where the hulking bulks of the Crocker Bank, Wells-
Fargo Bank, and the Crocker Building squat haughtily and turn
their cold shoulders on each other . . . The bright ring of lights
around the bases of the Bay Bridge towers, flickering across the
water like candles on a wedding cake . . . The lush little park on
the triangle at Union, Powell, and Columbus, with its big stone
bench and its high iron fence—a never-deserted island in a whirling
sea of traffic . . . The "raccoon man" who sprawls out in the sun
every day on the green northern slope of Telegraph Hill—dozing
away the hours while his pet raccoon dances around on the end of
a leash . . . A gay little carnival nestling on a North Beach corner,

in the shadow of the mighty twin spires of Saints Peter and Paul—
so aloof, so lost in the clouds above the tiny Ferris wheel . . . The
Alcatraz searchlight, shooting out its cold, rhythmic rays, each
flicker lighting up that stationary ship filled with men who aren't
going anywhere . . . Baghdad-by-the-Bay!

Well, I Liked 'Em   A columnist, if he is burning feverishly with the ambition to be widely read, soon learns to sublimate his own tastes to those of what he grandiosely terms "my great, average reading public, bless'm."

Translated a little less coyly, this means simply that he doesn't print everything that he, personally, thinks is a good or funny story. If he is endowed with even a smidge of intelligence—if he had more, he'd be out doing a man's work—he stops and thinks along these lines:

"This is indeed a grand little story, but will it appeal to Mrs. Zilch, who lives on Thirty-eighth Avenue in the Sunset District and leads a very sheltered existence?" Or he says to himself: "This story made me scream, but when I told it to Henry Falsetti, the average bartender, he just looked at me and said, 'Duuuuuh?'"

By weighing every item on the wide, insensitive scales of mediocrity, he manages to satisfy everyone, in a pale sort of way, while enthralling practically no one. And so, every now and then, he mutters to himself "T'heck with Mrs. Zilch and a pox on Mr. Falsetti" and prints a story for which he takes full responsibility. He happened to like it for itself, and, for the nonce, that was enough.

Here, then, are a few of the items that I printed without wondering who, if anyone, they'd appeal to. As I was saying, *I* liked 'em.

CONVERSATION PIECE   "Scotty" MacDuckston, owner of two San Francisco drive-ins, took his wife to see a play at the Curran Theater—and during the intermission, they stepped out to the side-walk for a whiff of air. While they were standing there, a curvy young doll, wearing an ultratight sweater, walked by, whereupon "Scotty" stared after her, whistled, and then asked his annoyed wife: "Y'think those are real?" Iced Mrs. MacDuckston: "Who'd buy 'em so small?"

On another occasion, Mr. and Mrs. MacDuckston were at the 365 Club, minding everybody's business, when over walked a Peninsula woman who proceeded to introduce her fourth husband. Gushed she to Mrs. MacDuckston: "Jo, I hope you and my wonderful new man get along just fine." "Of course we will, dolling," knifed Jo. "Any husband of yours is a friend of mine."

OF HUMAN INTEREST   Garfield Light and Otho Gardner, window washers with Crosetti Bros., were scrubbing the Market Street windows of Hale Bros. one afternoon. When they finished, they had a nice idea. They walked over to the little wood-and-glass sidewalk stand where Tony Barrett, the ancient "Lavender Man," has been peddling his sweet-smelling wares for countless years.

Carefully, Light and Gardner washed and polished the glass windbreak on Barrett's stand. "Now then"—they smiled as they left —"now you can see better."

"Thanks, thanks so much," murmured Tony Barrett, who is totally blind.

POINT OF VIEW   The racetrack characters who gather each 10 A.M. in John's Grill for their daily coffee-and-gabfests come up with some wondrous conversations—like, for instance, this.

Said one heavy bettor to another: "Say, Joe, I guess you noticed that that horse you gave me yesterday didn't come in"—whereupon a third hossplayer, name of Dave, cut in: "Joe, you give him a horse you didn't give ME?"

"Look, you heard what the man said," snapped Joe. "The horse didn't come in."

"I know, I know," said Dave reproachfully, "but Joe, we been friends a long time. You shoulda give it to me, too."

THE GALLANT   If you haven't seen William Saroyan lately, you might like to know that San Francisco's Pulitzer Prize–winning playwright and tireless novelist has grown the biggest, blackest mustache I've ever seen in all my bored days; makes him look like a cross between Groucho Marx and an Italian fruit peddler.

So one day, Saroyan was walking down Market Street when suddenly an old biddy caught up with him, fell into step, and kept peering at his face. At last she burst out: "Bill Saroyan! Y'know, for a minute I didn't recognize you with that mustache."

"Madam," said Saroyan gallantly, "I regret to say that I don't recognize you—without yours."

SHORTSNORT   This goes back to the time when Melvin Purvis, the famed ex–G man who killed Dillinger, was living in an apartment

on Telegraph Hill. He was a great one for avoiding social commit-
ments—hated cocktail parties more than gangsters—but one night a
determined hostess succeeded in luring him to one of her gather-
ings. Everything went reasonably well, except that the hostess got
a little flustered at having the great Melvin Purvis as her guest of
honor. "Attention, everybody," she cried out as he entered her salon.
"I want you all to meet Mervin Pelvis!"

QUOTE   Winston Norman, the widely known Montgomery
Streeter, got his annual stack of three hundred Christmas cards from
the printer last Yuletide season. With a sigh, he dug out the list of
his friends' names and addresses, got the stamps ready for sticking,
went to work on the first card—and then, suddenly swept the whole
shebang into the wastebasket with an exasperated gesture. "The
heck with it," said Norman firmly. "I'm not going to let Christmas
spoil my Christmas this year!"

INSIDE STORY   In search of the elusive item, I was walking
down Third Street one night—and bumped into an old friend who
plays the ponies pretty heavily. "Say," I asked him, "where can a
guy place a bet on a horse around here?" After looking this way
and that, he whispered: "In that restaurant right across the street—
and let me give you a tip." "Yeah?" I answered eagerly. "Don't eat
the food," he said. "It's terrible."

TOUGH GUY DEPT.   Lloyd Sampsell, the notorious "yacht bandit" and killer, was executed in April, 1952, at San Quentin—seventeen years after his partner in crime, Ethan McNab, died on the
gallows there. McNab, not as adroit at blocking justice as Sampsell,

was defended by Attorney Billy Southwell, who complained, shortly after the execution, that he hadn't been paid for his services. Southwell still has the letter McNab wrote him in reply to his plea for a fee: "Dear Mr. Southwell: I understand it is quite a jolting experience to be hung. The jar will probably knock my fillings loose. These you may have, in payment of the fee. So long. (Signed) Ethan McNab."

THE CHAMP   Edward "Bozo" Miller, the Oakland behemoth (three hundred pounds of dynamite) has a favorite indoor sport. Eating contests are his meat, and he is still undefeated, untied and unbelievable. His most recent challenger was an Oakland trencherman who bet him a big chunk that he could outeat "Bozo" in any language, especially Italian. Bozo accepted, and they started off with minestrone. After Bozo had downed his seventeenth bowl of soup and was ready to start on his eighteenth, the challenger threw in his spoon. "I quit, Bozo," he groaned, paying off. "Let's get out of here."

"Oh no," said Mr. Miller, summoning the waiter. "Not until I finish my dinner."

CHARACTER SKETCH   Perhaps the most Lincolnesque figure in town is tall, gaunt Judge Julian Goodell of the District Court of Appeal. He looks like Lincoln. He talks like Lincoln. He quotes Lincoln at length. He presides over occasional Lincoln Day activities at the Bohemian Club. And whenever someone is needed to play the role of Lincoln in a Club play, Judge Goodell naturally gets the call.

Some of the Bohemians were discussing this Lincoln-fixation one day—and Federal Judge Edward P. Murphy put the capper on the conversation. "Y'know," he said, "I don't think Julian will ever be completely happy until he's been assassinated."

QUESTION   You know how it is with professional comedians. People expect everything they say to be a howl, a yak, a gasser. So. So Morey Amsterdam, the ex–San Franciscan who's now a leading TV funnyman, ran into a friend on the street—and the friend said cleverly: "Hiya, Morey, how ya feelin'?"

"Not so good," said Morey. "Tired. Smatterofack, I've been thinking about going into the hospital for a week."

The friend thought hard for a second and then said sharply: "What's so funny about THAT?"

DIRECTIONS   In Alameda Naval Air Station's PX, a young sailor was wandering around, all alonely-like. Then, at last, in walked the traditional Beautiful Blonde. After staring at her for a few seconds, the sailor sidled over to her and ventured: "Uh, pardon me, miss, but I'm a stranger in town. Could you direct me to your house?"

LADIES' DAY   Ah, what is so inspiring, in its way, as the clear, cold logic of a woman? As, for instance:

Two matrons started to jaywalk across Stockton Street between the City of Paris and Macy's. A cop, seated in a nearby patrol car equipped with a microphone, said pleasantly over the loudspeaker: "Ladies, if you're from out of town, I'd like to tell you that it's against the law to cross in the middle of the block. Please go back and cross at the intersection."

The two ladies stopped dead in the middle of the street. Then one shook her finger angrily at the cop and rasped:

"I'll bet we've lived here longer than YOU have!"

THE PEARL   Tom Rickey, the big pottery man, has lunched on 10 oysters every Friday in the Clift's Redwood Room for the past 10 years—and, as he complained to the headwaiter one day, he has never found a poil in all those ersters. So, the waiter found a big, phony pearl and placed it in one of Rickey's oysters. Then the whole staff hid behind pillars and posts to watch the proceedings.

When Rickey came to the pearl, he laid down his fork, looked around surreptitiously, and then popped it into his pocket without a word!

SHORT AND SWEET   One of the witnesses during a recent Grand Jury investigation of Attorney Jim McInnis was his ex-secretary, Doris Purdy—who was asked by Assistant U. S. Attorney Joe Karesh: "Do you like Mr. McInnis?"

"Well," answered Doris, "I do and I don't."

"Aha," snapped Karesh, "and what DON'T you like about him?"

"His conceit," said Doris. "He's conceited about his looks."

"And what DO you like about him?" continued Karesh.

"His looks," said Doris.

BAGHDAD BAGATELLE   The waitress in the St. Francis Grill leaned over and whispered into Capitalist Herbert Fleishhacker's ear. "Would you mind giving me your room number?" she asked, her pencil poised over the luncheon tab he had just signed. Fleishhacker, who has lived in the St. Francis since 1908, was mildly surprised. But she was a new girl and it was her first day on the job. "My dear," gently smiled the eighty-year-old financier, "I don't think Mrs. Fleishhacker would like it—you give me yours!"

NATURE'S CALL   When Skipper Kent owned the Zombie Village in Oakland, he had a shrunken head on display. He took it with him when he opened his new restaurant in San Francisco. A few nights later, a sailor walked up to the Zombie Village's new owner, Mrs. William Hislop, and asked the usual sailor question: "Where's the head?" Answered Mrs. Hislop: "Skipper Kent took it with him to San Francisco." "Oh," said the slightly baffled sailor. "Well—uh— is there a service station near by?"

EAST BAY BAGATELLE   What happened to my friend Homer over in Oakland shouldn't happen to a dog—and it didn't. It happened to Homer.

He went across the Bay to meet a friend (male) in a bar. When he got there, what ho, the friend had two gals on his hands. After they'd had a couple of dull drinks, one of the girls said to my friend Homer: "Wouldja mind driving me home? I live in Alameda."

"O.K.," shrugged Homer, who couldn't care less. "Let's go."

As they drove into the Posey Tube toward Alameda, Homer glanced into the rear-view mirror and noticed a car pull out of a side street and get on his tail. In Alameda, the strange car stuck right with him, no matter which way he turned.

"Y'know," Homer said nervously, licking his lips, "I think we're being followed."

"Well," shrugged the girl, "I don't know who it could be—except maybe my husband."

"Yiiiipe!" yelled Homer, stepping on the gas and slapping himself on his dunderhead. Careening through red lights, sideslipping around corners, darting down alleys, our boy finally managed to lose the following car. Then he dumped the gal unceremoniously in front of her house and sped back toward Oakland.

As he neared the Tube again, he glanced back and found a pair of strange headlights on his trail again. Gritting his teeth so hard he sounded like a Waring mixer, Homer raced through the Tube and roared into Oakland, still being followed. Desperately, he zoomed into an alley and—zounds—dead end! Homer screeched to a stop against the wall, and the other car slid to a halt right behind him.

"Well, he's got me now," sighed Homer, getting out of the car and preparing to face her irate husband. Instead, out of the other car stepped a boiling traffic cop, who snapped: "You always drive like that?"

Almost fainting in relief, Homer blubbered: "Sorry—didn't hear your siren."

"Can't blow sirens in residential districts," said the cop. "I suppose you didn't see my red light?"

"What red light?" asked Homer. The cop got a funny look on his pan and walked back to his spotlight. He clicked it a few times. Yup. Out of order.

There was a moment's strange silence, and then the cop walked over and put his arm around Homer's shoulder.

"Whaddya say we go have a cup of coffee," he suggested.

HOMECOMING   A wounded Air Force sergeant from Korea, hobbling on crutches, dragged himself aboard a jam-packed No. 45

bus on Sutter Street. None of the men aboard made a move to help him, so McCann-Erickson's Isabel Brindley got up, took his arm and smiled, "Here, Sergeant, please take my seat."

The sergeant squared his shoulders, shook his head and gently shoved her back into her seat. "Thanks, lady," he said proudly, "this is the first time I've had a chance to be a gentleman since I got back!"

SCENE   A traffic copper, mounted on his dashing little tricycle, took the corner at Geary and Taylor just a little too fast one day, and thereby provided the sightem-of-the-week. His three-wheeler bike tipped over. He was thrown to the ground. And—oops—out of the box on the back of his vehicle tumbled a case of beer!

COMEDY OF ERRORS   Harrison "Bid" Bidwell of San Anselmo, who works for Standard Oil in San Francisco, was riding to town aboard a Greyhound bus, reading his morning *Examiner* and minding his own business. But not for long.

The woman sitting next to him put a cigarette in her mouth and began fumbling with her lighter. It wouldn't work. So "Bid" gallantly whipped out his lighter and lit her cigarette. He also lit something else—the veil on her hat.

As the flames flared around her face, Bidwell flung himself into desperate action. He snatched the hat off the gent in front of him and began beating her furiously over the head to smother the flames. The gent in front yelled "Hey—what's the idea!" and reached for his hat.

Well, this commotion awakened a guy who'd been dozing across the aisle—and it didn't take him long to size up the situation. Here, obviously, was a maniac attacking a woman with a hat. So he leaped across the aisle, grabbed Bidwell, and hurled him to the floor of the bus.

Now things were really rolling. A woman passenger, seated near by, decided she'd seen enough, so she grabbed for the emergency door handle. The bus driver, 'way up front, figured there really WAS an emergency, and slammed on the brakes. Two cars promptly smashed into the rear of the bus.

The saddest wail of all came from the young woman whose veil had been set on fire. With her eyebrows and lashes singed all to heck, all she could do was moan over and over: "What'll I tell my husband? He TOLD me not to smoke while I was wearing a veil!"

PURELY PERSONAL   For reasons that escape and annoy me, people have confused me for years with Ira Blue, a funny-looking duck who makes a doubtful living on TV and radio. Shucks, I'm a much handsomer feller than this Blue, as any old fool can plainly see, and I can—but now I wonder. One recent night, Ira wandered into the Mark's lower bar, and was promptly felled by one blow from the fist of a gent who snarled in cultured tones: "That'll learn you to write things about my wife!"

I'm very flattered that some people think I bear a striking resemblance to Ira Blue, handsome, attractive, brilliant young star of radio and TV. He'll go far, that boy, but if he does, I'm going with him. Right behind him, in fact.

PERSPECTIVE   Dong Kingman, the San Francisco Chinese artist whose water colors have won him international acclaim, lunched at the Palace Hotel with his sister, Esther Fong, a recent arrival from

Hong Kong. "Is your brother famous in China?" she was asked by Photographer George Shimmon. "Well, let me put it this way," answered Mrs. Fong. "Over there, they know that he's famous over here!"

ONE MAN'S FAMILY   Spring has come to little San Carlos, down the Peninsula. The soft, rolling hills are brightly green, and the big oak trees are beginning to lose their winter bareness . . .

Harrison Alper, thirty-three, who lives in the White Oaks section of San Carlos, arose early. He opened the bedroom window and sniffed the morning freshness appreciatively, and he noticed that the rose bushes in his garden were sprouting leaves.

Then he tiptoed into the next bedroom, where his three daughters —Pat, eight, Lynn, five, and Liz, three—were still asleep. Quietly he sat down and stared for long minutes at their faces, as though memorizing every feature.

After that, he was ready. "Let's go," he said to his wife, Miriam. They walked slowly out to the car and drove to Green's Hospital in San Francisco—where his left eye was removed. He had lost his right eye a year before, after thirty-five futile operations to stem an infection.

These spring days in San Carlos, Harrison Alper is going on with life as usual. He still attends his Lions Club meetings. And every day he goes to work at his successful sportswear shop, where he is learning to read the price tags in Braille. And his wife, Miriam, is able to muster a half-smile as she says: "At least, he won't have to have any more operations" . . .

BIG NAMES   One of San Francisco's Great Stories in 1951 concerned the marriage of Robert Gump, scion of one of the city's most cultured and respected families, to Sally Stanford, who won her doubtful reputation as a keeper of plush houses of ill fame.

Which is why I almost exploded with laughter when I overheard this conversation between two tourist ladies in Gump's world-famed store one afternoon:

First lady: "You say the Gump family is quite important here?"

Second: "Oh, quite. Why, one of them recently married into the Stanford clan!"

Joe   Joe Jones (we'll call him that) will be happy to know that
a lot of young-oldish San Franciscans haven't forgotten him—for Joe
couldn't stand to be forgotten, completely.

In his own way, the way of an era that has vanished like Atlantis,
Joe was memorable. He was tough, hard, and flashy, in a manner
that kindly biographers like to remember as "colorful." The following incident might inspire you to think of a more accurate
adjective:

Among his other activities, Joe had a few girls working for him.
One afternoon, he was making the rounds of the houses, collecting
his share of the proceeds from the night before, and grumbling
about the size of the take.

"Lazy, that's what they are," he spat as he walked up the sleazy
stairs of a Columbus Avenue "hotel." "Just a lazy buncha dames."

At the top of the stairs, a tired blonde was waiting for him, a
thin blue wrapper drawn tight around her skinny body.

"How much ya got for me?" asked Joe.

"Thirty-six dollars, honey," she said, handing over a roll of
bills.

"Thirty-six lousy bucks," he snapped disgustedly, stuffing them into his pocket. "Why, I oughta——" And he pulled back his right arm in a threatening gesture.

As he started to walk down the stairs, she clutched at his well-padded shoulder. "Joe," she whimpered. "Joe honey, I saw the cutest dress in a store on Market Street yesterday. You know how I need a dress. And it's only eighteen dollars. Willya give me the eighteen?"

"Colorful" Joe Jones stood stock still on a step, his hands on his hips, his eyes flickering with contempt and disbelief. "Eighteen dollars!" he exploded at the quaking prostitute. "Do you think I'm MADE of money?"

And he turned on his heel and stomped out, shaking his head over the incredible gall of the woman.

In the days when Gus Oliva, an extraordinary politician, was riding high in the San Francisco saddle, Joe Jones was his "fix," his boy-about-town, the guy to see if you wanted Something Done.

Joe made a lot of money and spent a lot of money—mainly on himself. He wore the sharpest clothes in town (one night, in the St. Francis, he saw a man wearing a suit like his, whereupon he stalked out, changed his clothes, and gave the offending suit to a surprised bellhop). And he held court every morning in John's Grill on Ellis Street, where he had a barber come in daily to singe his hair.

"Nobody's ever gonna catch ME looking like I just had a haircut," he'd boast, while his cronies would look on and beam approvingly.

But Joe Jones, the man with 30 suits in his closet and 30 dames on the string, was bound to get into trouble sooner or later. The reckoning came later than the law would have liked, but they finally landed him on something or other and shipped him off to Leavenworth Federal Penitentiary.

On his first day in prison, he went to the barbershop. "Just a singe around the edges," he told the barber loftily. The barber blinked incredulously, and then grabbed the clippers and ran them across the top of the new prisoner's head. White-faced, Jones leaped out of the chair and floored the barber. For that, he spent his first thirty days in solitary.

Old Gus Oliva, who has fallen on evil days, too, might like to know that Joe Jones, His Boy from the halcyon days, is back in San Francisco for the first time in a long time.

He still has a touch of class, visible through his stubble of beard and his tattered, slept-in clothes. And now and then, he wanders around to the old tailor shops where he spent so much money on himself once upon a time. Only now, he isn't after a suit with hand-picked edges.

All he asks for is a handout.

"You remember me—Joe Jones," he says with a crooked smile.

And some of them—the ones with the kindly memories of a "colorful" guy—do remember him. Unlike a certain Joe Jones, they don't spread their arms and demand heatedly: "Do you think I'm MADE of money?"

Pop (Lucien Caen, June 25, 1877–June 6, 1950)   There was nothing very remarkable about the way he died—in the transparent solitude of an oxygen tent late one Monday night in Sacramento's Sutter Hospital. And, if you look at it in the light of significant things, there was nothing very remarkable about the way he lived, either. And yet, as any one who knew him will tell you, he was a pretty remarkable guy. He could laugh—and he did, right down to the very end. He could make jokes—pretty bad ones, sometimes— and he was straining for the bright crack at a time when everything he did was a strain that finally got too intense. Even the young nurse on the night shift at the hospital knew he was something sort of special.

"We try to smile at all the patients," she said quietly, "but not very many of them try to smile back. He did."

I guess there's no reason, really, why I should try to load you with words about my father. He lived almost seventy-three long years and he worked hard during most of them and got by financially and then he died. He leaves a widow for whom life will never be the same, and two children who loved him for the delightful man he was.

That's one way of summing up the life of a person whom the dispassionate observer would describe, quite accurately, as "an average American." But that's what makes him an item. That's the gimmick. For the story of my father—the average American statistic of 1950—is the story of millions who never imagined that their lives would lead them into the pattern that ends with peaceful death in a peaceful American city.

And the great thing about these millions of Americans is that they fit so well into the pattern. They become a snug part of a new world. And they make such an imprint that when they die, they are missed, and their communities are less, and acquaintances walk up to you on the main street and say as they grab your hand:

"Your old man was a great guy. Why, I knew him for forty years, I guess. Won't seem quite the same, not seein' him around any more."

My father was born in Alsace-Lorraine when that stormy strip of land was under the German flag, but he always considered himself a Frenchman. (I guess he read every book ever written about Napoleon—and he thought Bonaparte was a pretty good operator until a general named Patton began whipping his tanks like race horses across France. From then on, he was strictly a Patton man.)

He came to the United States in the early 1890's, and, being a Frenchman, he headed for San Francisco. He got here like a typical greenhorn from the old country, too. A travel agent, or what corresponded to one, succeeded in convincing him that the only direct route from New York to San Francisco was via Canada.

But in spite of the grand circle tour that took most of the money, he fell in love with San Francisco. That was always "his" city. He knew the Poodle Dog and Techau's and Newman's and the old

Palace. He loved the rollicking ritual of lunch at Herbert's bachelor grill and a matinee at the Orpheum. And he always had a bag of peanuts in his pocket for the squirrels in Golden Gate Park—the squirrels that somehow don't seem to be quite as friendly and tame as they were in the days when everything was a little friendlier and a little tamer.

Not that my Pop had money to burn. Far from it. His first steady job was on the road as a whisky salesman, in the days when "the road" was a tortuous, winding thing that you covered in dusty old trains and jolting buggies rattling through mountains and deserts to villages that couldn't have been worth all the trouble.

But I guess they were. He "made" them all, and forever after, when he'd be introduced to somebody from Maricopa or Cupertino, he'd settle back, puff on his cigar, and twinkle: "Oh, sure, know your town well. Covered it back in '04, or maybe it was '05. Jake Meyers still running the saloon there?"

And he'd be surprised, and a little saddened, to find out that Jake and his saloon were long gone, and that the streets were now paved, and the old boardinghouse replaced by a motel.

A few sentences ago I referred to my father as "Pop." You know how that is, I guess. Some fathers are "Father," and a few are "Pater" and a very few are "Sir" or "Governor," and a lot are "Dad." And then there are the ones you wouldn't think of calling anything but "Pop."

He seemed to fit the name, and vice versa. A big, easygoing baldheaded guy with a fair-to-middling midriff and an expansive walk. You know "Pop." Sometimes he forgets and lets the cigar ashes dribble onto his vest. His tie usually looks like he tied it blindfolded. You send him to the corner grocery for a loaf of bread and he comes back with a quart of milk.

But he doesn't forget your favorite candy bar. And he surprises you with your first baseball mitt. And when you want a quarter to go to the movie, he slips you four bits and whispers: "Don't tell your mother."

That's "Pop." Anybody's Pop.

There was the time I wanted a new baseball uniform. It was beautiful and it had orange and black stockings and I'd never grow up to be another Babe Ruth or George Sisler without it. I think it cost about seventeen dollars. And I sneaked down to Pop's office— he was in business in Sacramento then—and poured out my story. He seemed to be only half-listening because he was engrossed in the front page of a newspaper, but suddenly he reached into his pocket and counted out the money.

I remembered later that the month was October and the year was 1929 and the headlines said something about a stock-market crash. There were days after that when the seventeen dollars I was wearing on the corner baseball diamond would have been useful for something more important. Food, for instance.

Well, I won't bother you with more. It's just that I'm proud of the man who came from Alsace-Lorraine to a wide circle of warm, grieving friends in Sacramento. Right now I'm thinking of Father's Day—and if he were still around and I could ask him what he'd like as a gift, he'd still say:

"Aw, don't be silly. I don't need anything."

And he doesn't.

Down the Old Skid Road

Skid Road. It has a smell all its own. Of poverty and dirt, of cheap wine and disinfectant, of frying grease and coffee that has been boiled twice too often.

It has a look all its own. Of pawnshops and saloons, of employment agencies and flophouses, of dusty windows and dark alleys, of neon signs that sputter and flicker and look like they're about to go out.

It has a population all its own. Of hollow-eyed old men who talk of the better days they once knew, of blowzy old women who sigh for the better nights they never knew, of sauntering cops who aren't half as tough as they try to look, of neat old pensioners who have never lived anywhere but on a Skid Road because they feel at home —and slightly superior—in the atmosphere.

San Francisco's Skid Road has all these things, and more, in its dozen or so blocks just South of Market and between, roughly, Second and Seventh Streets. It has all the traditional trimmings—drunks in the gutters, grifters lounging in doorways, half-starved dogs sniffing around garbage cans, and, at regular intervals, Outraged Public Officials who cry out: "This Skid Road is a disgrace to the City and County of San Francisco, and Something Must Be Done About It."

But nothing is ever done about it. Like the common cold, there will always be a Skid Road. If only because misery loves plenty of company.

The people come and go on Skid Road—looking alike, talking alike, smelling alike—but the legends remain. Of Spud Murphy, in and out of jail all the time, and the toughest guy on the Road before he got old. Of Tom Sharkey, the prizefighter who fought all the great ones when they had great ones, and who lived for years in a Skid Road hotel, and worked at odd jobs. Of Nellie Richardson, who ran the Denver House for years and who treated everyone so sympathetically that she is known as "The Great Lady of Skid Road." Of the "Thieves' Market" that flourishes along the sidewalks, with the peddlers shouting their wares in whispers, offering the passer-by everything from a "hot" pair of false teeth to a packet of razor blades.

And now and then, along the Road, they sing the legend of "Tough Tessie." Even the cops around the Southern Station, Skid Road's own, talk of her when the nights are slow and the memories are long.

"Tough Tessie" was a prostitute back in the 1920s. She was big and strong and she could fight like a man. And the men she liked to fight best were cops. They came to respect her, in the grudging way that one heavyweight respects another. After the first few tries, the cops gave up trying to arrest her. It wasn't worth the trouble, and the wear and tear on uniforms.

Tessie loved men's money, but she hated men. She climaxed many a business relationship by picking up her customer—naked—and throwing him down the stairs into the street, where he was certain to be arrested. One guy who made the mistake of trying to avoid payment was beaten so badly that he probably was never the same. At the risk of sounding ungallant, I would like to say that Tessie waren't no lady.

She loved street fights. One night, at Third and Howard, she was busily engaged in a brawl with two cops who were trying to arrest her. Along came a Catholic priest who stared aghast at the scene for a moment, and then threw himself into the middle of the melee, roaring at the officers:

"Take your hands off this woman!"

Tessie stopped swinging for a second, shouted "You stay out of this, Father!" gave him a shove that sent him sprawling, and resumed the battle.

One night in Southern Station, the cops were talking about Tessie, and a rookie, kibitzing, sneered: "Aw, she ain't so tough. I'll catch her and bring her in myself." The desk sergeant phoned a warning to Tessie. But an hour later, the rookie returned with her, and the description of his entrance will live forever in the annals of Southern.

There were great red gashes on his cheeks, and his eyes were puffed. His uniform hung in shreds, his gun was missing, his star was gone—but he had Tessie. Naked. And draped over his shoulder.

He tossed her to the ground in front of the desk sergeant and grunted weakly: "See, she ain't so tough." And then he slumped to the floor, alongside Tough Tessie, in a dead faint.

As I said earlier, the cops who patrol the Skid Road beat aren't as hardhearted as they pretend to be.

Two of the best are a couple of wise old-timers named Red Moriarity and Gene Clancy. They have the judgment that comes from years of pounding the hardest stretch of sidewalk in San Francisco. They know who to run in, who to shove aside, and who to lend a helping hand to. But even they make mistakes once in a while.

One night, Red and Gene arrested a drunk on Howard Street, and the next morning in court, the Skid Rowgue wailed to the judge, Eustace Cullinan: "It's all Red Moriarity's fault, Yer Honor. If he hadn't give me four bits yesterday morning, this would never have happened to me!"

On another occasion, Red was a little tougher. After warning a panhandler repeatedly to stop breaking the law against mooching on the streets, he ran him in. And in court he testified with a sad shake of his Irish head:

"Judge, I hated to do this, but I've told him time and again to cut it out. So I finally had to arrest him, that's all."

"You heard what Officer Moriarity said," Judge Cullinan snapped at the culprit. "He has given you a lot of breaks—and I'm going to give you one more. I'm dismissing the charge this time, but the next time, it's jail for you."

Mumbling his thanks, the panhandler scuttled out of the Hall of Justice.

Later that evening, as Judge Cullinan was leaving for home, the same panhandler accosted him.

"I know this might mean jail for me, Judge," he said sadly, "but I haven't got a nickel, and I'm getting desperate."

Judge Cullinan looked up and down Kearny Street. Then he reached into his pocket and pulled out a fifty-cent piece.

"Here," he said in a conspiratorial tone, putting the four-bitter in the panhandler's palm. "Just do me one favor. Don't tell Officer Moriarity!"

Another Skid Rowgue who makes regular appearances at the Hall of Justice is a gent known as "The Lonesome Swede," a solitary individual who apparently never meets anyone except officers who arrest him for various petty offenses.

One day he made one of his many official visits to Judge Leo Cunningham's courtroom, and the judge looked down at him with some irritation. "Look, Swede," he rasped, "how many times have you been before me this month?"

The Swede shrugged his shoulders with magnificent unconcern.

"Ay don' know, Y'r Honor," he said, "Ay t'ought YOU been keepin' score!"

Ah yes, the characters . . .

There's "Hemstitch Nettie," the Road's most widely self-advertised dopehead, who cackles that she's so full of holes (from the hypo needle) that she never goes swimming "because I'd sink." And the double-buddies whose nicknames are "Left" and "Right"—because one has his left leg off, and the other his right; one reason for their close friendship: their remaining feet are the same size, and they can buy one pair of shoes between them. And the girl known simply and colorfully as "Maybe Hey Bernice," whose conversational gambits are limited to "Buy me a drink, maybe hey?" and "Wanna maybe hey walk me home, hey?"

A character called "The Shammy Kid" makes a pretty fair living off the sentimental gentlemen of Skid Road, because he has discovered that most of them—if they're not flat broke—hang on to their watches. Family watches, they are, handed down from their fathers or grandfathers, and they cling to them stubbornly as the last ticking tie with so-called normal life.

So "The Shammy Kid" wanders along Automobile Row on Van Ness Avenue, picking up old chamois skins discarded by the men who wipe off the cars. He takes these back to his little hotel room on Howard Street, and sews them into tiny sacks—which he sells to his customers as protective "pockets" for their ancient timepieces. The last pockets on the Road to be emptied.

Another figure you're likely to run across in the Third and Howard wilderness is called "Velvet Fingers" Joe.

His Mission District family was poor, but Joe had such long, beautiful fingers that his mother decided he had to be a concert pianist. So the family hocked everything to get him a piano and lessons, but it was no use. Joe didn't have it. A flop.

Eventually, he drifted down the scale to Skid Road, where his long, beautiful fingers make him a dangerous living. "Velvet Fingers" Joe is now a pickpocket.

Most of the denizens of the Road know "The Sandwich Couple"— a husband and wife, both white-haired and gentle, maybe sixty or seventy years old. Every other Sunday morning, they show up around Fourth and Howard, each carrying a big shopping bag stuffed with thick, homemade sandwiches. Smiling and friendly, they walk slowly along the sidewalk, passing out the food to the poor and the hungry, and saying "Goot morning!" in rather heavy German accents.

But they won't give their names and they won't tell why they make their little expeditions to the Wrong Side of the Tracks. Only once did the woman drop a small clue. Her eyes looked far across the ocean to a Germany that knew the terror of hate and fear, and she said slowly and tonelessly: "We know what it is like to be hungry."

Among the charter members of the Skid Road Mooching and Chowline Society is a bleary-eyed individual with the wondrous name of "Palm Sunday" Burke.

Brother Burke, who has a wooden leg with an Argyle sock painted neatly around the ankle, sits on the sidewalk near churches. In one hand he clutches a bundle of pencils. The other hand he holds out, palm upward, to passers-by. Tattooed in bright blue letters on the palm are the words "God Bless and Thank You." And if you happen to see an occasional tear in "Palm Sunday's" honest brown eyes, it's because he keeps a chunk of onion concealed in his handkerchief.

One recent Sunday, he'd had time to massage only one eye with the onion when he looked up and found a woman staring sharply at him.

"Why," she asked perceptively, "is only one eye watering, my good man?"

"Palm Sunday" Burke thought fast.

"Dear lady," he explained politely, "one eye is crying about my plight, which is sad indeed, but the other eye is rejoicing because there are so many good people to help me."

He got her quarter. And earned every cent of it.

Off the Beaten Path You can never tell where you'll run into them—the "uncommon" people whose activities, whose thoughts, whose personal histories make item-fodder for the columnist's mill.

Take, for example, the balding news "boy" at the corner of Fourth and Market. Thousands of people pass him daily without a second look—if, indeed, they favor him with a first. Scores buy their newspapers from him without bothering to learn his name. A few, who watch him more closely, are mildly amused because when he gets tired of peddling his papers, he turns his corner over to his "first executive assistant" and ambles into a nearby saloon for a quick drink or two.

It so happens that his name is Chester A. Arthur. And he's the grandson of the twenty-first President of the United States, "Arthur the Magnificent," who wore fur robes and ruled in Washington with baronial splendor and kingly dignity.

However, life has not been as kind for his fifty-two-year-old grandson. My first contact with him came when he telephoned and complained that the authorities were attempting to evict him from his home, and couldn't I help?

"Home" turned out to be an eighty-year-old barn in a Mission District alley called Mersey Street, near Twenty-third and Chattanooga. And inspectors from the Health Department, after looking it over, decided the place was "non-sanitary and unfit for human habitation."

"Pfaw," snapped back Chester Arthur, who lived there for two years. "I've never been healthier. Why, I don't even have a cold. And I don't want to move."

But they closed in on him. First, the electricity was cut off, and he had to read by candlelight. His hot plate no longer worked, and he lived on cold food. There was no heat in the place, and he shivered by night in the ancient hayloft he used for a bedroom (it was reached by the companionway off the old ferryboat *Vallejo*, given to him by his friend, Artist Jean Varda).

However, that old barn on Mersey Street has seen gay parties and bright nights, for Chester Arthur has friends everywhere except in the Health Department. Moira Shearer, the British ballet queen, was the honored guest at a soiree there on her last visit to town. Dorothy Thompson has been a visitor. And countless others whose names are famous have found their way to "the second barn on the left" in that Mission District alley.

But established authority always wins. Chester Arthur at last admitted defeat, and moved out of the alley—"my colorful, picturesque alley"—and into a prosaic hotel room.

He enjoys selling newspapers because it keeps him in the fresh air—"and besides, everybody says I'm too old for anything else." And on the night that Dwight D. Eisenhower defeated Adlai Stevenson for the Presidency of the United States, Chester was hollering lustily at Fourth and Market:

"Eisenhower wins—just like Grandfather!"

Nobody asked him to explain that statement, and it's just as well. If he had, they wouldn't have believed him anyway.

One of San Francisco's more oddly named citizens is a Stanford graduate named Zeppelin Wai Wong—and naturally, everybody wonders how come. Very simple, really. Zeppelin (or "Zep") was born in San Francisco on September 1, 1929, while the German dirigible, *Graf Zeppelin* was droning overhead—and he thinks the strange name (his father's idea) is O.K. "Could be worse," he points out. "Suppose it had been the *Shenandoah?*"

Among the heart-cuddling things that make San Francisco "different" is the tidbit about the little old Italian lady in North Beach—who has the usual terrible trouble with the English language. Every morning for years, she has phoned to her four married daughters to see how they're feeling, etc., but the intricacies of the dial telephone are beyond her too. She simply dials "Operator" and the patient phone girls listen to her broken English, figure it out, and make the calls for her.

This has been going on so long that as soon as she dials "0" these days, the operator greets her cheerily with "Good morning, Grandma. Who d'you want first this morning—Rosie, Lorraine, Annie, or Bernice?"

The tenderloin district giggled over this incident—one which proves that the Turk-Eddy-Ellis sector still has its share of 14-karat karakters.

Seems that "Jelly" Korper, a 350-lb. buddy of the bookies, has owed a little money for some time to a retired gentleman named Alvin Koenigsberg, who is seventy-seven years old and weighs at least 110.

On a recent day, the word got around that "Jelly" had won a bundle on the ponies, so Koenigsberg walked up to him on Ellis Street and said: "Jelly, how about my money?"

"What money? Who's got money?" answered Jelly cleverly—a response that infuriated Koenigsberg. Without another word, the seventy-seven-year-old 110-pounder swung on Korper and knocked out a front tooth, by golly—at which point Jelly hollered to the howling mob of bystanders: "Protect me, protect me!"

As tiny Koenigsberg kept swinging, Dapper Dave Falk finally stepped in with a word of advice.

"Look," he said to the embattled 350-lb. Jelly. "Just fall on him."

Frank Lake has had something on his mind for a long time. He runs the service station at Third and Townsend—and for years he has wondered about those two big bells hanging atop the Southern Pacific Depot across the street. Are they real bells or fakes? Metal or papier-mâché?

One recent morning, Lake couldn't stand it any longer. He came down to work with his B.B. gun, took a careful bead on those bells, and fired away, round after round. They're real, all right. In fact, their sudden clanging had S.P. officials scampering out of the depot like late-to-work commuters.

Anyway, Frank Lake is now satisfied.

For some twenty years now, Louis Graffe has been trying to get back to his native Tahiti—but I'll be surprised if he ever makes it.

It's like this: In 1933, a wealthy American brought his yacht into Papete, and Louis shipped aboard as a deckhand. Eventually they got to Marseilles, France, where the yachtsman gave Louis enough money to get back to Tahiti.

Well, you know Marseilles, and if you don't I'll give you an idea: Four days and forty bars later, Louis Graffe was broke. Tahiti faded away to the back of his mind, and he knocked around France for a few years. Then he shipped aboard the French liner *Creman*—which planned a stop at Tahiti.

It never got there. In December, 1941, with war raging everywhere, the U.S. confiscated the *Creman* at Manila, and Louis Graffe became a seaman on an American merchant ship. Peace came, his ship idled here, and all of a sudden, Louis found himself a San Franciscan.

Someday, maybe, he'll return to the Tahiti he left in 1933. But meanwhile, Louis Graffe is working happily here as a bartender in a little place on Leavenworth Street named—"The Tahiti."

"Coattails" Mulloy runs a lugubrious saloon in Colma, across the road from Holy Cross Cemetery—and his jukebox contains such appropriate maladies as "Goodnight Irene," "It's Later Than You Think," "Are You Lonesome Tonight?" and "I Don't Care if the Sun Don't Shine." If you're wondering how "Coattails" got his colorful nickname, we've got the answer. The sign outside his joint used to read "Cocktails," but that is now against the law in California. So he changed it to "Coattails."

Well, I guess it's time you were hearing about Horace Brooks "Hitch" King, the No. 1 suit salesman up at Roos Bros. Ol' "Hitch," a bachelor, lives in the most comfortable rut in San Francisco. He has eaten at the Fly Trap every night for the past twenty-one years, arriving exactly at 6:50 P.M. "We set the clock by him," the waiters say. Only on Sundays does he vary the routine. That day, he arrives at the Fly Trap at exactly 4:30 P.M., "just to show that I'm still flexible."

"Hitch," who lives on the twelfth floor of the Elks Club, takes an annual vacation—and each time he goes through the same *megilla* he has observed for twenty years. He buys a new summer wardrobe. He consults travel folders. He asks his friends for resort suggestions. And then he leaves his twelfth floor room and is off— to the sun deck on the thirteenth floor, where he spends every day of his vacation. Every year.

Empires may crumble, thrones may totter, old soldiers may fade away, but one thing you can be sure of in these hectic times. "Hitch" King will be at the Fly Trap at 6:50 tonight—unless it happens to be Sunday. In which case he'll arrive at exactly 4:30.

Twenty-odd years ago, when he was a North Beach millionaire loaded with Transamerica stock, Gus Oliva was much more important than the Easter Rabbit in the eyes and hearts of San Francisco's children.

His Easter egg hunts in Golden Gate Park cost him $25,000 a year, and attracted thousands of kids from all over town. For each hunt, he imported 30,000 chocolate eggs from a Fresno firm. And he hid 5 eggs with hundred-dollar bills wrapped around them, 100 eggs with twenties, and 200 with fivers and 500 with dollars. Gus's last hunt, in 1931, was staged in Civic Center, because the wild-eyed moppets were creating such havoc in the Park.

Then came the depression. Gus Oliva was wiped out—and every Easter since he has sadly reminisced about the era when he was King for a Day to the children.

On the Saturday before last Easter, a friend took him to Golden Gate Fields racetrack, and "Poor Gus" got lucky. He won seventy dollars on the first race, rushed back to San Francisco, and bought 240 chocolate eggs. And on Easter Sunday, in the rain, the man who used to give away 30,000 eggs each year walked from door to door in a poor neighborhood—handing out his little gifts to the children who had never heard of Gus Oliva.

Frank McAuliffe, one of the more historic salesmen at Shreve's noted jewelry store, was wandering through Union Square one afternoon—and paused to chat with an Old Philosopher type who has been sitting in the Square for years. "How d'you pass the time here?" asked McAuliffe. "Wa'al," answered the graybeard, staring up at the Dewey monument, " 'bout seven years ago, I saw a pigeon fly through that wreath up there—and I ain't never seen it happen again. But some day another pigeon's gonna fly through it, and by golly, I aim t'see it." So he went on looking, and Frank went on walking. It was a lovely day.

Papa Pierre   The city looks the same as it always did. The fog still ducks its head under the Golden Gate Bridge and slithers into the Bay on its flat gray belly. The setting sun still paints the hills a golden red before it vanishes into the Pacific, and the afterglow lives for long, hushed minutes along the shaded paths of Golden Gate Park.

But the city is a little older, a little less gay. For, after seventeen triumphant years as conductor of the San Francisco Symphony Orchestra, Pierre Monteux has gone away. In 1952, at the age of seventy-seven, the chubby little man known throughout the world as "Frisco's Frenchman" ("Frisco" in this case being acceptable) resigned his baton and moved East to find new challenges—and, indubitably, conquer them.

Pierre Monteux was the closest thing to a musical idol that San Francisco had known since the child prodigy days of violinist Yehudi Menuhin.

When he came to the city in 1935, the once-proud orchestra was in the last stages of decay. A succession of guest conductors had broken the morale of its musicians, forced the best men to seek jobs elsewhere, and bored the audience into setting new non-attendance records.

In an amazingly short time, Pierre Monteux changed all that. He proved to be a brilliant, scholarly conductor who was deeply respected by his orchestra—and yet he had universal appeal, too. He was a tireless worker who could put in longer hours than musicians half his age, and never lose the bubbling personality that kept the orchestra from feeling rebellious about his occasional slave-driving.

And best of all, as far as San Francisco at large was concerned, he fit in. Short and roly-poly, with apple-red cheeks, a constant Gallic glint in his eyes and an endearing French accent, he filled the popular concept of the symphony maestro to perfection. People who never in their lives attended a concert beamed with proprietary pride as they watched him walking his beloved poodle, Fifi, along the streets of Nob Hill.

"Hey, Pierre," they'd shout from a passing cable car, "kommaw sa va, Papa Pierre? And how's Fifi?"

And Papa Pierre, bundled up in his black overcoat, would smile from behind his startling white moustache and shake his long black hair in friendly amusement.

"Fifi, zay 'allo to za nize pippils," he'd say, picking up the tiny dog and holding her over his head. And the cable car gripman would clang his gong and everybody would wave back and forth and feel happy and proud that Pierre Monteux, the big-league conductor, the Joe DiMaggio of his particular field, was "their" maestro.

Like all genuine idols, Pierre Monteux in San Francisco was blissfully unaware of his own importance—or the importance of other celebrities.

On his seventy-fifth birthday, he received a long, warm letter from Al Jolson; after reading it, he turned to his wife, Doris, with a puzzled look on his face and asked: "Who izz ziss Ahl Jolsaw?" At a fashionable cocktail party, he was introduced to Hildegarde, the noted supper room entertainer, and after a long conversation he bowed and beamed: "Verree hoppee to hov met you, Miss Garde."

And when he returned to San Francisco to begin his last season as conductor, the city's fireboats advanced across the Bay to meet his ferryboat, filling the air with glittering streams of water. The maestro watched them in fascination, and then sudden fear. "Mon Dieu," he exploded to Doris, "you dawn't suppose our boat is on fire?"

The warmhearted city showered him with affection. Keys from the Mayor, proclamations from the Board of Supervisors, thousands of letters from well-wishers on his birthdays, and standing ovations from his audiences; this was Pierre Monteux's golden life in San Francisco.

"Eet ees too much," he wept one day in his dressing room, surrounded by flowers and telegrams, "eet ees too much for a poor viola player from France."

But nothing was too much—and besides, he wasn't a poor viola player. He was excellent. When he wasn't busy with his orchestra, he performed with various string quartets at private recitals. And now and then he'd walk to the piano and play—rather badly—the single jazz selection he had mastered: "Crazy Rhythm."

Popular music he had little ear for, but his grasp of the classics was astounding, even to the most seasoned critics. He almost always conducted from memory. His conception of the standard classics was as sound as his interpretations of the most modern works. And he seemed never to lose his enthusiasm for either.

A whole generation of symphony-lovers will remember the tingling thrill of Monteux dashing out of the wings at the back of the Opera House stage, half-running swiftly around the orchestra, making a wide sweeping turn at the front of the stage—like a racing car at Indianapolis—and hopping nimbly onto the high podium.

For years, the audiences marveled at his whirlwind entrances. And there was sadness and much headshaking when Monteux finally confessed that he wasn't quite as young as he used to be, and agreed to let the Opera House carpenters add a step to the podium.

"However," he added, referring slyly to the speed with which he steamed onto the stage, "I refuse to let zem bank ze turn!"

The Monteux sense of humor always flashed through at the right time, the right place.

In 1950, after an exhausting guest-conducting tour of Europe, the maestro and his wife returned to New York and, hard on the heels of a harrowing twenty-two-hour flight, boarded a train to San Francisco.

Shortly after, they were stalled for seven hours behind a broken-down freight train. "You know," sighed fiftyish Doris Monteux as they waited irritably for the track to be cleared, "I'm too old for all this traipsing around."

"Eet's funny you should say that," twinkled the then seventy-five-year-old Monteux. "I was just zinking zat I ought to get myself a youngaire wife!"

At a dinner party one night, the conductor found himself seated next to an attractive and ambitious young singer who wanted desperately to appear with the Symphony. She used all her feminine wiles on the maestro and, at one point, leaned over and cooed in his ear: "What would you say if somebody whispered to you, 'Darling, I love you'?"

"I would say," shrugged Monteux, "that eet ees too late."

One time at Trader Vic's restaurant, a mutual friend of the Monteuxs rushed over to their table and planted a big kiss on Mme. Monteux's cheek.

"Don't evaire do zat again," raged Monteux in mock anger, and when the friend looked surprised, he smilingly explained:

"You see, I am a Frrranchman. Eet ees okay eef you kees ME, but not my wife!"

At the conclusion of Monteux's final season as conductor of the San Francisco Symphony, the members of the orchestra gave a farewell party for him at the Fairmont Hotel—and, during an impromptu show, the women members of the orchestra trooped out in daring costumes and danced a can-can.

"Amaaaazing," chuckled Monteux from behind his white moustache. "I have conducted here for seventeen years, and zis is ze first time I knew ze ladies in ze orchestra had legs!"

When word of his resignation became public, he was flooded with farewell gifts, none of which touched him more than an elaborate painting. It showed various San Francisco landmarks, surrounding a wonderful likeness of Papa Pierre—and it was painted by a famous local artist named John Paul Chase.

It's possible that you never heard of Artist Chase. He was a Gangster Era pal of "Baby Face" Nelson's, a close associate of the late John Dillinger, and the convicted slayer of an FBI agent. Chase, who took up painting a few years ago to pass the time, has plenty of time to pass. He's in Alcatraz—for life.

"Dear Mr. Monteux," read the note accompanying the painting, "This is a going-away present, from a guy who isn't going anywhere. (Signed) John Paul Chase."

Holiday at Half-Mast   Now it's getting harder to remember . . .

In the Presidio's tree-fringed cemetery, the white crosses stretch across the slopes to infinity, while the Flag hangs in mournful folds and the sound of "taps" fades away into the still air.

Another Armistice Day, and the city and its people pause to remember the end of "the war to end all wars," and the speeches are full of fine, ringing phrases about sacrifices and peace—but there is no peace. There are only the realities of the men who are still marching away to fight, and the fitful memories of thousands before them who marched away and never returned.

World War I—how long ago it seems, and how pitifully gay it began. The young men from the Mission and the Richmond, from St. Francis Wood and Presidio Heights, marching ramrod-straight down Market in their high-buttoned tunics and their quaint leggings and sailing away on a ferry boat while the band played "Over There."

"And we won't come back till it's over Over There."

But they didn't all come back. Soon the cheers were replaced by anxious silence, and the kids threw stones at dachshunds, and the old folks ate "Liberty Steak," and the Hof Brau restaurant on Market, where the booths were named after German cities, became the States, with its booths rechristened Maine and Texas and California.

But the only names that really counted were the Marne, and the Meuse-Argonne and St. Mihiel, and they became commonplaces— like the telegrams from the War Department and the gold stars in the windows. But in the end, it was all worth while, for the world had been made safe for democracy and there would be no more war.

Armistice Day, every November 11, year after year, and always the banks closed and the flags at dutiful half-staff and the speeches about the men who laid down their lives so that we might live in comfort, free from fear.

November 11, 1942—and already thousands of young men had marched away from San Francisco, like their fathers before them, and the white service stars blossomed bleakly in windows from Hunters Point to Land's End.

But this time it was different. This time there was no naïve bravado in the air, for already the German and his allies stood supreme over half the world, and the people remembered how hard it had been once before. There were no cheers as the draftees straggled away in their civilian clothes to faraway camps, and there were no stirringly simple songs like "Over There," no songs like "Roses of Picardy" to get sentimental over, no poems like "In Flanders' Fields" for the children to learn.

There were blackouts and rationing, and on Sundays, the people gathered in tense knots at Ocean Beach, as though expecting to see Japanese planes flying overhead. Half-lighted Market Street was thickly alive with sailors and their "sea gulls," and the Japanese Tea Garden became Oriental, and there was some talk that the Symphony should drop Wagner from its repertoire.

But the kids from the Mission and the Richmond, St. Francis Wood and Presidio Heights, came through again. And this time the geography lesson was more extensive—Bizerte and Truk, Hill 609 and the Solomons, Bastogne and the Coral Sea. And this time there were many more white crosses, and they grew in fields from Normandie to the Philippines.

And thousands came marching home again to San Francisco, without jubilation—vaguely wondering why they had been spared when Joe from Twenty-sixth Avenue had got his at Anzio, and Mike from Castro Street had gone in with his flaming plane at Guam, and Pete from Columbus Avenue had stopped a sniper's bullet near St. Lô.

They came back, and they listened with only half an ear and half a heart to the Armistice Day speeches about the war to end wars that had made the world safe for democracy. All they knew was that their war was over and they were safe—and that already a new menace was rising redly on the horizon.

Armistice Day, 1952—and the great city pauses and bows its head and tries to remember its fighting men in their flat, British-style tin helmets, and dry, dedicated Woodrow Wilson and the evanescent joy of 11 A.M., on November 11, 1918, when it was all over and all was finally right and right had triumphed and they'd be hanging Kaiser Bill in the morning.

But they didn't, and besides, it seems so long ago—now. So long ago that Armistice Day no longer means "the end of the war," but merely the end of a war that has never ended.

And so, on this thirty-fourth Armistice Day, you stand in the Presidio Cemetery alongside the aging men with the American Legion button in their lapels as they pay homage to their fallen comrades. But now it's hard to keep your thoughts on them—the men who died so long ago when the world was young and you could still thrill to the bright promise at the end of "Over There."

You look out over the gray city, and you can see them marching away once again—the kids from the Mission and the Richmond, St. Francis Wood and Presidio Heights. And again the white stars and the gold appear in the windows, and the carefully worded telegrams arrive from the War Department, and this time the geography lesson has been extended to include Seoul and Pyongyang, Inchon and Triangle Hill.

The heart-twisting notes of "Taps" ring out over the Presidio's rolling hills, and the words of a thousand speechmakers hang heavy in the air: "War to end war . . . safe for democracy . . . that they shall not have died in vain."

And in the Bay a troop transport moves slowly toward the Golden Gate, and on the waterfront, the rough wooden coffins are stacked high. For they won't all be back—if it's ever over, Over There.

Footnote to a Police Action   The war that isn't a war seemed awfully close to home, one day at the Fort Mason embarkation docks.

Ready to sail for overseas was a jampacked military transport, its rails lined with sober-faced troops. And on the dock—waving, smiling, crying, looking desperately for Their Familiar Face—stood the women who were left behind; the wives, the mothers, the sisters.

And then, in majestic silence, the great ship began to inch away. There was a frantic urgency, suddenly, in the hands that waved farewell, and then fell back in limp resignation.

And as the ship moved out into the stream and the crowd began to drift away, a very young mother, holding her baby boy in her arms, crushed her face against her son's cheek in fierce tenderness and sobbed: "Please—please—don't ever grow up" . . .

They Called It Frisco   Market Street resounded with the "Roar of the Four" as they raced along the quadruple streetcar tracks; the Sunset was merely a wide-open space where the wind blew sand into your eyes; and you could sit at the revolving counter in an O'Farrell Street restaurant called "The Merry-Go-Round" and eat all you wanted for fifty cents . . . The "real" Russian Hill, populated by real Russians, was high on the Potrero cliffs, and whenever one of the colony died, the casket was lowered over the side on ropes—for no car could make the grade . . . Lombard Street's curlicue road, between Hyde and Leavenworth, was used as a testing ground for automobiles; there was dancing in the penthouse atop the Clift Hotel; Jimmy Rolph, cowboy boots and all, would undoubtedly be the Mayor forever, and everybody was young and in love with the world of San Francisco.

Marquard's, at Geary and Mason, was the place to go for tea dancing on a Saturday afternoon, for the Nicest Girls went there alone to be Picked Up in the nicest possible way . . . There was a thing called Prohibition, but nobody paid much attention to it—and even at the extremely correct Palace you could get your grog by asking

the waiter for some "flowers"; he'd come right back with a flower
box containing the bottle . . . All you needed to be a big man
about town was a wallet full of "membership cards" to the 1001
speakeasies—for example, the Swastika Club at 49 Maiden Lane,
the Chapeau Rouge at 2215 Powell, the Royal Camel at 723 Filbert,
or the Town Club at 2796 Hyde . . . The streetcars were a nickel
and the cabs were a quarter, and a dollar went as far as you'd care
to throw it.

So much to see, so much to talk about in the bright-eyed days and
sparkling nights of a city's yesterdays . . . Trumpeter Bill James,
with Anson Weeks at the Mark, tearing down the house with his
version of "Margie." Arthur Cunningham stopping the show for sixteen solid weeks by singing "My Own United States" in *When
Johnny Comes Marching Home.* "Turn Around Dan" Camp jigging
wildly at the old Chutes, while the crowds roared "Turn Around,
Dan!"—and he would, to display a silly patch on the back of his
silly pants. Will King at the Casino, singing "I've got a girl who
paints her cheeks, another with a voice that squeaks, they both ran
away with a pair of Greeks—I wished I owned a restaurant!" (Now
he does) . . . These were the things that made San Francisco
laugh, easily and lightly, and anyway there wasn't much time to
get serious about; the stocks were higher than the Russ Building,
dashing Bert Ellison was the peerless leader of the Seals, and you
could eat your head off at Sanguinetti's for six bits, plus a dime tip.
Wine included.

The good gray city, always alive with memories, no matter what
your age or your era or your interests . . . How they crowd your
imagination: The waterfront a tangle of masts and spars (and Poet

George Sterling bringing the city to life with lines like "At the end of your streets are stars"). The newsboys riding the cable cars for free and throwing their papers onto the passing porches (and remember fancy Tom Williams, the racing magnate, who lived in a big house at Pacific and Divisadero? His son had a pony, with a special permit to take it to school each day on the cable car's "dummy"). No gleaming white tower on Telegraph Hill—it was just plain "Nannygoat Hill" then (and there was a slaughterhouse at Bay and Webster, with sheep grazing on the nearby hills among the wild artichokes) . . . A small, friendly city, where you knew your neighbor and liked him, and if you didn't you could always move; maybe all the way out to the new Richmond District, where rents were as high as twenty dollars a month. But furnished, of course.

So easy to put your mind into neutral and coast down the hills of the past . . . Then your mind's eye plays tricks and the days you remember shimmer in eternal sunshine. The Bay much bluer than it is now, with the S.P.'s white ferryboats sliding past the Key Route's orange ones and the wake sparkling with foam. The Ferry Building, a shining beacon at the foot of Market, the most important building in town, and alive with people rushing importantly around. Golden Gate Park was greener than the pastures of Heaven, and you could buy the biggest and best peanuts in the world for a nickel and feed them to the friendliest squirrels that ever lived. And at the end of each endless day the sun would sink dramatically in the very center of the Golden Gate, to the lapping applause of the waves . . . There was some wild talk about building a bridge there, but that could never be. Spoil the view.

You know how it was, even if you didn't live it yourself—for the past is always present in San Francisco . . . The "true" San Franciscans of the Missions, deigning to cross Market, speaking their own language and poking fun at anybody from the other side of the streetcar tracks. The fresh kids who'd sneak up behind a Chinese on a cable car and tie his queue to a post so that when he got up he'd almost break his neck; then the kids'. "Wallace," the biggest lion in the world, out at the Chutes with Cannon the Fat Man, who weighted 780 pounds. Everybody talking baseball and no wonder; the manager of the winter league teams were such titans as George Sisler, Harry Heilmann, Ty Cobb, and Rogers Hornsby. Joaquin Miller, "The Poet of the Sierra," back from the Klondike and parading up Post Street in a suit whose buttons were solid gold nuggets. If you wanted to drive your girl to the Cliff House in style, you could rent a hack at the Fashion Stables on Ellis between Mason and Taylor—and you could keep it out until morning. The hack, that is.

That was San Francisco . . . Kindly Matt Brady would always be District Attorney, and you could get the "fix" any old time from Pete McDonough in his bail bond office (but, now, alas, they are gone). There would always be parking places and a nickel glass of beer and plenty of space to build a home and dozens of old friends to wave to as you walk along Geary (but where are they now?) . . . The city changes and grows away from you even as you live in the middle of it. Only the memories get longer and refuse to die.

Vacation Blues   Tahoe, Carmel Valley, Russian River,
Santa Cruz, Santa Barbara, La Jolla, Reno, Las Vegas . . .

"Rest, Relax, Enjoy!" cry the siren voices of their travel folders—
but the San Franciscan listens with only half an ear . . . No matter
where he goes, in this world that is running away from itself, his
city will always be with him . . . High in the mountains, under the
wide summer sky, he will feel the cold breath of the fog and in his
mind's eye he will see the mist crawling with pale fingers over Twin
Peaks . . . Stretched out by a distant sea, he will hear a far-off
whistle and close his eyes to picture a dark freighter inching past
Alcatraz, with a cloud of sea gulls screaming around its masts . . .
Wherever he goes to get away from it all it will still be with him—
for there is no getting away from San Francisco.

Sun Valley, Banff, Victoria, Ojai Valley, Sea Island, Catalina Island,
Balboa Island, Hawaii . . .

"See New Places and New Faces!" chant the drum-beaters for the
great ritual of the Annual Vacation—and the San Franciscan goes
and looks and listens, and he sees the places and the faces . . . But
nowhere does he see the view from Top o' the Mark, where you

order a drink and get drunk on the scenery. Nowhere does he find
the glorious greenery of a soft meadow in Golden Gate Park. Nowhere does he find a street as crazy as Lombard's curly-cue, doing
its snake dance from Hyde to Leavenworth. And no, nowhere does
he see the faces that are San Francisco—the leathery features of the
Powell Street gripman, squinting uphill from Pine at the California
Street signal-box; the white-capped, wide-open faces of the long-
shoremen, swaggering along the Embarcadero as though they
owned it (and why not?); Archie the El Prado doorman, playing
his daily game of traffic chess along Post Street, moving his customers' cars from one space to another, always one move ahead
of the cop; "Tiny" Armstrong, the walking novelty shop, making
his strange noises on Powell Street—secure in the city where characters are laughed with, not at.

Guerneville, Juan-Les-Pins, Capitola, Cap d'Antibes, Martha's Vine-
yard, Boca Raton, Monte Rio . . .
    "This Time Get out of Your Rut—The Other Half of the World
Is Waiting for You" . . . And the San Franciscan, who never has
time to see the other half of his city, wonders vaguely if he is in a
rut, and he follows the crowds . . . He threads his way through
customs and road maps—he who gets lost in the Ingleside District.
He argues in bad French with the concierge at the Paris Ritz—he
who is baffled by a Deep Mission accent. He struggles from crag
to crag in the High Sierra and manages to get back safely—he who
has never climbed Mount Davidson, couldn't find Pine Lake if he
had to, and doesn't know Visitacion Valley from Noe Valley . . .
He does all these things in a fever and a fury, all the while prom-
ising himself that someday he'll take advantage of the rut he loves

and explore the Montgomery Block and bicycle in the Park and fish in Lake Merced and maybe even climb the inside of Coit Tower.

Tahoe Tavern, El Nido Rancho, Robles Del Rio, Soda Springs, Mount Rose, Hoberg's, Sonoma Mission Inn, Brookdale . . .

"Brighten Your Perspective—a Change Will Do You Good!" they tell you in challenging tones, and of course they're right . . . But perhaps they have never seen the challenging tones of a sunset outside the Golden Gate, filling the skies with blues and pinks that glow and fade before your eyes. They've never seen the far-off windows of the East Bay, touched with fire for an instant by the dying sun. They've never seen the fog of dusk, filtering through a Chinatown sidestreet and transforming it from a drab byway into a mysterious setting for secret dramas. They've never listened to the thick hush of a clear dawn over the Bay, when the waters are still asleep and even the Ferry Building seems to have its tower tucked under a wing. They've never turned an ordinary street corner to find a sudden view that makes you stop dead in your tracks—proud in the discovery of a fresh perspective on the old city that is always new.

Feather River Inn, the Riverside and Mapes, El Rancho, Heavenly Hana, Carmel Valley Inn, Cal-Neva and Stateline, Squaw Valley . . .

"Sunny Days, Starry Nights, Wonderful Food, Reasonable Rates!" —the vacationland has many voices, and whether they whisper or shout, they make their point . . . And so the San Franciscan trades his sunny days for other sunny days—and while he simmers in oil

at the grim business of getting a tan, he knows that the discreet
San Francisco sun is playing delicately across the green of Union
Square, resting lightly on the furs of Post Street's perennial "best-
dressed women," chasing the shadows out of Montgomery Street's
dark canyon . . . And at night, his flaming skin athrob, he knows
that his magic city is coming to life in the ritualistic pattern—at the
Palace Corner and the St. Francis Grill and the Mark lower bar and
the Cirque Room; at Veltri's and Amelio's and the Blue Fox and
the Papagayo and Vic's; in front of the Geary and the Curran and
the Opera House, and at the 365 and Forbidden City and Sinaloa,
and in tiny theaters in the Mission and tiny bars in the Richmond;
and the night won't be over until the scavengers play their alarm
clock chorus of rattles, bangs, and crashes.

This is the San Francisco that the San Franciscan deserts every
summer—to sizzle under the vacation sun that is now (according
to the advertisements) shining everywhere, day and night . . .
Good-by, cool world!

As you can see from the foregoing, the average San Franciscan—
this one, anyway—has all the makings of a happy stick-in-the-mud.
He is in no hurry to get away from it all, and the more he has seen
of the world, the less of a hurry he is in.

Let me say in all modesty that I've been around a good deal for
a guy who wears a Buster Brown collar, bulldog shoes, and double-
breasted vests festooned with buttons reading "Oh You Kid,"
"Chicken Inspector," and "Twenty-three Skiddoo."

My intimate friends know me merely as a boor who wears ladies'
hats at parties and can recite the Gettysburg Address in pig Latin,

but the cold truth is that I know the four corners of the world as intimately as any other square who ever pasted a "Raffles Hotel" sticker (obtained in a Powell Street travel agency) on his wicker luggage and tipped a redcap by flicking a cigarette ash into his outstretched palm.

There is hardly a fashionable watering spa on the Continent in which I have not had a bag of watered spa dropped on my head. The far-flung beaches of the Riviera (the one in France, not the restaurant on Columbus Avenue) have felt the impact of the sun-bleached torso which has won for me the cognomen of "The Beached Whale."

I have dined surpassingly on breast of pheasant and a frosty magnum of Coq d'Cola ('29) at Maxim's in Paris, not even blanching at the three-thousand-franc check. I merely passed out on the spot, which is marked to this day with a plaque reading, "À bas les Americains" (trans.: "Down with Les Cain," sic).

In Berlin I have danced on a table top with Marlene Dietrich, or perhaps it was her cousin by a previous marriage, and in Rome, I have been greeted by a clamor reminiscent of the first days of Pompeii or the last days of Mussolini.

In fact, there was even some talk along the Vittorio Veneto of stringing me up by my heels at the nearest gasoline station, but fortunately a counterpart of Clara Spetacci couldn't be found. Besides, the station was so busy pumping lasagne (well-known Italian gasoline) into Fiats that they had no time for me. Suffice to say I exited hastily on a bicycle, singing "Don't want me 'cause my Fiat's too big."

Yes, friend, I have been around.

I have worked in the Safeway in Skagway, Alaska. I can pronounce Reykjavik, Iceland, with my mouth closed and one head tied behind me. I have supped on baksheesh (rare Indian rice) in Bombay and thrown pilaff (Armenian money) at William Saroyan in Nazdi Novgorod. I have been around Lowell Thomas four times. I have marveled at the strange images in Grauman's Chinese Theater and I have ridden a commuter train to Redwood City and lived to tell the tale.

I have even been kicked out of the El Rancho drive-in theater in Sacramento for flashing my spotlight on the screen.

Why, you ask, am I telling you all these incredible tales? Ah, if you but knew. I am asking myself the same question.

Well, for one thing—twenty minutes elapsed between the last sentence and this one—as vacation time approaches on little cat feet—say, that's a good line, must remember to tell it to Carl Sandburg some time—as I was saying, vacation time is approaching and my thoughts invariably turn to memories of past adventures and the contemplation of approaching ones.

Where shall we go this year on a limited budget and a '23 Harley-Davidson motorcycle? To Lake Tahoe, perchance, to gambol on the green with the gamblers and plunge, feet first, nose between thumb and forefinger, into the icy blue waters? To Pismo Beach, the Uncultured Pearl of the Pacific, to dive for abalone and old tires? To the golden strands of Waikiki, there to marvel at the picturesque natives attired in Aloha shirts manufactured in Biloxi, Miss.?

But no. After a hurried check with the American Trust Co. and the neighborhood Collector of Internal Revenue, these worldly pleasures hold no allure for me. Let the others pile into their cars and head for Yosemite and the Grand Canyon, sweet. Let somebody else be barred from the Stork Club and "21," for a change. Let not the siren call of far-off Fresno, California, be picked up by my intelligent, clipped ears.

This year I want to realize the ambition of all world travelers and visit magical, mystical San Francisco, land of the summer fog, home of the Seals that are forever on the rocks, enchanted city where even the ferries have a building, Broadway has a tunnel, and the Mayor has ulcers.

The things I have heard about San Francisco are enough to fire anyone's imagination, and I plan to fire mine almost immediately.

I want to stand in Golden Gate Park and look at the Golden Gate. Climb Twin Peaks and stand with one foot on each peak, like the Colossus of Rhodes. Cross the Bay Bridge and sniff the wonders of Oakland. Go down to Fisherman's Wharf and listen to the colorful Italian fishermen, their feet encased in stocking caps, singing the songs of their ancient heroes, DiMaggio, Lazzeri, and Crosetti.

I want to browse through the markets on Market Street, spend a Saturday Evening on Post, and send a wire from Telegraph Hill. Put on a babushka and sandals and join in the wild peasant dances on Russian Hill. Ride out to the Cliff House on a cable car and watch the ships unloading along the Embarcadero. And perhaps, if luck is with me, although I usually travel alone, I will become the first man to jump onto the Golden Gate Bridge.

In short, I want to spend three glorious weeks in San Francisco, getting to know the city, the REAL city, as intimately as I know London, Stockton, and Lodi. And I want the city to know me. I want to be called Jackson on Washington, Eddy on Ellis, and jerk on Turk. Then, and only then, will I be satisfied.

Come to think of it, I feel pretty satisfied already.

And despite all his talk, his genuine, go-away-and-leave-me-alone satisfaction with his city, the San Franciscan does know his way around.

There is quite a winter exodus to Palm Springs and Las Vegas, and to the spectacular snow country of the high Sierra. Thanks to an excellent plane schedule, thousands commute weekly to Los Angeles, there to stare at Lana Turner and Kirk Douglas as unabashedly as the most saucer-eyed tourist from Fairmont, Minnesota. Matson's great white *Lurline* and the American President Lines' *Wilson* and *Cleveland* are jammed whenever they set out across the Pacific. And there is seldom an empty seat aboard the Mexico-bound planes of American Airlines, Pan-American, and Philippine.

Yes. The San Franciscan, including this one, does manage to tear himself away every now and then, and he reports as follows:

NEW YORK TO ME   What is New York? It's the biggest, smallest, dirtiest, shiniest, meanest, most openhearted city in the world . . . The incredible tower of the Empire State Building gleams in the night like a shower of rockets—in full view of the bums of the Bowery, who stumble around with their eyes glued to the sidewalk . . . At No. 100 Park Avenue, a vertical searchlight knifes into the blackness to guide helicopters to a landing field on its roof, but no helicopter lands there—it's all for show . . . The biggest city in the world, and yet one of the smallest—for all the activity that makes it exciting, romantic and colorful takes place within an area no larger than downtown San Francisco . . . A city its bards sing of as cold, cruel, and hard—but the cabdrivers are always ready to strike up a friendly conversation, the phone girls are cheery and

polite, the cops have a warmth in their smile, and I haven't seen
a grumbling elevator operator yet. Or a panhandler, for that matter.

Midtown Manhattan, with its endless rows of soaring apartments
and hotels, housing the leading talents in every field you can think
of—the Nation's wealthiest, wisest, and most successful people, living at each other's elbows . . . Herbert Hoover walking into his
"home" at the Waldorf, Bernard Baruch sitting arrow-straight on his
bench in bleak Central Park, Hattie Carnegie at lunch in the Colony
—these are the vignettes you stumble across merely by accident here,
hinting at other exciting people in exciting places, right around any
corner. The breakneck pace that you can feel and hear at all hours,
day and night—the earthquaking of the street beneath your feet as
a subway train races by far below; the taxi horns, as insistent and
imperative at 4 A.M. as they are at 4 P.M.; the unceasing, indefinable
hum of millions of people and machines at work and at play in the
smallest possible space—a constant buzzing in your ears, a perpetual
cinder in your mind's eye.

Broadway with its pulsating acres of neon signs and huge marquees and tiny orange juice stands and smelly hamburger shops—
San Francisco's Market Street, magnified out of all proportion to
reality, so that somehow the people look too small . . . Fifth Avenue—a Post Street lined with oversized shops, each corner crawling
with knots of fur-bearing animals, the sidewalks wider than any
sidewalks you've ever seen and still not wide enough to take care
of the pushing, prodding pedestrians . . . Wall Street—a Montgomery Street as seen in your nightmares, the skyscrapers careening
crazily into the sky and leaving just a narrow slot for sunlight, for
air, for falling ticker tape, falling bodies . . . Central Park—A
Golden Gate Park in the finest part of the city, but without the

warmth, the softness, the never-ending charm of John McLaren's miracle; an expanse of cold, winding roads and trees shivering in their nakedness.

In many ways, New York is, I suppose, the cliquiest and most caste-conscious city in the world. The New Yorker who is in a certain high-income bracket and holding down an important job in the executive world has ironclad, unyielding notions about everything from the "right" hotel to the "right" restaurant to the "right" clothes —and no amount of ridicule or sarcasm will make him change. The government might put a freeze on prices and wages and anything else it may think of, but it will never have to freeze the opinions of the midtown Manhattanite. They've been frozen tight for years, and there's no chance of a thaw.

This ultraparticular group—and this is the so-called "smart" group that sets the pace around town—considers only a few hotels to be worth while, for instance. The Plaza, St. Regis, Pierre, and Sherry-Netherland are approved, maybe, plus a few of the smaller, equally chic ones on the quiet side streets. But the famed Waldorf they liken to Grand Central Station—except for "the towers." The towers are O.K., but just barely. The vast Statler, run by ex-San Franciscan Jimmy McCabe, is fine for convention delegates, but who wants to be a convention delegate? And so it goes, right down the line, snobbish and sniffish as you please.

There aren't too many restaurants and clubs that meet the mysterious requirements of the "right" people. The "21" passes the test, of course, and so, to varying degrees, do Le Pavillon, Voisin, the Colony, Quo Vadis, and a few steak houses, like Gallagher's, McCarthy's, etc. But, on the other hand, the Stork Club, which is con-

sidered absolutely absolute in some parts of the world, is regarded
with mild suspicion by the group. They have a feeling that the proprietor, Mr. Sherman Billingsley, isn't quite one of them. If they do
go there at all, it's with an air of slight condescension. In fact, I'm
not sure whether the Stork people and the "21" crowd, if we may so
lump 'em (and you may) actually speak to each other with anything
like sincerity. It's more of a cold nod.

It's a legend of long standing, as you might have heard, that it's
pretty tough to get into the "21"—which, of course, is one of the
anomalies of the age. Why should it be tough to get into a bar and
restaurant that charges you more than plenty for everything? You'd
think they'd have the door wide open and the welcome mat out for
anybody willing to meet their prices.

But the Kriendler brothers, who run the jernt with a hand as iron
as the gate out front, have played it smart through the years—so that
now, when you're allowed in, you consider it a great privilege to
be permitted to spend your money. They've achieved this happy
state by stationing a full complement of steely-eyed gents at the
front door, and at various intervals inside, who are trained to inspect
you carefully as you walk through the door. This is about the same
thing as trying to sneak past ten sets of electric eyes with your
pockets full of silverware—sooner or later the buzzer's going to go
off, but you don't know when, or which one. If you can run the
gantlet with a sufficiently matter-of-fact air, nobody will blow the
whistle on you. However, if you turn red and fidget with your
clothes and look down a couple of times to see if everything is
properly buttoned, you're dead. First thing you know, one of these
inspectors will tap you on the shoulder and say: "Do you have a
reservation?" In which case your only recourse is to say, "No, do
I look like an Indian?" and turn on your heel and walk out.

I've managed to force my way into "21" a couple of times without being halted, and I guess this sort of scotches the whole legend. Any place that would let me in would let anybody in.

I don't know whether you're aware of this, but there's a certain group in San Francisco—very much like the bunch I've just been talking about—which figures that what our town needs most of all is a place like "21." So I was properly amused, at the bar of "21," to hear one Frank Young, a member in good standing of the caste-conscious set, remark with a painful sigh: "Y'know what New York needs most of all? A place like Trader Vic's."

See? It all depends on your warped point of view.

They say New York is the greatest party town in the world—and one morning I awoke with the head to prove it. For the night before, fellow workers, I attended a party in a penthouse high atop the surtax brackets overlooking Park Avenue.

Now you know that a party in a Park Avenue penthouse has to be something pretty special, and this was. In fact, it had everything. Celebrities. Large open terraces for drunks to fall from. Two large dogs (the host's) for drunks to fall over. A solemn reason for the party to be given in the first place: The launching of a brand-new Steinway grand piano in the drawing room (I guess a living room is a drawing room when it's in a penthouse).

And besides all that—Tallulah Bankhead.

After watching her in action, I'm convinced that every party should have Miss Bankhead as the life of it. She was everywhere at once, drinking, smoking, shouting, mumbling, fighting, tossing her hair, rolling her *r's* and flattening her *a's*. And she was dressed for comfort—in a black sweater and black slacks and black slippers and black circles under her eyes. She wears slacks to parties because then she can fling herself into sofas, chairs, walls, floors, guests, etc., "without worrying about anything."

Just what she has to worry about in the first place I wouldn't know. Come to think of it, I wouldn't care, especially.

But let us get back to the central theme of the party—the christening of the new piano. All the action, and there was plenty of it, was staged around its smooth, flowing lines, and by the time the little clambake was over, there were enough alcoholic rings on its expensive surface to mark it as a very ancient piano. "That's the idea of the party," said the host bravely, smiling through his pallor. "Wanna make that li'l ol' piano look like it's lived a little."

So the party was a success. At the end of the soiree, the piano could have passed for a relic of the Barbary Coast, or at the very least a graduate of the old Sally Stanford School of Advanced Social Studies at 1144 Pine Street.

If you will sit still for a little wild name-dropping, I would like to tell you that the piano was broken in by a veritable Who's Who of the stage, screen, television, and allied polite larcenies.

Joe Bushkin, café society's favorite pianist (and a protégé of Tallulah's) was the first to have a go at the keyboard, and he wasn't much fun. He merely plays very fine piano. However, whenever he'd get up to stretch his fingers around a highball glass, Ed "Archie" Gardner, of Duffy's Tavern renown, would fling himself into the pilot's seat and try to play "La Vie en Rose," which he couldn't play at all. Only the first few notes. Then he'd fall off the seat. Just for laughs, of course.

In between these hilarious goings-on (hardly anybody noticed me with a cuspidor on my head and my pants rolled up), Abe

Burrows, writer of the big Broadway hit, *Guys and Dolls,* played a few notes. Bill Gargan, the actor, hit the keys now and then. Conrad Hilton, the biggest hotel man in the world (he owns the Waldorf, the Plaza, the Roosevelt, and the Sunshine Motel near Milpitas), lounged comfortably against the now famous piano, looking every bit as distinguished as he has a right to look. Eileen Wilson sang a few songs. So did Jane Morgan, who sings with éclat and finesse (a French vaudeville act) in the more elegant saloons. San Francisco's Carol Channing, the big blonde of *Gentlemen Prefer Blondes,* preferred to sit in a corner with her husband, whose name nobody caught.

Sounds pretty exciting, doesn't it? But you soon discover that a party is just a party, whether it's in a Park Avenue penthouse, crammed with stars, or on Telegraph Hill, crammed with people. Nothing happened here that couldn't have happened in San Francisco, and frequently does. Drinks were knocked over. Runs ("damn") appeared magically in nylons. Cigarettes smoldered on coffee tables. Men flirted with their best friends' wives. Women argued, vowed never to speak to each other again as long as they lived, and wound up with their arms around each other, crying and kissing and pledging eternal friendship. The frankly bored ones slipped away without saying good-by to the host. And so the ice melted in stale drinks and the night wore on and the people gradually wore out.

The party dissolved around 3 A.M. in a sudden flurry of good-bys and struggling overcoats.

The aforementioned distinguished Mr. Hilton disappeared with a striking red-clad brunette young enough to be his ex-daughter-in-law—and the disappointed younger gents, who'd also had their eyes on the brunette, made the usual sighing remark about "How you gonna fight the Waldorf-Astoria?"

Miss Bankhead broke off an angry argument with a wan, long-haired, strangely attractive girl and strode over to the piano, where she crashed out the opening chords of the Rachmaninoff Prelude in C Sharp Minor. But the notes were all wrong, and in a sudden frenzy she ran her fingers crazily up and down the keys, in a cascading cacophony. The notes burst out through the open French doors, out over the terrace, out over Park Avenue, and lost themselves amid the sleeping skyscrapers.

The dogs, which had been dozing in a corner, lifted their heads and barked.

Tallulah arose from the piano and walked rapidly toward the door.

The party was over, and I shook hands with the host, whose name I never did catch, and who didn't get my name, either.

But whoever he is, he has one heckuva well-broken-in piano.

In the interests of pure scienic research, and also because I had nothing else to do at the moment, I took a ride on a subway.

After all, there's been a lot of talk through the years about a subway for San Francisco, and I wanted to find out, firsthand, about life in the metropolitan underworld. It was exactly the way I remembered it from a few years ago, when I had to ride the New York subways out of necessity. Undoubtedly the fastest way to get around in a big city—but murder in the worst degree anyway.

I waited until the 5 P.M. rush hour began, and then joined a mob of wilted white-collar workers scrambling toward a hole in the ground at Forty-seventh Street and Sixth Avenue. The irritation began immediately. Everybody tried to be first down the stairs, men kept shouting "Awright, awright, stay in line," and on the third step, I got my first elbow in the ribs.

Sharp elbows are something no subway rider should be without, if you want to get ahead in the underworld. Unless you've got 'em and use 'em—offensively and defensively—you'll never get through the turnstile, never get onto the platform, never get into the train. You'll merely be squeezed to a pulp, trampled on and left behind, flatter than the Marina.

You get to know people very well in a subway train. Sometimes you ride for miles snuggled up against an imperfect stranger, standing there nose to nose with a silly grin on your face. You can't say anything bright, like "Nice weather we're having," and you can't even shift your position to something a little less confining for fear that he (or she, as the case may be) might take it personally. All you can do is stand there stiffly, gazing into a pair of eyes approximately one-half inch from yours. And whatever you do, don't drop your eyelids, even for a second. No room to bend over and pick them up—and besides, I shudder to think about bending over in a subway.

Everything happens fast in a train hurtling through the Manhattan blackness. The cars take off with a jet-propelled whoosh that hurls you back against a dozen elbows aligned in a solid row by veteran subway riders. As the train gathers speed (it cruises at what seems to be ninety miles per hour) you slowly regain your equilibrium and begin wondering how many strange hands are in your pockets. Then, with a painful squeal, the train slides into a station— and stops on a dime (they used to stop on a nickel, but the fare has been raised). And when a subway train stops, the passengers keep going for several feet, willy and nilly. In fact, both Willy and Nilly went for my feet, and landed on them accurately, too.

The most remarkable thing about a subway crowd is that these highly personal contacts—the kind that would inspire a girl to yell for the police in San Francisco—are made in the strictest deadpan. It's part of the rules and regulations, I guess. Nobody smiles in a subway. Everybody wears the grim, never-changing expression of a crowd watching *Das Rheingold* at the San Francisco Opera House.

All the poking, hauling and elbowing is taken as matter of course, and I was quite relieved to discover that I wouldn't have to marry the girl standing in front of me. Nice girl, weight about 120, and all real, but our relationship seemed purely physical.

Femininities aside, the most fascinating figures in the subway world are the old hands who somehow manage to read a newspaper between Forty-sixth and 125th—from cover to cover, without once opening the paper. They merely fold it around and around until it's hardly larger than a postage stamp, flip it this way and that, and produce a tiny area of type suitable for reading at a point directly below the tip of the nose. Hard on the eyes, of course—and, whenever the train comes to one of its sudden stops, a little hard on the nose, too. You've read about people whose noses are buried in newspapers. The New York subways are full of them.

By the time we reached the 125th Street station, all the fight had gone out of me. The doors slid open and I decided to go along with the crowd. Completely relaxed, I was carried out onto the platform with my feet a good three inches off the ground. Then the crowd dispersed toward the exits and I came back to earth with a thud.

Despite the slight inconveniences—the back of my coat was dotted with lipstick from the impetuous girls behind me (impetuous every time the train stopped, that is) and my shoes looked like Washington's at Valley Forge—despite these minor inconveniences, the subway had proved itself a real little speed-burner. From Forty-seventh to 125th in less than twenty minutes during the rush hour is pretty good going—and let's face it, the irritations are just as plentiful in a Muni bus in San Francisco.

For a few minutes, I stood on the underground platform, watching the locals and expresses rattle by, jammed to the doors with dead-eyed New Yorkers. Should I sacrifice myself further to scientific research by riding back to midtown on a returning train, or should I——?

Suddenly a train stopped in front of me, and as I stood there wavering, I was surrounded in a trice by a wall of flying elbows and knobby knees. "C'mon, c'mon," the irritated voices rasped in my ears, and the strange hands began kneading my back, exploring my pockets, locating my wallet and pinching it speculatively.

My mind was made up.

With the cry of a wounded bookie, I broke away from the New York Neanderthal mob and raced up the iron, debris-strewn stairs.

Outside, in the fresh cold air of the night, I stood on a corner and uttered my first plaintive word since disappearing into the underground twenty long minutes before.

"Taxi!"

If I may make a slightly stuffy pronouncement, it's "color" that makes a city great—the color of picturesque people and places, of foreign colonies ranged side by side, of frenetic activity and unceasing movement.

San Francisco has "color" to an almost overwhelming degree. New Orleans has a slight touch of it, in a very special Frenchified way. And New York is loaded with it, from the Battery to the Bronx, from the Hudson River to the East.

Not all of it is pretty—but all of it is real, all of it memorable. The sagging old tenements of the Lower East Side, whose odor grabs your nostrils as you drive past—these have a grim color. Rickety, dirty Pell and Mott Streets in the heart of New York's Chinatown—this section has a powerful something all its own. It's a far, far cry from the prettified Chinatown of San Francisco, with its gay tourist trappings. The New York Chinatown is smaller, darker—an unsmiling few blocks bogged down under decades of grime.

And Third Avenue around Bleecker Street in the Bowery—here are all the Skid Rows and flophouses in the country, rolled up in one ugly bundle. Here, on block after block, you see misery on parade—the canned-heat bums staggering around the sidewalks, muttering their gibberish and waving their scarecrow arms. The tattered old dolls with the scraggly teeth and the straggly hair, staring at you through half-dead eyes and teetering slowly on the edge of the gutters, their feet dragging, their arms hanging straight down in the age-old gesture of despair.

The secondhand stores in endless array, the flophouses, the panhandlers, the sauntering, hard-eyed cops—and over it all, in an iron counterpoint, the rattle and roar of the elevated trains. And standing strong and serene in the background, that crowning anomaly in this brutalized little world: the Bowery Savings Bank.

The Bowery, the Bowery . . . I'll never go there any more.

Metropolitan color; it abounds in every corner of Manhattan.

On Mulberry Street, where the Italians have their little colony and the tinny tones of a far-off accordion hang heavy in the air. On Central Park West, where the high and mighty live high and mightily in skyscraper apartment houses overlooking the park.

There is color galore in Rockefeller Center—which old-hand New Yorkers call "Rock Center," and where the gaily attired children ice-skate to and fro in the shadow of endless buildings. And along Fifth Avenue, with its breath-takingly beautiful St. Patrick's Cathedral, and its world-famed temples of commerce: Bonwit Teller, Bergdorf Goodman, Saks, Cartier's, Tiffany's, Peck & Peck, Best, DePinna— the names that spell Fifth Avenue everywhere.

A strange, attractively repellent city . . .

Your heart turns cold and gray in the alleys of the financial district, where the sun seldom shines and the rushing workers seldom smile and the massive buildings, rusty and crusty, glower impersonally at the passer-by.

And yet, only a few blocks away, you have to smile a warm, friendly smile at New York's City Hall—the old, pretty little two-story building that is so dwarfed by its towering neighbors, so small, so quaint, so obviously an amusing little irony in the world's greatest city.

And down at the tip of Manhattan, surrounded by ugly warehouses and ramshackle buildings, you can stand and thrill to the sight of the Statue of Liberty, hazily outlined in the harbor, and I don't care how cynical you are, I don't care how many times you've seen her, how many pictures you've looked at—she is always exciting to look at. Here is the symbol supreme of a new land, and your

mind wanders around to the huddled millions who've sailed past
her to start life afresh, from scratch, in America. New York—with
liberty in its harbor. San Francisco—with Alcatraz. America—from
A to Z.

Colorful New York—and you're impressed anew as you speed along
the Henry Hudson Parkway, overlooking the great piers with their
great names. Cunard White Star, United States Line, the French
Line. Over there, the twin red stacks of the mighty *Mauretania* flare
up, with the thin line of Jersey in the background, across the river.
Here, the "queen" ships of the Atlantic are berthed—the *Mary*, the
Elizabeth—and here is the sleek *America*, the slick *Ile de France*,
the *Liberté*, all the names that mean de luxe travel on the high seas.
New Yorkers see these great ships every day, nosing through the
harbor and into the Hudson, and they no longer look twice. A San
Franciscan is as casual about his two bridges.

And speaking of color—how can you top the theater district west
of Broadway just before curtain time? Cops, cabs and customers in
a furious knot along Forty-sixth and Forty-seventh, where the leg-
endary names sparkle in lights above the marquees: Ethel Merman,
Paul Lukas, Rosalind Russell, Jose Ferrer, Clive Brook, Louis
Calhern, Carol Channing, Celeste Holm, on and on, bright in the
night, and where else are you going to find such an array?

You can even find a certain quaintness in the metropolitan magic
of Manhattan, almost a small-town quality. The parents with their
children at the Central Park Zoo on a sunny Sunday, chattering
away like parents everywhere. The cabdrivers, almost pathetically
eager to talk to their customers, as friendly and outgoing as kids.
And, of course, New York's answer to San Francisco's cable car—the

ancient horse-drawn hansoms lined up in a picturesque row along
Fifth-ninth Street, ready to take you for a clattering spin through
the park. It's a wonderful, relaxing way to spend an hour—in a hack
that's a hundred years old, jiggling pleasantly around the easy
curves at a pace even slower than that of a cable car. Seven dollars
for the ride, and worth every nickel of it.

That's New York—brimming with color, and pulsing with life, from
the subways far below your feet, to the Empire State, far above the
clouds. And besides all that, as Toots Shor brayed exultantly in front
of his Fifty-first Street institution:

"Besides all that, m'boy, this is the big leagues—the biggest big
league in the world. This is the town of champs, and if you don't
know it, you're a chump."

I'm no chump. I know it.

MEXICO TO ME   The tourist's first tip from the American foreign
colony set: that you never refer to Mexico City as Mexico City; just
plain Mexico, please—and why, I have no idea . . . The first view
of Mexico (the city) from a circling American Airlines plane at
midnight: a shimmering sham of endless lights, cloaking the heady
daytime spectacle of luxury and squalor that makes it indeed "The
City of Contrasts" . . . The drawling hordes of wealthy Texans
who make regular week-end junkets to the Mexican play places—to
the point where they are singled out, not always kindly, as "those
Texicans" . . . The peons, with their bare feet, battered old hats,
and dirty serapes, wandering along the elegant Avenidas Juarez and
Reforma, looking as weirdly out of place as Ozark hillbillies lounging
at the corner of Post and Grant . . . Hotel Del Prado, the swank

mecca for Americans, with its lobby four stories high—and its urbane, "English-speaking" clerk who raps smartly on the bell and purrs: "One moment, please, and you will be shown to your rooms by a boybell."

The sad-eyed, undersized children, some of them carrying babies, who cluster at the entrances to the tourist traps, form a circle around you and wail for your pesos—whereupon the doorman rushes out and chases them away with a ferocity that makes you want to hit him over the head with the nearest Texan . . . The constant warnings, on all sides, to "stay away from the drinking water, it's dynamite"; so the first word you learn is "Tehuacan," a bottled spring water guzzled so assiduously by Americanos that I wish I owned a few shares in the outfit . . . The wonderful Mexican telephone operators, who take hours to get your number, but keep you amused meanwhile with such assurances as "I weel hov eet for you een a moment, señor. Don't hang!"

The old, French-style buildings along the main boulevards of Mexico City—giving it a truly continental air—which are slowly disappearing to be replaced by the neon-and-chrome modernities which remind you too strongly of Main Street, U.S.A. . . . The taxi drivers, heavier-footed and wilder-eyed than their Parisian counterparts, whipping their Fords and Chevvies and Buicks through the heaviest traffic with both hands on the horn and no hands on the wheel. Mexico City's cabs must have the best brakes in the world. They've never been used . . . The familiar names like Joan Crawford and Elizabeth Taylor, springing out of the theater marquees from a welter of Spanish that probably means nothing more important than "Movies Are Your Best Entertainment" . . . And the Mexican radio programs, which make your ears feel like they never left home; singing commercials, blatant comedians, and orchestras that play such fine old Mexican melodies as "Begin the Beguine," "El Rancho Grande," and "Harbor Lights"—the latest hits from Teen Pon Olley.

The Trader Vic's of Mexico—Les Ambassadeurs restaurant—where the waiter captains wear cutaways and striped pants and the menu features pâté from Strasbourg and sole from Holland and where, if you order Mexican food, you're likely to get nothing more than a lifted eyebrow, very well done . . . The Cadillacs parked three deep in front of the popular 1–2–3 restaurant, giving you a faint idea of the wealth that abounds somewhere in this overwhelming tangle of tumble-down houses and jumbled-up poverty; a Cad costs $10,000 American in Mexico . . . The tireless touristas, armed with dictionaries and printed cards that compute dollars into pesos (a peso is approximately eleven cents), trooping from one luggage-and-silver shop to the next, buying hard bargains from the soft-spoken proprietors; the luggage is cheap, and rather looks it on close inspection, and the jewelry is no doubt fine if you like silver jewelry. You do? Fine. I left it all for you.

The main highway to Cuernevaca, a two-lane, twisting thing that writhes through tiny villages of wooden shacks, snoozing natives full of pulque, and strips of beef drying on clotheslines in the beating sun; only the flies get fat . . . The wandering street musicians in Cuernevaca—the mariaches—who play cute little games with the gringos. Two of them ask if you'd like to hear a song (it's usually "Guadalajara," of course) and when you dumbly nod yes, they let out a whistle—and out from behind a corner troops the rest of the family, nine strong, packing the oddest assortment of instruments that side of Spike Jones: one-string violins, big mandolins that have seen pluckier days, and guitars filled with lost chords. But when they get together, which is not often enough to become monotonous, the music adds up to a charming little concert, at strictly non-union rates . . . The dignified, impassive old women who peddle their odds-and-endless arrays at the street corners—earrings, bracelets, knives, razor blades, jelly in chunks, fountain pens, and, above and below all, gum, gum and more gum; Cheeklets, who'll buy my Cheeklets?

Warm days and cool nights, skyscrapers and hovels, colorful street loungers who look like bit players in Mexican movies, fat Americans tsk-tsking piously over emaciated dogs asleep on the sidewalks, Mexican restaurants that don't serve tortillas, history slowly falling apart on all sides, expatriates who are more Mexican than the Mexicans, hordes of workers taking their siesta in the shadow of buildings they are either tearing down or putting up, it's hard to tell which . . . That is Mexico, to me.

They start talking about it days in advance—like baseball fans discussing a coming double-header, or football followers chattering about The Big Game. In the bars, on the streets, in the taxis, you hear the names of the matadors so often that they become familiar, like Joe DiMaggio and Frankie Albert.

For on Sunday, in the Plaza Mexico, the world's biggest bull ring, Matadors Martorell, Aparicio, and Velazquez will kill six bulls in the final spectacle of the Mexican major league season. And everybody, my dear, simply everybody will be there.

Starting the Wednesday before, the lines are long and restive at No. 9 Izzaga, where you buy your tickets for a price that depends on how inexperienced you look to the gimlet-eyed seller. I must have looked pleasingly green, literally and figuratively. He soaked me 140 pesos for two seats (about $15.50) and succeeded in making me feel pretty lucky to get them, too. This is known as killing the toro Norteamericano, and I showed no fight whatever.

By early Sunday afternoon, the whole great city—not including the six bulls whose fate has already been decided—is caught up in the fever. The fashionables, powdered, perfumed and dressed to kill, eat a leisurely prefight luncheon in the sunswept patio at 1-2-3, or at Les Ambassadeurs or the Jena or Hotel Del Prado. The touristas are busy getting loaded, with cameras to match. The cabs and Cads are lined up, ready to go. And already the cheaper seats on the sunny side of the arena are beginning to fill with the native aficionados who walked miles to get to the strange spectacle which adds up to sadistic cruelty for some, a traditional, stirring experience for others.

All roads lead to the Plaza Mexico on Sunday. And whether your steps are swift or faltering depends strictly on your point of view.

It was hot and windy in the Plaza that Sunday afternoon at four —the time when the trumpets sound and the air is thick with sweat and the hint of blood to come.

A self-appointed guide, apparently as lost as I, led me up countless stairs to the top of the arena, a dizzying vantage point looking down into the ring. From there, the fifty thousand seats seem to slant straight down, and straight down I walked—for our seats were in the fourth row, and already occupied, of course, by two Mexicans whose expressions indicated that anybody who comes late to a bull-fight shouldn't come at all.

At that point, I was inclined to agree. Walking down three hundred vertical steps, on a full stomach and everybody else's feet, is enough to make you want to trade places with the bull. After all, HE doesn't know what he's doing.

But it was worth all the trouble. Plaza Mexico, with its fifty thousand "olé"-shouters and its colorful Latin-American signs advertising Seagram's Seven Crown, Red Hackle Scotch, and Nescafé, is an inspiring edifice in a country whose buildings all lean suspiciously to starboard. The action in the ring was memorable. And I was fortunate enough to be seated next to a Texas couple who know all about bullfighting and were anxious to cut me in.

The most heroic figure at a bullfight is the bull—and these were 1200-pound La Puntas, massive of shoulder, noble of head, speedy of hoof.

Your sentiments are with him as he charges out of a chute into the center of the sandy ring, looking around coldly, sneering at the fifty thousand gapers. Already there are two beribboned barbs in the hump of muscle on his neck.

"Purty, those ribbons," drawled the Texas girl. "Colorful touch."

Every classical move that takes place thereafter is designed to make the bull lower his proud head and to weaken his muscles— so that the final job of the matador, the killing thrust of the sword over the horns, can be accomplished with a minimum of risk.

I don't mean to sound snide. The bull's goose might be cooked beyond the shadow of a doubt, but the matador is risking his life, too—against 1200 pounds of perfectly conditioned muscle. A fighting bull has a short life—about four years—but up until the last fifteen minutes or so, he has been living on the fat of the land, waiting only to die miserably in the warm sands of Plaza Mexico with the gloating cheers of fifty thousand thrill-seekers fading in his prized ears.

A brave bull dies slowly and fights hard. First against the taunting peones, who flaunt their capes in his face and then leap to safety over the fence or behind a barrier when he charges. He fights against the drab, fat-haunched picadors who ride in on mattressed horses and plunge their picks into his neck as he drives his horns into the frightened, well-protected horses. When the picador lances the bull too often and too deep, the crowd hoots—for then the bull has little fight left for the matador. Nobody loves a picador, I'm sure. It's the lowest form of employment.

Then come the dancing banderillos, who, in a fine show of grace and daring, run at the bull, sidestep his horns, and place their gaily colored darts in his neck. ("Colorful," sighed the Texas girl again. "Picturesque.") And finally, La Suerte Suprema, "the moment of truth," has arrived for the agonized, hard-breathing animal whose sides by this time are streaming with blood.

The matador makes his accomplished passes with the cape, weakening the bull to the point where sometimes he falls to his knees and can barely arise. Matador Aparicio wowed the mob by getting on his knees, too, and then walking away with his back to the toro (loud cries of "Olé! Olé!" and "Mucho!"). Matador Martorell was butted once, but he was unhurt, and the camera-toting Texan on my left complained: "That's nothing. I like to see the horns go into the man's groin. I got a great shot once, with the horns in six inches, great shot." Matador Velazquez tried to kill his bull twice, but failed both times, and when he walked away I figured he was going to come back with a gun. But an assistant delivered the coup de grace with a short dagger.

The three matadors each killed their two bulls, and it's not a pretty death. The great beasts, after receiving the sword thrust, don't fall in their tracks and die on the spot. Some stand blankly for long seconds and then collapse majestically, like a building toppling. Some thrash around, gore flooding from their throats. Some die methodically, first getting on their knees and then rolling slowly over, as though going to sleep for the night.

And then, while the matador walks around the arena, bowing to the crowd—if a patron throws his hat at him, he has to pick it up and throw it back—three horses come in and drag the bull away, and a ground crew with rakes spreads fresh sand over the blood-spattered mess.

Two hours later, it was all over. The six bulls had paid the price for four years of easy living. Matador Aparicio had won a pair of ears for his distinguished efforts. Matador Velazquez had really been beaten by the bull, but he was still alive. Matador Martorell had a bruise, of the kind a quarterback gets twenty times every Saturday during football season. And in the setting sun, the fifty thousand aficionados trooped slowly out of the great bowl, having passed two pleasant hours.

When I looked back at the entrance to the arena, the Texas couple was buying a couple of souvenirs—plastic fighting bulls, with slits on top so they could be used as piggy banks. "The children will just love 'em, honey," she was saying to her husband, who still looked disgruntled. He hadn't seen a horn enter a man's groin, and for him, death had been incomplete that Sunday afternoon.

A few short years ago, they tell me, Acapulco was a tiny Mexican village sleeping in the sun on the shores of the Pacific. Then some enterprising operators discovered that there's gold in them there white sands—and today, therefore, we have the "new" Acapulco,

world-famed resort, mecca for sunnymooners, and enchanted land
of gleaming white luxury hotels, tourists who prey on sailfish, and
shopkeepers who prey on tourists.

All this is not without good reason. Even the approach to Acapulco is designed to knock your Yankee eye out. The plane from
Mexico City comes in low over the mountains—and there, un-
folding suddenly, are strips of gleaming beach, a gentle bay dotted
with yachts, and hotels that crown the hilltops and crowd the blue
waters.

And if that isn't enough to take your breath away, the plane
daintily skims over the waves and lands on a beach. Absolutely.
You can step through the door and throw yourself right into the
Pacific, but that's the coward's way. Instead, we chose to face the
rigors of Acapulco, a decision that proved to be character-building,
even for a couple of characters.

The denizens of Acapulco are divided quite roughly into three
groups. There are the natives, who drive you crazy in taxis and
operate shops featuring merchandise lately imported from the shop
next door. There are the semistylish "regular" visitors from Mexico
City and Texas, who have their own houses and form a tightly knit
social group that gets tight nightly at cocktail parties which are
like cocktail parties everywhere, only more so. And there are the
blinking, white-skinned, first-time tourists, looking like they'd arrived on the noon bus from Hammond, Indiana, or Chillicothe,
Ohio. One, who shall be forever nameless, looked like he'd just
arrived by jitney from San Francisco—although in fairness, I must
say he bore the unmistakable stamp of the world traveler. On his
suitcase, at least.

For the accommodation of these poor souls, simmering away in their Aloha shirts and sandals, Acapulco provides a dozen hotels that look almost as impressive as their colored photographs on the airline calendars. Most favored, perhaps, is Hotel de Las Americas, on a hilltop overlooking the ocean on one side, the bay on the other, and very little in between. The only thing I can say against the Las Americas is that the walls are thin and the acoustics are strange, which gives you the impression that you're living in the midst of two hundred conversations, most of them pretty dull.

Atop the next hill, with a sweeping view of the unreal harbor, is the noted A. C. Blumenthal's fortresslike Casablanca, and further on, at the other end of town, is the Mirador, built on rocks above the ocean and containing La Perla, the outdoor night club owned by Miss Hedy Lamarr's most recent reject, Ted Stauffer. Scattered around and about these institutions are a dozen other inns—with names like Caleta, La Playa, and Club de Pesca—but even so, it isn't enough.

Acapulco is so crowded that tourists fight to rent bunk space aboard fishing boats in the harbor, and the hotels are booked solid for days in advance. This'll give you an idea, maybe. To go somewhere else.

I don't want you to think that everything is slick and super in the "luxury" spots of Acapulco. The place grew too fast, and after all, it's Mexico and nobody's in a hurry. The hotel staffs are painfully eager to please, but the room service coffee is likely to arrive in a chipped old pot or a blackened tin pitcher that has seen better days, probably on Howard Street. And the chambermaids cutely indicate their eagerness to make the beds (with you still in 'em) by forming choral groups outside your door at 8 A.M. and singing Mexican folk songs interspersed with hysterical laughter. I know

what they were laughing about. They knew how much we were
paying for our room.

However, there's plenty to get up early for in Acapulco. For instance, conversations with room service. I called one morning for
orange juice and asked: "Is it fresh?" "Is it fresh?" came the
wounded reply. "Why, we open it every morning!"

And a tour of the downtown shops, where the shopkeepers insist
that they speak English, and get angry if you can't understand
them. They wrap your purchases in bags that are undoubtedly
printed in English, though. One read: "We Deliber. All Oders."
Another features "Beach Ware." And in a third shop, a very old,
very sweet woman sits at a counter with a pencil and painstakingly
crosses out an *n* and scribbles in an *r* on each bag so that "Beach
Wean" becomes "Beach Wear."

The weather and the beaches are magnificent. In fact, there are
two beaches sizzling under the full impact of the angry sun—one
called the "Morning Beach," the other the "Afternoon Beach"—and
I can testify that there is no hour of the day in which you can't
get a third-degree burn. Even though there are friendly beach boys
who'll turn you over every few minutes for a handful of pesos, you
can't stay ahead of the ultraviolet rays. The only solution—and I'm
sure all Acapulco will be happy to see me try it—is to skewer yourself on a spit and revolve slowly, all the while basting yourself with
coconut oil and shouting, "Vive San Francisco!"

Small wonder I was unanimously voted the tourist least likely to
cement inter-American relations. In my small circles of enemies, I
became known as the man who put the half-Nelson on Rockefeller.

Night falls slowly and dramatically over Acapulco, with a sunset
that writhes into the Pacific and leaves in its wake a breathless

ceiling of warm stars a scant few inches overhead. Then there are long, tall drinks on the Las Americas terrace, or dancing in the sand at the Copacabana night club, or clinging to a windswept table at La Perla to watch the superb divers plunge a hundred feet off sheer cliffs into the boiling waters below.

This is Acapulco—if you can forget that behind the thin line of garish hotels and fat tourists exists the real town, the town of poverty and dirt and undersized children and bony dogs and the inescapable stench of raw, red meat hanging on clotheslines in front of the slanting wooden shacks.

It was easy to leave Acapulco. But then, any place is easy to leave —when you're returning to the cool, clean magic of Baghdad-by-the-Bay.

HAWAII TO ME   The cynics call it a "tourist trap"—but what's wrong with that?

It's one of the most beautiful, and beautifully run traps in the world. The waters off famed Waikiki are a heady swirlpool of blues, greens, ambers, and purples, shimmering like sequins in the sun. The temperature is an even 75 the year around, and the flowers all look like they were invented by Salvador Dali in a particularly surrealist mood. In the three big beachfront hotels—the Royal Hawaiian, the Moana, and the stunning new SurfRider—the service is flattering and the food is fattening. Upon your arrival, you are throttled in orchid leis up to your ears and kissed on both cheeks by hula girls wearing just enough to keep cool. When you jaywalk across Kalakaua Avenue, traffic immediately screeches to a respectful halt, for the tourist is the Islands' No. 3 industry (after sugar and pineapple) and it's considered very bad form to mow down the guy who brings in the loot.

This is a tourist trap? Look, I'm trapped. Just don't let me escape.

THOUGHTS WHILE TANNING   *Aloha* is the handiest word in the Hawaiian language (which, yawn, has a twelve-letter alphabet). It means anything and everything—hello, good-by, I love you, good luck, drop dead. However, nobody speaks Hawaiian except the tourists . . . Everybody says "I'm going to Hawaii" but hardly anybody goes to Hawaii ("The Big Island"); the island of Oahu, and specifically the Waikiki sector of Honolulu, gets practically all the business . . . If you're allergic to pineapple, the Islands are not for you. You can't escape the stuff. Your old-fashioned is garnished with pineapple slices. When you awaken in the morning, you discover that some pixy has stolen into your room and left a whole pineapple, with its innards sliced into long sticks. A cottage cheese and pineapple salad consists of a huge chunk of pineapple, with a dab of cottage cheese, instead of the other way around. The orange juice? Canned or frozen . . . The Islands are more like America than America, except for one notable item. No billboards. They're forbidden because they'd spoil the flower-happy vistas . . . Practically everything in Hawaii is imported—even the famed banyan trees. There is no indigenous plant life, and every flaming flower came from elsewhere. Most of the food is flown or shipped in. The grass skirts come originally from Samoa, the ukulele is a Portuguese invention, all the songs were adapted from missionary melodies (and are titled "Lovely Hula Hands"), and the tradition of casting leis from your ship into the waters off Diamond Head was invented by a lazy steward who got tired of cleaning dead flowers off the deck.

WAIKIKI WICKI-WACKI   The tourists, who spend at least fifty million dollars a year in Hawaii, are, for the most part, a pretty harried lot.

They tumble off their ship or plane, fall into a $1.98 Aloha shirt, load their cameras, and are off in a trice, whatever that is, to see the sights, whatever those are. Fresh from Kokomo, Muncie, or Ashtabula, they are pushover prey for the energetic wiles of the hotel social directors and tour conductors, and the next thing they know, they are weighted down with schedules and hurrying to grab planes for the other islands, busses for Koko Head and the Blow Hole, and rushing to go on a picnic. A picnic, incidentally, is called a "Piki-niki" in Hawaiian, which has an unfortunate tendency to sound like baby talk.

Some of these tourists, who never sit still long enough to get a sunburn, go winging off for a couple of days to see the volcano on the island of Hawaii, and return, tired and pale, to gasp, "Unbelievable! Indescribable!" I'm willing to take their word for it. I missed Vesuvius and the last days of Pompeii, and they ain't gonna rope me in for no minor league spectacle.

However, even the wariest tourist in Honolulu is a cinch to be trapped, sooner or later, into attending a luau—and I was no exception.

After nimbly sidestepping the volcano junket, the Koko Head tour, the Elks Club hei-ride, and the three-day course in outdoor lei-making, I found myself surrounded one night by a man named Don the Beachcomber, who tore off my city clothes, wrapped me in some colorful cloth, and cried: "Come to my luau!" And the next thing you knau, there I was.

Mr. Beachcomber—for this is his legal name, Mr. Don Beachcomber—stages a luau, pronounced "lu-wow," each Sunday night in his grass-covered restaurant on Kalakaua Avenue, and while it's not a fête worse than death exactly, I don't think it'll ever replace food.

What happens at a luau is that the men all wear long cloth gadgets tucked in around their fat middles, and the women all wear sarongs that make them look like road company Dorothy Lamours, and then everybody sits on the floor at low tables and eats with his fingers. Not having eaten with my paddies for some years now, I chewed my index finger down to the second joint before Don straightened me and it out. However, for an index finger, I must say it wasn't too bad. Just a touch gamy, perhaps.

The big deal at a luau, aside from aching backs and sticky fingers, is a whole pig roasted underground in a nest of preheated rocks. This tastes exactly like roast pig. The rocks aren't served. Then comes some raw salmon mixed with chopped ice and a very good deal indeed called laulau, which happens to be pork, butterfish, and beef wrapped in a bunch of leaves and cooked with the pig. Mighty tasty. In and around these items are sprinkled the omnipresent pineapple and the most appalling of Hawaiian staples, poi.

There probably are people in the world who honestly enjoy poi, but I doubt it. What's to like? Poi is taro root pounded to a gray, ghastly paste, and in this country we would use it to put up wallpaper. In Hawaii, they eat it with the same little cries of pleasure that a bookworm must emit upon coming across a jar of Stanford's Library Paste. Like everything else at a luau, poi is eaten with the fingers, and it comes in two consistencies: one-finger and two-finger. And it's murder on manicures.

As I was leaving the luau, bent of back and drippy of digits, I noticed a man being ejected rather peremptorily by Mr. Beachcomber and his staff. "Catch him wearing a necktie?" I asked. "Nope," hissed Mr. Beachcomber. "Trying to smuggle in a fork." Oh, the poor sane fool.

ALOHA   If you don't watch out, you can get pretty sentimental about Hawaii. It's a lush, friendly place, and the perfume of hibiscus and ginger is always in the air, and there is always a steel guitar sighing somewhere in the far-off night. Crusty Mark Twain felt the charm to the point of describing the Islands as "the loveliest fleet anchored in any ocean." And Poet Don Blanding caught the warm, flowery mood when he dreamed: "If moonlight were fragrant, it would smell like white ginger blossoms."

It's a soft place to live and a hard place to leave, but leave it I did early one morning, with my Island treasures, stamped Made in Kokomo, clutched to my overweight heart. Nine hours later, as the DC–6 flies, I was back where I started, watching my sunburn fade before my eyes. The eyes will fade later.

But there's one thing you can always say for San Francisco, and I'd like to say it right here: You're so nice to come home to.

Minnie   Ah, the strange and wonderful people of Baghdad-by-the-Bay . . .

You wander around the town and you meet the squares and the characters, and then, 'way out in the 6100 block on Mission, you run into somebody like Minnie Amos.

She was born Minnie O'Hara, fifty-four years ago in Ireland, and she still has a delightful brogue, the twinkle in her eyes, the up-turned nose. But these aren't the things that add up to her story—a story even her neighbors don't know.

When she was a girl, Minnie of Mission Street started working in the kitchen on the estate of Sir Humphrey Martin of England—near Ascot, where the Prince of Wales spent a lot of his time. And because the Prince used to drop in on Sir Humphrey a lot, and because he liked curry and chutney, Minnie learned to make those dishes.

That's why she's still alive and working and reasonably happy.

One day she married a British civil servant named Amos. They went to India. Then they moved to Manila, with their young daughter. And then came the war and the Japanese. Her husband "disappeared," never to be heard from again. Her daughter was killed—

beheaded before the agonized eyes of her mother. And through a series of million-to-one happenstances, Minnie Amos escaped to San Francisco.

Here, she didn't know a soul, but eventually she got a few odd jobs in hotel kitchens. Frankly, she didn't care whether she lived or died. Then, one dismal night, she remembered about curry and chutney.

In her tiny kitchen out on Mission Street, she experimented. All by herself, she began packaging the stuff, making her own labels, doing her own packaging, her own selling. Every morning at 5:45, she's down at the produce district, buying her ingredients. And every day, she works till midnight—her hard, hot work filling the Mission Street air with the spicy aromas of India, the land where she once knew her small measure of happiness. Understandably, the name on her labels read "Dream of India."

Minnie is getting along all right now. Some of the best restaurants, from here to Carmel, are using the products of her one-woman "factory." And once again, she feels like she has something to live for. "Everybody's so nice to me," says Minnie O'Hara Amos, whose strange life led her around the world to San Francisco—the hard way. The very hard way.

The Sunshine Spreader   Every once in a while—
every once in a great while, I should say—I find myself suffocated
by that feeling described so aptly by the Germans as *Weltschmerz*.
The woes of mankind weigh heavily on my sloping shoulders, and
I feel that I must fulfill my function as a public servant by Doing
Something for Somebody.

As anybody in the newspaper business will be only too happy
to tell you, this is usually a mistake.

First, before printing a story designed to tug at the reader's heart
—and purse strings—the Pitiful Case must be investigated to make
sure it is also a Deserving Case.

In the second place, the self-appointed Do-Gooder must be pre-
pared to handle the contributions, thank the donors, and see that
the funds are spent properly by the grateful, tear-stained object of
his affections.

And in the third place, it's important to find out whether the
person being helped wants to be helped in the first place.

All this sage counsel was forgotten one day, however, when
I heard about the case of Lydia Radich. This story I
printed:

"OF HUMAN INTEREST   She was only sixteen, she had a new dress, it was Easter Sunday, and she had her twenty-year-old fiancé by her side, to hold her hand and tell her sweet and wonderful things. Outside, the rain had finally let up, so they decided to go for a walk, hand in hand. Then it happened. A truck, out of control, skidded through the intersection, hit them in the pedestrian crosswalk, and carried them thirty-five feet, where it pinned her against a wall.

"That is the story of Lydia Radich, who has been crippled from birth. She was saving her money for an all-important third operation that, doctors hoped, would allow her to walk without braces by June, when she would step to the altar with Noilden Robinson. Now, the doctors are hoping to save one of her legs, almost severed by that truck. If they fail, she'll spend the rest of her life in a wheelchair. Meanwhile, young Robinson is in the hospital, too, with a possible broken back. And her widowed mother is praying for both of them.

"I don't often make an appeal for financial aid. But if anybody deserves help, it is sixteen-year-old Lydia Radich, whose dreams were smashed all over again—on Easter Sunday."

The reaction to that item was gratifying, to say the least. Over five hundred cash responses poured in from all over California, and even from Honolulu and Alaska. A week later, I went out to the San Francisco Hospital and presented a check for $3040 to Lydia, a small, dark-haired girl with a wistful smile and great black eyes.

"This is the nicest thing that ever happened to me," she said, and then she cried a little, the tears trickling slowly down her pale cheeks.

Perhaps it was the nicest thing that ever happened to little Lydia Radich. I don't know. But I do know that the money worked its immediate and inevitable change in the surrounding atmosphere.

Before the kindly thousands rolled in, Lydia's family and friends had kept her buoyed up with their courageous, chins-up attitude. Her widowed mother had mortgaged their home to help pay for Lydia's operations. Her sister worked after school to help out. Her boy friend was kindly, courtly, and considerate.

Suddenly, there was a change. The sister quit her job, and told Lydia in the hospital that she'd like to buy some clothes and charge them—to Lydia. Lydia's mother was besieged by a casual friend who turned into an ardent suitor overnight. And Lydia's boy friend thought it might be a good idea if they got married immediately. Things rapidly got to the point where nobody was talking to anybody.

Then, reluctantly, the Radich's attorney told me it might be a good idea if I made the financial decisions—a touchy job, at best. Part of the money, I decided, should be used to pay off the mortgage on Mrs. Radich's house. Some went to the sister for clothes. A radio was purchased for her boy friend who was still in the hospital, too. And the rest went toward a home for Lydia and Noilden, to live in after they were married.

And married they were, about a year later. They have three children. They have separated once, but are now together again. It's difficult to say whether little Lydia Radich is as happy now as she was when nobody on the outside was trying to help, and she and her family and friends were working long and hard by themselves to bring her back to health.

It seemed like such a simple thing—asking the readers for a little money to help an unfortunate girl. It turned out to be cold, hard, calculating work in an atmosphere that changed, with shocking speed, from warmth and directness to suspicions and tensions.

I first heard of Anna Johnson just a few days before Christmas.

There was embarrassment in her faltering stride and drooping shoulders as she walked into my office—a big, rawboned Norwegian girl with watery blue eyes and dirty, wispy blond hair. She was wearing an old blue dress with an interesting collection of stains across the bosom, and a thin beige overcoat decorated at the collar and cuffs with ratty fur.

Anna Johnson looked to be about thirty, and pregnant.

"I'm sorry to bother you," she said in the singsong of her native tongue, "but I don't know where to turn. I got a little boy. I'm going to have another baby any minute. I got no money and no friends. I been everywhere and talked to everybody—all those charity people—and nobody will help me."

I looked at pale, pregnant Anna Johnson, and I listened to the sounds of the Christmas bells in the streets outside, and I forgot the cynical advice of a dozen city editors: Stay out of other people's troubles, a newspaper has enough of its own.

Then she said thickly through her prominent teeth: "It's going to be such a terrible Christmas for my little boy. And the place we're living in—it's miserable, awful."

It was that, all right. A back room in a Mission Street heartbreak house called, for want of a more accurate name, a hotel. The room had no windows, but the rug was more than adequately ventilated. The bed was a wired-together nightmare of broken springs, covered with blankets that must have accompanied Napoleon's army in its march on Moscow. The smell of undisturbed dirt and abject poverty hung heavy in the stale air.

Anna Johnson gathered her happy four-year-old son onto her knee and told her simple story, all the while staring dully at the blank, streaked wall. She had been married to a farmer in Nebraska, but now she was divorced. She had managed to get a waitress job in a San Francisco cafeteria, and she had met a bus boy—the father of her unborn child. When she told him she was pregnant, he had patted her on the shoulder and had said that she could count on him. Then he quit his job and disappeared.

"Ah, I don't care about him," she said, her chin resting atop her smiling little boy's head. "But who's gonna take care of Jimmy here while I'm having the baby. What do I do with the baby? How do I buy Christmas presents? What's to become of us?"

She looked around the stifling room, so far from the wide fields of Nebraska, so far from the Norway of her childhood.

I went back to the office and wrote a story that implied, in my labored prose, that only a Scrooge could turn a deaf ear to the plight of Anna Johnson on the eve of Christmas. Then I called my friends to see whether they could take care of her boy while she was having the baby. Each of them—false friends!—managed to invent a satisfactory excuse on the spur of the moment, and I had a dismal mental picture of my own Christmas Eve, to be spent pacing the hospital corridor with Anna Johnson's son while she was in the delivery room.

The next morning, my story appeared in the paper, and by night-fall, $520 had rolled in, plus dozens of telephone calls pledging more. Plus a telephone call from Community Chest headquarters.

"It is nice of you to help Anna Johnson," said a cool, Community

Chest voice, "but it isn't really necessary, you know—unless, of course, you were just trying to print a sob story for Christmas. We are placing her little boy in our home on Nineteenth Avenue, and we are arranging for her hospital stay and a place for her to live afterwards."

When I explained all this to Anna Johnson, she looked more perplexed than pleased.

"I can't understand that," she said over and over, her fingers wandering aimlessly through her thin hair. "I didn't think they were gonna do anything for me. Say, I saw your story about me this morning, and it was swell. I liked it. Uh—how much money did you get?"

"Anna," I said, arising to leave, "I got $520. And I'm giving it to the Community Chest—to help people like you."

Anna Johnson didn't say anything. She just looked at me with her wide, watery, expressionless eyes. Then she looked at her little boy, sitting on the floor and playing happily with the holes in the rug.

"You win, Anna," I said, and I gave her the money and left in a hurry.

"Merry Christmas," she sang out, her voice echoing down the long, drab hall.

I found out later that I'd done the right thing, at that. The Community Chest really hadn't heard about Anna Johnson—until they'd read her story in the newspaper.

Late one dark night, on the eve of Thanksgiving, a woman I'd never heard of before became a widow—suddenly and shockingly.

Her husband, a cabdriver, picked up a fare who ordered him to drive to a remote section of the city. Then he held a gun at the back of his head and ordered him to turn over his money. The driver complied.

And then, for no apparent reason except fiendish whimsy, the bandit pulled the trigger and the cabbie died instantly. The murderer was never caught.

Once again I felt the urge to help. The widow, I wrote, was destitute—a living, innocent victim. And again the readers responded, to the tune of $1593. Deeply pleased, I obtained a cashier's check in that amount and hurried out to her house.

But she wouldn't see me.

"Nobody," she said coldly through an intermediary, "is going to call me a destitute in print and get away with it. I won't have my morals questioned."

She got the money, anyway, through some cabdriver friends of her late husband. I sincerely hope it helped.

Call Me Al For a lot of San Franciscans, it was a night they'll never forget—a Pearl Harbor of show business.

As news, and it was stop-press news, it was the kind of story nobody wanted to believe. It had that prime requisite of high tragedy—a bolt-from-the-blue suddenness that stunned people into silence. And, to heighten the shock effect, it all started as such a routine matter.

Al Jolson, the man Irving Berlin must have had in mind when he wrote "There's No Business Like Show Business," came to San Francisco to appear on a radio program.

He was in soaring spirits from the moment he arrived in "aaaah, my favorite city in the whole world." For lunch, he went to North Beach, in search of a tiny restaurant where, he bubbled, "I had the greatest meal in the whole world, ten years ago, for fifty cents." That night, he dined at Tarantino's on Fisherman's Wharf, where Dan Sweeney, the owner, greeted: "Hello, Mr. Jolson, how are you?"

"Never felt better in my life," beamed Al.

And as he ate, he kept humming a few bars from the then current hit, "Sentimental Me."

Ironic. The man who had entertained millions sang his last song in public—to himself. For two hours later, back in his hotel room, Al Jolson died.

No sooner had the Jolson story come to its untimely end than everybody had a memory about the minstrel man.

Old-time San Franciscans remembered him singing in front of lantern slides in a theater at Twenty-second and Mission. Not-so-oldtimers recalled the San Francisco opening of *The Jazz Singer,* highlighted by a "Jolson Imitation" contest on the stage. A dozen youngsters got down on their knees and spread their arms in the manner that became a classic overnight. The winner was Tommy Harris, now a prosperous restaurant owner, who still has the tarnished cup proclaiming him San Francisco's best imitation.

The cup was likewise.

When Showman Sid Grauman opened his National Theater at Post and Steiner Streets after the earthquake and fire, he hired young Jolson, who complained one night about the noise of the rain beating down on the tin roof.

"The people can't hear me," pouted Al.

So Grauman had a runway built out into the audience, and Jolson thereupon discovered the technique that carried him to fame—the way to get closer to the audiences he loved as much as they loved him.

But life was generally rough for Al during his early days in San Francisco. He recalled, on one of his last visits, that he had lived for months on the free lunches in a saloon at Powell and O'Farrell— the Barrel House, I believe it was.

"I patronized that place every day," he smiled. "They had the freest free lunch in town."

Typically and respectfully, Jolson's San Francisco admirers stayed in the shadows after his death. No mobs stormed Hotel St. Francis, pushing and shoving ghoulishly for a glimpse of his body. No crowds tried to jam into the funeral parlor where his body lay before its removal to Hollywood.

This was the quiet background for one of the most moving stories I ran into during those few moving days.

On Central Avenue in San Francisco lives Mrs. Mabel Tico. When she was only nine years old, she fell in love with Jolson, through his pictures in newspapers and on sheet music. Ever since, she remained one of his most devoted fans, buying his records, seeing his movies, listening to him on the air.

But she never saw him in person.

On the morning after Jolson's death, jolted and weeping, she hurried down to N. Gray's funeral parlor. She asked if she might see her idol. Yes, she could. And for the next thirty minutes, she sat all alone with the man she had worshiped for thirty-five years, but had never seen. No one else came into the room where the greatest entertainer of them all lay in death on a cot.

Then Mrs. Tico went back to her little house on Central Avenue. "I still can't believe that out of the millions who loved him," she sighed, "I could have been fortunate enough to have had thirty minutes alone with Al Jolson" . . .

But next day in Hollywood, twenty-two thousand fans rioted at his funeral.

By way of a footnote:

Since Jolson died, a new kind of character has developed in San Francisco. He's the old-time theaterman who had never so much as met Jolson, but who was quick to confide: "Y'know, if it wasn't for me, Joley prob'ly wunna gotten no place. I gave the kid his first break in show business, and y'know, he never forgot it. Always writin' me letters, or calling to see if I needed help, things like that" . . .

I've added their names to my list of "Famous San Francisco Firsters." You've met them all, at one time or another.

There's the man to whom Enrico Caruso said on the morning of April 18, 1906: "I'll never set foot in this city again." And there's the oldster who caught the rose thrown by Luisa Tetrazzini after she sang "The Last Rose of Summer" at Lotta's Fountain in 1910. And the guy who got drunk nightly with Jack London. And the fellow who knew Emperor Norton so well that he was bitten regulary by Bummer and Lazarus—and has the scars to prove it. And the unsung sandlot scout who first saw signs of greatness in a kid named Joe DiMaggio. And, most numerous of all, the first man to drive across the Bay Bridge and/or walk across the Golden Gate Bridge.

What a town. We've got a million of 'em

For Future Reference   It's just a matter of time.

One of these not-so-fine mornings, San Francisco will wake up and discover that the manic-progressives of public transportation have finally achieved their secret ambition.

There will be a strange new silence in the air. The slotted streets will seem uncomfortably quiet. And the people will look at each other in sudden consternation and gasp: "The cable cars—our cable cars—they've taken them away!"

It's inevitable—as inevitable as that bridges should replace ferryboats and that busses should supplant streetcars. Once there were a dozen cable car lines in San Francisco. Now there are three, attacked from all sides by those clear-eyed thinkers who point out righteously that the cables lose money—while closing those clear eyes to the fact that the hinky-dinkies are worth millions annually in publicity, good will, and the kind of unique color that is disappearing all too fast from "different" San Francisco.

So, while there still is time, let's take a ride on a Powell Street cable. Not the last ride, to be sure, but closer to the last ride than I care to think. For, as I was saying, it's just a matter of time.

The conductor sings out:

"Fares, please, fares . . . Wanna transfer? . . . No, lady, you can't stand on the outside step. Men only . . . 'Board!"

Wonderful, the way the gripman climbs aboard the Powell cable after it has been swung around on the turntable, with all hands helping. The passengers are clinging to the steps and the seats, awaiting the magic moment, and then he strides majestically to the grips—like a pilot climbing into his airliner . . . And there's always the tourist staring in slight disbelief from the sidewalk by the Bank of America, while a native knowingly points out the grip and the slot and dispenses clouds of misinformation ("That gizmo there goes down through the gimmick and grabs the dingbat, you follow me?") . . . The women tuck their skirts under their legs, the gripman clangs a final warning clang-clang, and we're off with a jerk (how do you do) past the corner sidewalk stand whose proud address is No. 1 Powell.

("Let 'em through, let 'em through . . . Plenty of room inside, don't shove . . . That's right, lady, you transfer to the B car at Geary" . . .)

There's something open, aboveboard, and pleasantly small-townish about a cable car . . . You can smell the food being cooked in Moar's and Bernstein's and Bunny's and Omar Khayyam's. You can wave, Main Street style, as you bounce past Saloonkeepers Baron Long and Harry Walsh on one side, and Florist George Arabian and Fight Promoter Bennie Ford on the other, mixing with the broken-nosers and the gamblers and the town characters who give Powell Street its Runyonesque flavor. You can stare smack into a hotel lobby, where a lounger sits and stares right back at you. And if Lefty O'Doul's newest Cadillac is parked in front of the saloon that bears his name, you can lean out daringly from the bottom step and take a mock kick at it.

Then there's the St. Francis's distinguished doorman, blowing his taxi whistle in the middle of the street and almost getting clipped as you rattle past. And the Gray Line busses, loading up with sightseers who look out of their windows at their first strange sight—you on a cable car . . . You turn and glance inside the car at the people sitting behind the glass doors. You don't see anybody you recognize—and you reflect for a second on the old tale that these aren't real people who sit inside of a cable car; they're built in at the factory!

("Coming out, let 'em out! . . . Give that lady a hand with the baby . . . Awright, fasten your safety belts, we're going up . . . Whatzat? Nnno, bud, you don't get no flying pay on THIS trip" . . .)

The University of California Extension—its campus a slanty sidewalk where the students stand, with one leg longer than the other, and puff cigarettes and flip the butts at the slot . . . Sears, of tiny pancake fame, and the Family Club, with its prim row of clipped trees starting with precision at one boundary of its property and marching to the other—you count them as you roll by . . . And always, the intriguing windows of apartment houses passing right in front of your nose, making you a Peeping Tom whether you like it or not, and you're afraid you do, a little . . . The welcome plateaux of Bush and Pine, where the phalanxes of autos, four abreast, stop respectfully because they know that a cable car can't; they don't need that automatic signal to tell them that the immovable object is coming with irresistible force, and a bell to match . . .

The gripman playfully raps out the rhythm of "California, Here I Come," and you're at——

"California Street . . . Fairmont, Top o' the Mark . . . Transfer to the Cal cable . . . How many transfers do you WANT, lady?" . . .)

One of the nicer things about a cable car is that everybody helps drive it. When it pauses for a double-parked auto, the guys on the lower step lean out, survey the clearance with gimlet eyes, and coach: "O.K., O.K., yer gonna make it—all clear" . . . Then the slow dip down the other slope of Nob Hill, the smart apartment houses melting into not-so-smart ones, the French laundries and the Chinese, and a snifter of garlic from nearby North Beach at Jackson—where the conductors get off to throw the hand switch and then leap back on as the car rattles, with the verve of a roller coaster, around the famed "'Kout-fer-da-curve!" turn . . . Jackson Street, with its minor miracle of two slots and three rails so that two cars can use it by sharing the middle rail—and suddenly you "'Kout!" again, this time into Mason Street, and you notice the dead rails of long-dead cable lines, indecently buried under pavement that covers its steel bones only in patches.

("Yeah, we stop near Fisherman's Wharf, Mister . . . Huh? Sure, you can come back on the Hyde Street line—just a couple of blocks over . . . Awright, here we go, over the top" . . .)

At Vallejo Street, you suddenly nose into space and then start down—frighteningly fast at first, until the grip takes hold . . . Ahead, the Bay and the stacks of streamers nuzzling up to the piers near Fisherman's Wharf . . . The big, raw hill near Green Street, with its hundreds of wooden steps going up and up while the tourists follow them with their eyes as far as they can, and then stop, out of breath . . . The swing into Columbus Avenue at Mason, where, for a block, you'll find four streetcar tracks, just like Market used to be; past the big night clubs and the little bars, and then the flat home stretch along Taylor Street and the final, slow clatter onto "the forgotten turntable" at the corner of Bay.

Grizzled Gripman Earl Hugh takes off his gloves, leans on his lever and grunts: "Me? I been running one of these things for thirty years. Started out on the old Castro line, ran into the Mission. Great, those Mission people. Why, the women used to jump on and off while we were running, with their arms full of babies and bundles. Yeah— I was on the Pacific Heights run, too. Women sure are different out there. Useta get sore if you didn't let 'em off right at their doorstep. What'll I do if they take these cable cars off? I know what I'll do. I'll get out of the transportation business!"

And so will thousands of other San Franciscans who feel exactly the way he does—that the cable cars are their personal transportation system, unique and irreplaceable. They'll get to work some other way, course, but it won't be the same. Frieda Klussmann, head of the Citizens Committee to Save the Cable Cars, puts it this way: "How can you fall in love with a bus?"

Dearie, Do You Remember? When men were men, and they fought over their women—the hard way. Example? Well, In June, 1892, Palace Waiter Harry McBride and Poodle Dog Waiter Frank La Rue (no, he was not a poodle dog) discovered they were going with the same girl. Challenges were exchanged and they met on June 10 in a gym to settle it—with bare fists. McBride died the next day, but La Rue didn't get the girl anyway. Seems she'd liked McBride better all the time . . . When one of the more unimportant (and unexciting) acts in Will Morrisey's revue at the Capital Theatre—this was about '27—was a thing called "Two Boys and a Piano." The other boy (the one who didn't play the piano): Bing Crosby . . . When, if you rented an apartment and had small children in the family, the landlord made you tack cheesecloth on all the walls so the kiddies wouldn't smudge 'em . . . When Columbia Park, on the site of today's run-down Columbia Square, was one of the town's gayer places: a dance hall, German band, beer, pretzels, bratwurst, and indigestion—in short, fun for all, followed by a few free-for-alls . . . When, in the era of horse-drawn wagons, draymen loathed making deliveries to the mansions atop Nob Hill; because the horses couldn't scale the steep slopes directly, they had to drive out Bush as far as Hyde, turn up to California, and then clatter back to the top of the hill. The original Grand Circle Tour.

Them was the days—when the great Luisa Tetrazzini and her almost-busted operatic troupe straggled into town for her first appearance; opening night tickets went for four bits, but it didn't take long for the town to hear about her magnificent voice (second night, seats sold for two dollars, if you were lucky enough to get one) . . . When the Old Poodle Dog, in its heyday of heavenly food and naughty nights in upstairs dining rooms, hired one guy whose sole job it was to loiter out front—and keep his eyes peeled for irate wives; grateful customers still claim he could spot an angry Mrs. at 100 paces . . . When the waterfront was enlivened by the steam calliope on the deck of the ship *S.M. Whipple*—loudly playing "The Girl I Left Behind Me" as she sailed out into the stream and headed Gateward . . . When the Bay was full of Japanese shipping—but no three ships alike (bad luck, according to a Japanese superstition); and so whereas the *Asama Maru* and the *Tatsuta Maru* were two-stackers, its "sister" ship, the *Chichibu Maru,* was only single-stacked . . . When the States Hof Brau restaurant on Market featured a superb concert orchestra (musicians worked for peanuts in those days)—and a dozen brands of imported beer on draft, served by rootin' Teuton bartenders with handlebar moustaches and thick accents with necks to match.

Yes, dearie, I don't remember—when downtown's No. 1 character was a shabby old frau named "Princess Margaret" who peddled gum nightly from the St. Francis to the Techau to Tiny Holmes's to

Herbert's to Coffee Dan's—and (between 9 P.M. and 1 A.M.) averaged twenty dollars nightly; Tiny Armstrong should do so good yet . . . When Ted Lewis headlined the last show at the old Orpheum, on the night vaudeville died, and cried unashamedly on the stage; he had plenty of company—the whole audience . . . When the happiest ferry on the Bay was the 5:15 P.M. to Marin County, which sailed gaily into the setting sun with the same band of commuters for years—all of whom were close friends in the faroff Maroon County of the pre-Bridge years . . . When the empty lot at Powell and Clay was jammed each night with dope addicts, all waiting nervously for the little hotel at Sacramento and Powell to open; that's where they bought their Stuff, in the days before the firequake . . . When Geary, west of Central Avenue, was known simply as Point Lobos Road, because that's where it ran to, and that was the ONLY thing it ran to; in between, nothing but sand—and is there anything that adds up to less than lots of sand?

They called it "Frisco"—when, if you wanted a downtown snack, you could choose between Maskey's, Gruenhagen's, and the Orange Blossom for a cup of hot chocolate topped with whipped cream and nutmeg (the popular snack of the day) . . . When doughnuts, snails, and butterhorns were ten cents a dozen, and you REALLY got a baker's dozen (and no, Junior, a "baker's dozen" is not eleven—it's thirteen) . . . When the place for a quick lunch was the Waldorf, on Market Street across from the Palace, where the Waldorf fizzes were the all-time end—and a great waiter named Noah kept you supplied indefinitely with slices of hot ham served on hot buns, for free . . . When, on a sunny Sunday, you could see as many as two hundred kids paddling in the Bay off Beale Street, all of them wearing bathing suits made from gunny sacks with the corners cut out . . . When Anna Held, 'way past her prime but still a French doll, made a triumphant comeback at the Cort Theatre, singing "Won't You Come and Play Wiz Me" and "I Can't Make My Eyes Behave" absolutely killing the people; the same Annforgettable Anna who made headlines in the nineties by splashing around nudishly in a pool of champagne at the old Almaden winery.

A city's heart was young and gay—when the fish peddlers were out and around each Friday in their horse-drawn wagons, followed inevitably by a long string of bony cats . . . When the sailing ships tied up along the waterfront had oh, such romantic names—like, for instance, *Three Brothers, The Falls of Afton, The Glory of the Seas,* and *The County Clare,* names full of salt spray and the snapping crackle of canvas . . . When the Hot Joke of the Moment went something like this: "Hey, haveya heard—Foster and Kleiser aren't speaking. All they do is make signs!" . . . When Tod Sloane, the famed jockey, had his baggage attached at the Baldwin Hotel—for, despite all his strutting up and down Market Street, he couldn't pay his bill . . . When the newsboys hurled their papers at your doorstep from passing cable cars, when gold and silver were the "only" legal money (if you tried to pay with currency, you needed identification, like a check casher today), and there was a saloon at 270 Brannan called the "What Ever's Right"—on account when you asked the bartender how much you owed, he merely said: "Whatever's right" . . . And there wasn't much wrong with a city like that.

It's Hard to Be Good   In the Department of Utter
Wickedness, it's quite true that San Francisco ain't what she used
to be.

The raucous dives of the Barbary Coast, which might have been
almost as bad as they were painted by zealous reformers, have
long since disappeared, to be replaced by a cheaply neonesque
carbon copy. The infamous "cribs," too, are gone with the cold
winds of righteousness, and tong wars and hatchetmen no longer
disturb the peace of the biggest Chinatown in the Western
world.

But don't get me wrong. San Francisco is still a far cry from
Chillicothe, Ohio, or Abilene, Texas. After all, it's a waterfront city,
with everything that implies in the way of illicit trafficking. It's a
hard-drinking city, with one saloon for every 600 people (and, it
seems at times, 600 people in every saloon). And it's a city with
a world-wide reputation for liberalism—in the old-fashioned sense
of that word—and the Leading Citizens and the law enforcers try
to keep that in mind, if only subconsciously.

For San Francisco, whether it admits it openly or not, knows it
has a reputation to live down to. It's a profitable point to remem-

ber, in a city that counts the tourist business high among its major industries.

Books that are banned in Boston are best sellers in San Francisco, and their merits are argued hotly in the finest salons. Plays that are run out of Memphis, Tennessee, as "obscene" are received with open minds, and broad critical appraisal, on Geary Street. Performers who are picketed in New York are unmolested at the Auditorium. Oh, the bluenoses and the do-gooders have their say, no doubt of that, but their voices carry no more weight than that of the next minority group. They get their say, and if they can say it loudly enough to win their point—fine.

However, the laissez-faire attitude of San Francisco has its inevitable evils, too, the evils that beset every great city. There is graft and corruption, and unsavory connivances in high places. The city "opens" and "closes" on a mysterious schedule, and when it is "open," the houses of prostitution flourish, the bookies are hard at work, gambling runs wild in the alleys of Chinatown, and the B-girls ply their sordid little trade in the saloons of the tenderloin district.

The B-girls are not, I suppose, peculiar to San Francisco, but they are believed to have been born on the Barbary Coast. In fact, nobody is even certain what the term means. But they are painfully easy to identify. They hang around bars frequented by lonely men anxious for company and conversation, and they "permit" these men to buy them drinks. At the end of the evening, the girls split the take with the house. And naturally, they don't drink hard liquor. Their glass usually contains colored water that looks like Scotch or bourbon. And the men pay Scotch and bourbon prices—doubled— for them.

I bought "drinks" for a B-girl named Mary one night in a seamy, smelly little bar on Third Street.

She was about twenty-five, and ugly as only an ugly girl who dyes her hair and wears too much make-up can be ugly. She had come to San Francisco from a small town near Sacramento, where I was born, and so we had a little to talk about. But just a little.

Mary was noncommittal. She sipped her colored-water "Scotches" (at seventy-five cents per) with monotonous speed for two hours, and she was addicted to the cliché, "Well, it's a living," as the answer to all my questions about her livelihood. She did confide, in a rare burst, that she had taken shorthand and typing in high school and had come to San Francisco in search of office work, but that's as far as she'd go. Conversationally, that is.

During the awkward silences as we sat at the bar, she'd nudge my elbow meaningfully or press her thigh against mine, all the while favoring me with what she undoubtedly thought of as an enticing glance.

As closing time drew near, a fantastic gambit—fantastic even for old San Francisco, I'm sure—was announced by the bartender. A beefy, red-faced character with piggish eyes, he rapped on the bar for attention and announced with a leer:

"Tonight, gen'lemen, we got a special door prize, yes indeedy. Come closer and lend an ear to the big deal."

The six other men in the bar looked uncomfortable and walked slowly to the bar.

"Now," went on the bartender, spreading his hands on the bar and bending forward confidentially, "see little Mary here? Ain't she a beauty?"

Mary smiled weakly and glanced around nervously at the circle of bemused faces.

"Well," finished the bartender, "whoever buys a quart of champagne gets to take Mary home for the night. How about THAT for a deal?"

A couple of the men snorted derisively and headed for the door. Another gave Mary an appraising look and shook his head. The other two put their heads together and began discussing the price of champagne and women.

"Come on," whispered Mary, digging an elbow into my ribs, "buy the champagne. Be a sport. I'm real nice, really I am."

For ten dollars—sometimes it's nice to be on an expense account —I got a four-dollar bottle of champagne. Mary and I solemnly toasted our new-found love, and we left the rest of the bottle with the bartender, who looked like he had the proper stomach for the horrible wine.

Together, we walked to the door, and I led her to an all-night lunch counter across the street.

"Well," said Mary dully, "where'll we go? I know a little hotel around the corner that's O.K."

"You go where you want," I said. "Me, I'm going home. Alone."

"Well, of all the jerks," spluttered Mary indignantly, arising from her stool. "So if you didn't want me, why'dja buy the champagne?"

"I don't know really," I said lamely. "I suppose I thought I was rescuing you from something."

"If you don't take the cake," she snapped, deeply insulted. And she stalked out on her thin legs, her high heels beating an angry tattoo on the cold, stone floor.

As I left, I saw her cross the street, talking earnestly to a sailor who had been waiting for a bus. I watched them walk away together, around the corner to the little hotel that was O.K.

Most B-girls have little to say about their racket. But Laura was different. She was fed up with the life, and particularly with saloon-keepers who did her dirt by shorting her on her pay. And so she came up to my office one day and had her little say.

Laura was a not unattractive blonde divorcee, twenty-seven years old, with small blue eyes and a rather direct, open manner. She claimed to be a college graduate, and was just illiterate enough to make that statement ring true.

"There's one thing I wanna get over to you right now," she said. "I'm through with the racket—but don't think for one minute I'm sorry for the men who come into those joints and get clipped. They know what they're getting into. Honest, I hafta laugh every time I read those stories about the 'poor servicemen' who get taken by B-girls for all their dough. A man's a man, and as far as I'm concerned, they're all fair game."

But, she was asked, how about the naïve servicemen from small towns, who've never heard about B-girls and the baby-buy-me-a-drink routine?

"There may be some guys like that," admitted Laura, "but I've never seen 'em. In fact, most of the servicemen I've hadda deal with are murder, strictly. I'd like to take all of 'em down to their last cent—including carfare."

Laura had no idea how many bars in town employ B-girls (in the parlance of the trade, when a place starts hiring girls, they've "gone B") but she thinks it's "forty or fifty at least, and hundreds of girls are working at it, off and on. It's not a bad job, if you can stand all the guff you hafta put up with."

There is no union for B-girls. They can work the 10 A.M.–6 P.M. shift, or the 6 P.M.–2 A.M. shift—or both, if they're strong of back, willing of mind, and have nothing better to do anyway. They get no guarantee—just a straight 50 per cent commission on every drink that is bought for them. And there's plenty of profit in those drinks.

"Naturally," said Laura, naturally, "we can't drink hard liquor all day and all night, and we're no good if we're drunk, either. Once in a while we drink wine or champagne—but most of the time, I drink water with a little Coke in it, or grenadine with water. We make up fancy names for 'em—otherwise the guys get mad at paying the dollar."

Besides patience and an insensitive ear, a B-girl—or just plain "girl," as they call themselves—has to have a staggering capacity for liquid intake. Laura, for example, averaged forty drinks a night, adding up to twenty dollars nightly as her share.

"However, sometimes things get going pretty good," Laura admitted. "My top night was ninety dollars, but the next day, when I thought about it, I got pretty scared. That's a hundred and eighty drinks, and that must be pretty hard on the old system. Girl friend of mine made a hundred and fifty dollars one day, though, working a double shift, and she came through it O.K."

How about income tax? Laura was asked.

Her answer was a superior, half-pitying smile—the kind she must have given any G.I. from Iowa who might have asked: "What's in that drink you're drinking?"

She didn't say so in so many words, but Laura implied that the profession of B-girls is overly maligned—and really quite a social necessity.

"After all, let's face it," she said. "This is a waterfront town, and every waterfront town has saloons with girls. New York, San Diego, Los Angeles, Frisco"—ah, that's where she cheapened herself—"they all have the same kind of joints. The guys expect it. They walk into a bar, and there's no girls, they walk out again, and what's the percentage?"

Laura was very firm on one point. A B-girl is not a prostitute. "Nobody wants them around a place—especially the owners. They cause nothing but trouble. We help spot 'em and run 'em out. And we don't 'roll' drunks for their dough, either. Only a few girls do that, and they're strictly no good. They get everybody in a jam."

When a saloonkeeper refers to a B-girl as a "good girl," he isn't discussing her morals, however. He means she sits with a lot of men, is dutifully pleasant, and gets them to buy a maximum of drinks with a minimum of fuss.

"Most of the girls are O.K., take it from me," reported Laura earnestly. "They're either married or living faithfully with some-one."

After a moment's pause, during which she sighed romantically, Laura confided: "Worst mistake a girl can make is to marry some guy she meets on the job. I've seen it happen a dozen times. Never works out. I can't imagine why, offhand, but it never does."

It's not an easy job. The hours are long and the drinks are weak and the men are problems, in the usual way. "They do get to be a drag, y'know," shrugged Laura. "But whaddya gonna do? And to make things worse, there's always competition."

Competition, to a B-girl, is a "legit." That's a girl who comes into a bar to pick up a man for no apparent commercial reason. "Sure burns me up," said Laura heatedly. "So she sits with a guy finally and he's buying her drinks, and she isn't making a penny out of it. What kinda sense is that?"

A good B-girl, according to Laura, is a girl who's "quiet and nice," who doesn't dress flashily or use too much make-up—"you should look like a secretary"—and who's a good listener without being softhearted.

"They've all got sob stories," said Laura, "and they're all the same. The only guys I feel sorry for are the old pensioners who live around the tenderloin. They know the drinks they buy for us are phonies, but they do it anyway, just to have company. It's a helluva world when you gotta buy conversation."

It sure is.

Sometimes you meet one that's a little different. June Byron for example.

She is about thirty and, as she says, "I guess you'd say that I'm attractive." I would, and so would you. She's a trim five foot two with the traditional eyes of blue, and she looks right at you while she talks, which is quite often and in a loud, clear voice.

Shortly before World War II, June came down from her home town of Yakima. "I thought I knew all about everything," she recalls, "but the first thing I found out is that I didn't know anything."

She started "learning" by going to work as a B-girl in a Market Street saloon. The boss liked her. So did the prosperous businessmen who occasionally dropped in. They bought drinks for her, but, as June puts it, "funny things kept happening."

The funny thing was this: "As soon as these men had one drink with me, they'd fall asleep. Then the boss and another guy would take him out for a walk, and the man would never come back—and the boss had his money in his pocket. So I said to the boss: 'I don't get it. You want me to get these men to buy me drinks, and then you go and put 'em to sleep and take their money.'

"And the boss said: 'June, you're learning too fast. Get lost.'"

June continued to learn. She worked in other tenderloin joints. She watched drinks being doctored, and dope being peddled. In her own words, "I was a little bit of everything." She married a North Beach guy, "a tough little monkey," and "he kept me in black eyes." She had it annulled and the Judge advised: "June, go back to Yakima and pick apples."

But June didn't go back. During the war, she married a fine young man who never returned; killed in action. And a few years back she bought a bar on Third Street and did very well at it. "But it was a place of filth and corruption. I knew I was doing wrong. I was fed up with the world. I had to get out and cleanse my soul." She sold the bar, gave up drinking and smoking, and joined a church.

Now, June Byron has a mission in life. "I've been called, and I know it!" she says, her eyes snapping. On Sundays she preaches at Third and Howard, not far from the saloon she once owned, and she tells her audiences about the evils of dope and drink. "I speak their language," she says. "They listen to me."

Other days, she waves her arms and exhorts her listeners in Portsmouth Square, across from the Hall of Justice, and in Jefferson Park at Eddy and Gough. When she runs out of things to say about vice and corruption, she attacks Communism, which, she says, "manifests itself everywhere like flies."

Pretty June Byron, war widow, ex B-girl, onetime saloonkeeper, now lives in a little house near the Cow Palace—and the girl who came here from Yakima "to learn about life" is happy at last. "I am telling the truth," she says quietly. "God will reward me."

And so, as you can see, there's something for everybody in San Francisco—the cool, the beautiful, the quaint city of winding streets and cable cars, of clean, white fog and colorful people who babble their friendship in a dozen foreign tongues . . .

Just South of Market, in the downtown area, is a quaint, colorful, friendly little place—the kind of place where a stranger might like to buy himself a quick drink. He wouldn't be a stranger long, though, especially if he happened to flash a sizable roll of bills. In no time, he'd find himself enmeshed in what the trade calls "the assembly line."

First, the B-girls get a crack at him. After that, if he's still willing and friendly, he's steered into a "nice" little game in the back, where marked cards are almost guaranteed to relieve him of any excess money. However, if he has the fantastic luck to win, he suddenly finds himself out in the alley, where a character they call "Big Joe" does the job directly and efficiently. "Joe" hits like a mule and is just as smart. But he knows his job and he does it well.

If, by some miracle, a cop happens along, "Big Joe" fishes a marked card out of the victim's otherwise empty pockets and grunts: "Howdya like this guy—tried to phony up our friendly li'l card game. So I slugged him." And with a kick in the pants to help him along, the sucker is sent on his way. He has been through the "assembly line" and has come out the other end—broke, and broken.

Quaint, colorful San Francisco, enchanted land of fog and cable cars . . .

On a Pearl Harbor Anniversary For all we knew, it was going to be just another Sunday.

The city was sleeping late, as usual, for Saturday night had been especially gay around town. There was so much to do, and we were all so young.

Henry "Hot Lips" Busse was playing for dancers in the Palace's Rose Room, with Headwaiter Adolph Steinhoff presiding urbanely at the door. Eddie Fitzpatrick's band and the elegant dance team of Harger and Maye (Harger was later to be murdered) were the attractions at the Music Box on O'Farrell—where the Duncan sisters had just walked out in a huff, causing much excited conversation in the downtown circle. It was really Hot News.

A roly-poly comedian named Romo Vincent was good for a few laughs at Gerun and Martinelli's Bal Tabarin—especially at the midnight show—and practically everybody wound up at Bimbo's 365, on lower Market for the 4 A.M. performance. Then the mob reported faithfully to Vanessi's for a Joe's Special, or something equally indigestible (at that hour, anyway), and finally—home, to stumble over the morning paper on the front step and fall into bed.

Life was like that. And to make it better, the prediction for Sunday was clear and sunny—just right for a drive through the Park, a stroll at the beach, a Ramos fizz at the Cliff House.

And there was nothing to do on Sunday morning except sleep, sleep, sleep.

I guess it was about 10 A.M. on that Sunday when the phone rang. I thought about letting it ring itself to death, but it refused to die. At last, I picked up the receiver—without knowing that the gesture symbolized the end of an era.

It was the girl in the apartment downstairs. "Hey," she said breathlessly, "I know you're an Orson Welles fan. Well, he's got a program on the air right now—something about the Japs bombing Pearl Harbor. Boy, is it realistic, don't miss it. Better than his man from Mars stuff."

I turned on the radio, but it wasn't Orson Welles. It was The News. The news that nobody wanted to hear. The story that couldn't happen to us, in our snug, smug, secure little world. The radio bulletin that couldn't be turned off, the newspaper headline that was bigger and blacker than reality—too big to comprehend.

In the Sunday morning stillness, a hundred thousand phones were ringing in San Francisco, each peal of the bell awakening the city from the long, peaceful sleep it would never know again.

At least the weather prediction had been right. The skies were clear, and the unknowing sun shone down brightly as ever. But all else was turmoil, for all of a sudden, nobody wanted to be alone. It was too much to live with—by yourself.

In an involuntary gesture, you pulled up the Venetian blinds and blinked out at the city. Everything was still there, as it had been the morning before—Coit Tower still on its hill, the cables still clearing their throats in the slots, the Top still o' the Mark. No columns of smoke rising from bomb-shattered ruins.

And yet, everything looked different, and you needed reassuring. Already the "Extras" were being shouted from the streetcorners, and people were gathering in the streets, looking at each other anxiously as though they were expecting to hear: "It's all a joke, don't believe it, another wild rumor."

But the hours and the bulletins and the headlines rolled on, and all escapes to yesterday were cut off. On Post, in "Little Osaka," a drunken Chinese had trouble convincing a Marine that he was really Chinese, and in the Japanese Tea Garden in Golden Gate Park, a customer suddenly and viciously swept the teapot and cups off his table and cursed loudly as he stalked away.

It was growing in the open now—the poison of hatred—and it would never end.

By sundown, the urge to get as close as possible to the scene of history was more than anyone could resist. Thousands of cars jammed the Great Highway, and thousands of people were silhouetted against the angry, setting sun, all of them looking West in bewildered silence and shaking their heads in frustration—and unspoken fear for their futures.

In the downtown dimout, the drama grew. Army and Navy sound trucks rattled past the half-lit streetlamps, their speakers blaring out orders that would have been mere theatrics, twenty-four hours before: "Report to your stations . . . Members of such and such Regiment, report to headquarters . . . Urgent . . ."

The saloonkeepers—that is, the more delicate among them—were a little ashamed to look happy at the sudden increase in business, but it was picking up fast. In the tenderloin and along Powell, there were noisy knots at every bar. "The Marines for me." "I think I'll try the Air Corps." "And me, they'll hafta draft, ha-ha." Older men were buying drinks for G.I.s they'd ignored (or complained about) for months, and already the word *Japanese* had disappeared from everybody's vocabulary. "Slap the Jap" was scrawled on a hundred walls.

And so the Sunday that started out to be just another Sunday came to an end.

In the crash of a bomb and the flash of a news bulletin, the San Francisco of our young dreams went up in invisible smoke and collapsed in unseen rubble. Even though the war was to remain far away from the Bay and the Beach, the faces and the places would never be the same again, for we would never be the same again.

And it all started on a Sunday morning with the ringing of a telephone that nobody wanted to answer.

Just Foolin' Around   All his harried life (oh, the poor feller), the daily newspaper columnist worries about running out of "news" for his space.

The fact that this "news" consists mainly of a prediction that seldom comes true, a divorce rumor involving two people you never heard of, the latest (if inane) wisecrack-about-town, and the signing of a third-rate act by a second-rate night club has nothing to do with his fixation.

"Some day," he cries neurotically at regular intervals, "some day I'm gonna sit down in front of this typewriter with the deadline staring me in the face, and have nothing to write about. Nothing. Let's face it. Who can fill so much space day after day?"

Certain less fortunate columnists have to moan in this fashion to themselves—or their pitiable wives. I happen to be lucky enough to have a bright assistant named Jerry Bundsen to sing the "nothing to write about" blues to. And on these occasions, he leans back in his chair, gazes at the ceiling and says, "O.K., so you got nothing to write about. So let's dream something up."

Through the years, we've dreamed up all manner of things to fill the voracious white spaces. We've dreamed up imaginary conversations between San Francisco characters, we've aired our pet hates in columns called "If I Had a Million," we've run into fantastic escapades via a column titled "The Walking Caen," and we've phoned everybody from the Governor to a callhouse madam to find out whether they chew their fingernails or bathe in bubble baths.

Once in a while, we dream up a thing called "Impossible Quotes," which runs something like this:

A Muni bus driver: "Don't crowd to the back, folks. Let's all stand around here where we can talk."

"Odds" Bodkin, who runs a cigar stand in the tenderloin: "Of course I handle horse race bets. Ya think I can make a living selling candy bars?"

Mayor Elmer Robinson: "Please send those photographers away."

Harry Bridges: "Sometimes I get so homesick for Australia I could just die."

Skid Rowgue on Third Street: "Hey, buddy, lemme have a quarter, willya—I wanna buy meself a slugga booze."

Carl Wente, President of the Bank of America: "No, let's not open a branch in Muir Woods. I think we have entirely too many branches as it is."

Henry Kaiser: "We can't handle it—it's just too big for us."

Attorney J. W. "Jake" Ehrlich: "I'm sorry, Sally, I won't be able to handle a case like that. It might damage my reputation."

Ben Swig: "Well, shall we all go over to the Top o' the Mark for a drink?"

The President of the Pacific-Union Club: "Then it's all set, fellows. We'll have an open house for the public every year from now on."

Cab driver: "Look, lady, that's only three blocks away—why don'tcha walk?"

Garage attendant: "Here's your car, sir—and see that scratch on the back fender? I did it."

Lobbyist Artie Samish: "My job consists simply of trying to ram through legislation favorable to my clients."

Dr. J. C. Geiger: "I have a small contribution I'd like to make to the scrap medal drive."

Paul Fagan, owner of the Seals: "Whaddya mean, will the Coast League ever be a third major league? We'll be lucky if we don't become a second Three-Eye League."

Elmer "Bones" Remmer: "I welcome this opportunity to explain the means by which I make my livelihood."

Traffic Director Captain Jack Eker: "If it weren't for the unfailing courtesy of our motorists, traffic conditions would rapidly become intolerable."

Bill Humphrey, President of the Olympic Club since 1907: "I'm not the only man who can run this outfit."

Edmond Rieder, general manager of the Palace Hotel: "Instead of putting it on the menu as 'Grenadine de boeuf haché sur le petit pain grillé aux oignons,' why don't we just call it hamburger?"

Glen Jamison, the Director of Internal Revenue: "So what if you ARE a few days late? After all, you're only human."

Waiter to customer: "I wish you wouldn't tip me quite so much, sir—it lowers my impression of you."

Visiting Hollywood starlet: "This is my first visit to San Francisco, and all I can say is feh. I'll take Los Angeles."

Henry Doelger: "Come to think of it, a twenty-five-foot frontage IS kinda small for a home."

Mayor Clifford Rishell of Oakland: "Unity is the most important issue of the day—and therefore I heartily recommend that Oakland change its name to East San Francisco."

F. L. Felton, San Francisco's chief weatherman: "Frankly I'm stumped. It could rain or shine, for all I can tell."

On another occasion, when all the established news sources were answering "What's new?" with "I dunno, what?" we got together with Gardner Dailey, the eminent architect, and produced something called "Let's Be Original," which rather deflated the pet theory that San Francisco is the nation's most "different" city. Some of our alarming discoveries:

The Fairmont hotel is a copy of the Royal Palace in Madrid . . . That Corinthian column in Union Square (the Dewey Monument) is a steal from the Hadrian Column at the East gate to Istanbul . . . The Ferry Building tower is an "adaption"—nice word—of the Giralda Tower in Seville . . . No. 333 Montgomery (the Pacific National Bank Building) is a duplicate of Chicago's No. 333 North Michigan Boulevard . . . The Palace of the Legion of Honor museum is a "replica" of the Legion of Honor on the Quai d'Orsay in Paris . . . Pine, Filbert, and Chestnut were named after streets in Philadelphia; Broadway, Lombard, and Greenwich were christened after dittoes in New York . . . The Carolands mansion down the Peninsula is a carbon copy of one of Napoleon's chateaux; and Nancy Ann Abbott's showplace in Hillsborough is a miniature of the White House (if you ask to see a picture of her home, she says "Look on the back of a twenty-dollar bill") . . . The Library in Civic Center is a duplicate of the Public Library in Detroit . . . The University of California's famed Campanile was "influenced" by the St. Mark's Tower in Venice—but the Campanile is ten feet higher . . . Even our fences aren't original; the ornate one between the Opera House and the Veterans Building is a copy of the fence in the Great Square at Nancy, France . . . The Levi Strauss Building at Pine and Battery Streets is a "close copy" (that's architectural double-talk) of the Marquette Building in Chicago—the original U.S. skyscraper, built in 1894 . . . Architect Willis Polk's noted "Water Temple" at Sunol is "in the image of" the Temple of Vesta near Tivoli . . . And most of the buildings along Howard Street resemble the Leaning Tower of Pisa—but only in the inclination.

It's standard operating procedure, among newless San Francisco columnists, to poke fun at the Pacific-Union Club, a haven for socially acceptable millionaires on Nob Hill.

The P-U, as it is known rather inelegantly to the public-at-large and the members-at-small, is housed in the handsome brownstone mansion built by James Flood, one of the "Bonanza Kings," and, according to reports filtering to the outside world, shelters the kind of thinking that was popular in Flood's day.

Hence, when the P-U built a parking lot behind the club a few years ago, all San Francisco was appropriately impressed. As someone inquired archly of Member Sydney Walton: "Has the P-U come to the conclusion that the automobile is here to stay?" Similar observations were inspired by the sight of a television aerial being installed on the club's roof, but I was eventually straightened out by a member who confided: "It's not for the club as a whole, you understand. One of the members has bought a TV set for his room. Naturally, the subject will come up for discussion at the next board of directors' meeting."

As you can see, the P-U, with its 450 members, its brownstone home, and its great bronze fence lends itself admirably to the kind of wealthy-old-men's-club humor purveyed in the cartoons of the slick magazines.

Whenever ex-President Truman or any other Democratic luminary arrives at the Fairmont Hotel, directly across the street, some newsman is sure to report next day: "And a gaunt white Republican hand reached up and began pulling down the window shades in the Pacific-Union Club."

The club's aging millionaires die off at such a steady rate that a standard San Francisco joke goes as follows: "Hey, did you hear— they just fired the bellboy at the Pacific-Union. He made a terrible mistake this morning. Ran the flag all the way to the top of the pole!"

In February, 1952, however, the club came brightly to life to celebrate its one-hundredth anniversary. For the first time in recent history, the membership announced bravely, women would be allowed to penetrate the Bronze Curtain for a gala dinner dance. Roger Lapham, Jr., son of an ex-Mayor of San Francisco, immediately wondered whether it would be called "The Moth Ball." And one of the younger P-Uers, a rather giddy sixty-year-old, issued the following stern injunction to the membership: "No member may bring his mistress unless she is the wife of a member."

Naturally, the P-U has its human side, too. The home of the Nobhillity has (or had, at this writing) a house cat, which a liveried footman places outside on the front stoop every morning for a breath of air and a look at life. However, you mustn't expect the club to unbend completely. This tomcat isn't named "Tom" like any other tomcat. Its name is "Thomas."

And the club does a nice thing with its leftover food. St. Anthony's Kitchen, on Jones Street, which provides hundreds of down-and-outers with free meals each day, gets regular food donations from the P-U, a fact which might be of interest to some of its indigent ex-members.

In passing, I'm reminded of one of my all-time favorite San Francisco quotes. It was authored by wonderful Mrs. James Flood, who once lived in the home that houses the P-U, and later in a mansion that is now Sacred Heart Convent.

"I am the only woman in San Francisco," she once said, "who had a son born in a girls' school, and a daughter born in a men's club!"

Sometimes, when the gossip has died down to an inaudible whisper and the rumors are dull enough to be true, Jerry and I get on the telephones and call everybody we can think of, gathering simple-minded material for columns we call "Little Things about Big People," or "Footnotes on Headliners," or "They're Only Human."

None of the results of these efforts will ever make journalistic history or win a Pulitzer Prize, but they are true to at least one principle of good newspapering: names, names, and more names. And if it is true that names make news, the following copy is stop-press news:

"Russian Mike," the noted Geary Street gambler, eats caviar sandwiches for breakfast . . . Lawyer Leo Friedman has to have lining put in the pants of his suits—otherwise he gets a rash, the delicate fellow . . . Robert Watt Miller, boss of Pacific Lighting Corporation, carefully checks every room in his Nob Hill mansion before retiring, to make sure all the lights are out . . . Emerson Murfee, the Peninsula restaurateur, had his twin-engined Beechcraft painted bluish-gray, to match his Cadillac.

Larry Metcalf, the socialite auto dealer, has a completely stocked bar and library in his bathroom; when he says "Excuse me, I'm going to the library," he means it . . . Louis Lurie is so rich that he can afford cuffs on the sleeves of his suits—but the drapes in his Montgomery Street office are tattered . . . I. W. Hellman, top man at the Wells Fargo Bank, drives chefs crazy; smokes cigarettes right through every course . . . "Lefty" isn't "Lefty O'Doul's only nickname; his other one is "Fuzzy"—and he hates it . . . Tiny Armstrong, who sometimes wears pajamas on the street, sleeps in his underwear.

All his close friends address Banker Parker Maddux as "Judge"— something he's never been (was a U. S. Attorney once, though) . . . Oscar Lewis, the noted author, does all his writing standing up (at a special typewriter table) so he can pace back and forth while thinking; claims he walked forty-two miles while writing "Bonanza Inn" . . . Mrs. Ambrose Diehl, who might be the town's No. 1 hostess and party-giver, amazes her guests by drinking one martini after another with no visible effects; no wonder—the "martinis" are pear juice.

George D. Smith, owner of the Mark Hopkins, has only one answer when somebody rushes into his office demanding a "yes or no!" decision; it's always "No!" . . . When Mrs. Elmer Robinson is vacationing at the Mayor's Grass Valley farm, the last thing she does each night before retiring is stand outside the house—listening to the "night noises"; and I don't mean snores . . . Kathleen Norris, who has made a fortune from her books, was fired from the old *Bulletin* shortly after the '06 firequake because, said her boss, she couldn't write . . . Barnaby Conrad, the author-artist-bullfighter-diplomat-lecturer–TV star, etc., wears evening pumps in the daytime and looks pretty silly.

Attorney Jake Ehrlich's wedding present to Dave Falk (when he married Margie Mueller) was a free divorce from Dave's first wife . . . "Original Andy" Lacbay, the Broadway master barber, trains his customers to come in weekly for a trim—but he gets HIS hair cut every six weeks . . . Anson Blake (of the Blake, Moffit & Towne tribe) graduated from Cal in '91—and still wears his tiny Block C on his watch chain, where it dangles just below his beard . . . Luz Garcia of the Sinaloa, one of our better language garblers, tells her dearest friends "I love you as never," and can't understand why they're slightly perplexed.

Playwright William Saroyan once bought himself a Soundscriber so he could avoid the job of typing his effusions—but he's now back at the typewriter; found he spent all his time dictating dirty stories to the machine, playing them back, and laughing his fool head off . . . Marvin Dito, the transportation executive, wears a bow tie made out of a silk map of France—carried by his brother, Frank, through Europe during World War II . . . The Gardner Meins, Jr., ranking members of the gay young married set, go to bed at eight o'clock every week night—but oof, what week ends! . . . Architect Gardner Dailey can't eat salads with dressing, so he eats salads without dressing. What I mean is, he's dressed while eating but he's allergic to dressing so he has his salads with his clothes on but without dressing and pfooie.

Edwin Berk, the furrier, and his brother Clarence (he makes Medico Pipes) are four years apart in age. They married sisters who are ditto; the marriages were four years apart—and their first children were born four years apart. The Berks are still seldom apart. The Edwins live at 1444 Jefferson and the Clarences live at 1455 Jefferson . . . Dr. J. C. Geiger, the Oakland Health Director, catches three colds a year every year, and would like to say a few words on the subject. "Ah-choo." Thank you, Dr. Geiger.

Mayor Robinson, whose doctor has ordered him to stop smoking, has five hundred dollars' worth of fine cigars stashed away in his home; every night he opens the closet where they're stored, takes a deep breath, wipes a tear from his eye, and tiptoes quickly away . . . Richard Gump has never won a prize at golf, but he holds the Lakeside record for throwing a driver; pitched it fifty yards off the seventh tee once in a fit of anger, and that's as far as he can drive a ball. Fore! . . . Socialite Mrs. Jackson Moffett is a fingernail chewer; but only her own . . . Captain Ralph Olstad of the Police Traffic Bureau is called "Snowshoes" by his fellow gumshoes —but he can't understand it. "After all," he says petulantly, "my shoes are only size twelve. Inspector Dan Shelley wears sixteens at least."

Supervisor John J. Sullivan takes his own made-in-S.F. French bread with him whenever he goes to Los Angeles; doesn't like the Smogland variety . . . Mason Geisendorfer, the customs broker, wears his hat all the time—indoors, outdoors, to bedcetera. Like I said, he wears his hat all the time . . . Bill Crawford, the retired rice tycoon who lives in Pebble Beach, is the best duck caller in the State. Just quacks away—without mechanical aids—and the quackers come fluttering in from all sides, they quackshilly do . . . Grant Avenue's Stella K. Johnson, the "grandmother of the corset business," has three Arabian stallions—and rides an hour every day . . . Shipwreck Van Nolan, the flagpole sitter, eats nothing but raw

vegetables for lunch—carrots one day, celery the next, and so on
and yawn; his foolosophy: "Either you gotta eat right or live
right" . . .

Mrs. Hans Klussmann, head of the Citizens Committee to Save
the Cable Cars, paints 'em too. Cable cars, I mean. In oil. Even
won a prize for same. For a painting of a cable car. Ding-ding . . .
Papagayo Al Williams has a cold all the time on account he refuses
to raise the roof of his Cadvertible, even when the fog is rolling in;
he's usually so full of penicillin that he looks moldy . . . Harvey
Riley, the customs marine expert, has 150 pipes and smokes a fresh
one every hour on the hour; his favorite: a five-cent corn cobber
. . . Hm: Dr. Laurance Cross, the Mayor of Berkeley, lives on Los
Angeles Avenue.

Millionaire Vincent Hallinan is so eager to impress the prole-
tariat with his sincerity that on his last trip to Europe, he took only
one suit in his baggage; figuring he'd look less capitalistic if he was
wrinkled? . . . Ted Friend has several paintings by "the well-
known Czechoslovakian artist, Zorg," in his beautiful Vallejo Street
home—and traps the phonies every time. "Of course, you've heard
of Zorg," he says. "Oh, of course," they nod, "love his work." Zorg
is Ted Friend . . . Tom Rooney, boss of the San Francisco Sports
Show, calls everybody "Sport." Ties in nicely with his business,
besides which he has a terrible memory for names . . . Thomas
Carr Howe, director of the Legion of Honor museum, hates baseball
as much as his wife, Francesca, loves it; they get along fine anyhow,
which disproves the old theory. Any old theory.

The Shah of Iran, according to my international sources (aw,
come off it, Caen), doesn't light his cigarettes with a gold Dunhill
or even a silver Ronson. He uses big, fat paper matches from

Tarantino's. He expressed great fondness for them on his last visit here, and the restaurant sends him cartons . . . Fine thing. He wants matches, they send him cartons.

A Virginia City gambling joint keeps one roulette table reserved at all times for Lucius Beebe and Charles Clegg, the town's most distinguished residents. And when they play at it, the peasants are ordered to maintain a respectful distance. Watch, but don't touch . . . Attorney H. Ward Dawson, Jr., picks his teeth in all the best places—between 'em, naturally—but it's O.K.; he uses a solid gold toothpick . . . Cecil Whitebone, the Van Ness automogul whose home is down the Peninsula, rides to work in style every morning; in a chauffeured Ford that meets him at the Third and Townsend station . . . Longest running gag in town: Attorney Jake Ehrlich's attempts to collect a one-dollar debt from Judge George Schonfeld —a debt that dates back thirty years to the days when Schonfeld was a lawyer and young Jake served a subpoena for him. And never got paid. The Judge keeps crying statute of limitations. Jake keeps crying.

Restaurateur Gene McAteer gets up every morning at six, puts on a sweatshirt, and jogs around the track at nearby Aptos Junior High; this keeps him in the pink of condition, and he can have it . . . Speaking of early risers, Dr. F. H. Redewill, chief of the County Medical Association's art section, arises every morning at five and paints until seven. He's great on dawns, no good on sunsets . . . On the other hand, "Champagne Dick" Jose, the bubbly salesman, likes to sleep—and he's got a wide choice of beds. He has an apartment in San Francisco here, a ditto in Burlingame, a lodge in San Carlos, and a home in Redwood City. And insomnia everywhere . . . Banker Jerd Sullivan and Lawyer Garret McEnerney II, who

are both six foot six ("Thirteen feet of nothing," they call themselves), use extra long golf clubs at the Burlingame Club, and have
to hire extra long caddies to carry their extra long bags. Extra! . . .
For years, Governor Warren wore only one kind of necktie—a solid
maroon job costing a buck (he bought 'em by the dozens). At last,
in desperation, Mrs. Warren got the children to complain, and after
a few months, the Governor got the idea. Now he wears splashy
jobs, and all is bright with the world of Warrens.

Henry North, boss of Metropolitan Life in San Francisco, is so
color-blind that his wife Barbara has to pick out his tie each morning; when they're feuding, she refuses to help—and he goes to work
with the straaangest combinations . . . Police Chief Michael Gaffey
insists "I don't have a single superstition"—but he refuses to make
a major decision or launch a project on a Friday; his unlucky day
. . . Ray Abbaticchio of the FBI hates mysteries so much that he
has never read a whodunit book, seen a mystery film or watched
one on TV; he has even been known to turn off "Ah, Sweet Mystery
of Life."

Ty Cobb, the baseball immortal who now lives in Atherton, has
told only a few old friends a "secret" of his diamond success: a
pint of chilled champagne before each game . . . Superintendent
of Education Herbert Clish is the bane of restaurant owners; scribbles (in ink) all over the tablecloths . . . Father William Dunne,
President of University of San Francisco, is such an accomplished
amateur chef that friends "borrow" him to cook for their social
affairs . . . Tommy Heath, manager of the Seals, refuses to change
his uniform while the team is on a winning streak. His uniform is
seldom dirty. The Seals don't win THAT often.

Agent Larry Allen consumes three cigars a day, via the chewing system; never lights 'em . . . Dr. Chester W. Johnson, the Sutter Street dentist, walks home for lunch every day—he's that mad for his wife's clear bouillon soup . . . Gambler Bill Graham has something to say about everybody, whether it's good or bad; his philosophy: "If you can't say something nice about a guy, rap him" . . . Tom Groody, the TV scientist, always has a pipe in his face, even in front of the camera; lights it all the time, too, even when it's empty.

Attorney Jerome White, who lives in Sea Cliff, is rugged; swims in the ocean there every day and plays golf without his shoes . . . Edmond Rieder, general manager of the Palace Hotel, owns only two hats—a Homburg and a beret . . . Millionaire Edmond Herrscher agitates the bubbles out of his champagne with a solid gold swizzle stick . . . Walter Glinsky, smooth-as-silk maître d'hôtel at El Prado, is so discreet that when he gets sore he excuses himself, sneaks behind the kitchen door, and swears.

Bert Gillespie, dean of S.F. exporters, has a beautiful home in St. Francis Wood, but is so stricken with wanderlust that he can't stay there longer than three weeks at a time—then off he goes; been around the world five times . . . Nancy Ann Abbott, the creator of Storybook Dolls, has only two dolls in her home, and both are imports from France . . . Ben Swig, owner of the Fairmont (where most of the top-drawer Democrats stay) comes from a family so staunchly Republican that he and all his brothers were named after Republican Presidents; Ben's full name, for example, is Benjamin Harrison Swig.

Dr. Ellis Sox, San Francisco's Health Director, plays classical records (loud) on turntables he built himself—after subscribing to every electrical gadget magazine in the country: "Ellis' Wonder-

land," his wife, Linea, calls the setup . . . Charlie Low, boss of the
Forbidden City night club, hasn't had breakfast at home in twenty-
three years; goes to a little restaurant on Jackson Street, where, for
all those years, he has always had the same meal—waffle and a cup
of coffee . . . Senator Gerald O'Gara is such an habitual hand-
shaker that he sometimes astounds his wife by shaking HER hand
as he leaves the house in the morning . . . George Killion, President of American President Lines, carries two rabbit feet in his
pockets all the time; rubs 'em behind his ears when he needs luck,
which isn't very often.

If you visit the home of Lee Giroux, San Francisco's top TV star,
don't be surprised if you're served hot dogs; his family is so mad
for them (morning, noon, or night, makes no difference) that they
buy them by the yard . . . Attorney Ernest J. Torregano is such a
Francophile that his letterheads read simply "Ernest J. Torregano,
Avocat" (this is French for lawyer, not avocado, and yrwelcome)
. . . Bill Kyne, owner of Bay Meadows, is so frantic to pick a winner that sometimes he bets three horses to win in one race—and
even then he's often wrong . . . Vic Gotti, owner of Ernie's restaurant, goes home every afternoon to play jacks with his daughters,
Vickie and Marlo, but he's getting too good for them. "Already," he
boasts, "I'm up to tensies." And so to bedsies.

Another "rainy day" column that Jerry and I enjoy putting together
—and the readers enjoy tearing apart—is called "Department of
Useless Information," and it's just that, to say the most. Among the
things we've discovered, as the result of practically no research
whatever, are these, to which you are quite welcome, thank you:
That stock jokebook character—the old-maid schoolteacher—is

rapidly becoming a thing of the past; exactly 54.1 per cent of all elementary teachers in San Francisco are married, and three thousand a year quit their jobs in California to go to the hitching post . . . Usually on hand in the San Francisco branch of the U. S. Mint: $1,200,000,000, give or take a few cents . . . The tooth is mighty dept: San Francisco's one thousand dentists yank a hundred thousand teeth each year—and, if they were stacked one upon the other, they'd reach to a height of 8887 feet and add up to a pretty silly sight; besides, it's impossible . . . More rex sole is sold at Fisherman's Wharf than any other kind of fish—especially barracuda; that's the most unpopular item on the Wharf menus, probably because the very thought of barracuda gives people the shivers . . . Going, going, gone: Back in 1945, San Francisco had 665 streetcars (of the traditional type) rattling around the streets; that number has now been reduced to 185—which means that they're going fast, in their own slow way.

The Gaines Dog Research Center of New York puts out a pamphlet called "Touring with Towser" (wow) which lists the hotels, motels, etc., which'll accept dogs (also people). Oakland cracks the list with three hotels. Our town, says the pamphlet, has none. Unlisted: cat houses . . . The most expensive item at Gump's famed art store is a pot—the kind you cook in. It's a tripod affair of bronze, made in 1500 B.C. (the Chou Dynasty), and although it's slightly corroded, it's price-tagged at twelve thousand dollars. Very modern design. As a Gump executive puts it: "Looks like it could have come from Kasper's." (That's a rival store, which makes this a very funny remark; so laugh).

You can buy almost anything in a Third Street pawnshop; for example, the Reliable has assorted false teeth, a wooden leg, an elephant tusk, some Nazi guns, and a few Japanese swords, plus all kinds of medals that meant a lot to somebody—once . . . The Bette Lane shop on Post, which features big clothes for big women (sizes up to 56), is run by Myra Lieber, who's five feet four, weighs 102, and wears a size seven . . . About 250,000 books are borrowed from the City's twenty-one public libraries each year—and 1200 are never returned. Take a bow, San Francisco. This is far below the national average . . . Don't ask me why this is—ask the SPCA—but anyway, long-haired dogs seem to be getting dumber all the time. That is, they get lost far more often than the short-haired variety. A few years ago, it was the other way around, with fox terriers leading the wrong-way pack. Today, getting lost is an old spaniel custom.

The pretty carhops at the drive-in restaurants (like Ott's, Mel's, etc.) have their own lingo—a little different from the usual waitress-type slang; for instance, "stretch one" means a coke; "red stretch" is a cherry coke; "J.B." (for jaw-breaker) is a steak sandwich; whole wheat is "W.W.," or "wobbly-wobbly"; a malted milk is a "mammy," a shortcake is a "shorty," deep-dish pie is a "D.D."—and hot chocolate, for reasons nobody can figure out, is simply "make one" . . . Old-timers who attended the long-gone Lincoln School here still tip their hats politely when they walk past the Dewey Monument in Union Square. That's because Ida Clark, eighth-grade teacher at the school in the early 1900s, was the model for the figure atop the monument (sculpted by Robert Aiken, one of her students)—and now we'll tell you why the old grads still raise their lids when they pass by. Quote from one (Frank McAuliffe): "You always tip your hat to your teacher."

The oldest active union man in town (if I'm wrong slap me with a union suit) must be John Glover, who belongs to the Ship's Clerk Union, lives at the YMCA—and works every day. He's ninety-four, and has voted for every President since Garfield . . . Henri Lenoir, who wears a beret, talks with an accent, but insists he isn't a character, peddles twenty-eight different kinds of beer in his Vesuvio bar—including Old Manx ale and oyster stout from the Isle of Man. Nobody ever asks for the stuff, but Henry stocks it anyway, for sedimental reasons. He went to school on the Isle of Man . . . Some delivery trucks around town (W. & J. Sloane's, for example), have a time clock gadget installed on the underside—and when the truck stops, so does the clock; a double-check against loafing, I guess, unless the driver has learned how to sleep at the wheel . . . The merry-go-round in Golden Gate Park is listed officially by the city as a "monument"; it was donated by Herbert Fleishhacker, who has been on a few merry-go-rounds (financially) himself. And Huntington Park, on Nob Hill, was a gift from Mrs. C. P. Huntington, of course, but she didn't donate the "Dancing Sprites" fountain in the middle; that was given by Mrs. James Flood, her old neighbor in The Great Days of the hill.

San Francisco proudly calls itself "The Financial Colossus of the West," but the biggest trust fund in these parts—the $33,000,000 Insurance Securities, Inc.—has its head office in Oakland . . . If you're looking for a $50,000 diamond ring, Shreve's has plenty, and they're going slow; they also have a $17,000 wrist watch—but frankly, my time isn't that valuable . . . Of the city's 68,272 public school students, 3,896 are absent each day on account of illness—and 1506 just plain play "hooky," or whatever the kids call it these days . . . And whereas The Emporium department store occupies the most expensive piece of property in town, the cheapest is a lot,

50 x 100 feet at the corner of Gilman and Boalt (assessed value: twenty dollars). Nice piece of property, and all that, but there's one slight drawback. At high tide, it's six feet under water.

When the worst comes to the end, Jerry and I resort to the most time-honored trick in the San Francisco columning trade. We take a ride on a Powell or a California Street cable, to see what we can overhear. Besides getting us out of the stuffy office and into the fresh air, it's usually time well spent.

Example: On a Powell cable one afternoon, a well-dressed, distinguished-looking man turned to the woman standing next to him and remarked warmly: "I say, that's a lovely camellia you're wearing."

"Why, thank you," beamed the woman.

They rode a block in silence, and then the man said to her in a rather embarrassed way: "Y'know, I wouldn't talk to a strange lady on the street or in a bus—but on a cable car, somehow, it seems all right."

"I understand," smiled back Mrs. Frieda Klussmann, head of the Citizens Committee to Save the Cable Cars. "I understand perfectly."

Example: Mrs. Harold Rome, wife of the noted New York musical comedy composer, took a ride on a Powell cable and enthused to the gripman: "Ah, this is my favorite city—next to New York, of course."

"Lady," grunted the gripman, "you've got great taste in seconds."

Example: One sweltering afternoon, Mrs. Cameron Robertson, of the Hormel Meat family, found herself the only passenger on a Hyde Street cable. At Union, the gripman pulled the brake, mumbled "Excuse me a minute," and galloped into Earle Swenson's ice-cream shop at the corner. In a few seconds, he was back with two ice-cream cones. One for himself. And one for his passenger, Mrs. Robertson.

Example: A Powell-Jackson cable was on its last run late one night, with only two passengers aboard, a young man and his girl friend. At Powell and Sacramento, he said to the gripman: "Would you wait here just a second? This is where my girl lives, and I'll be right back."

They ran to the door of her apartment, where he pecked her a good-night kiss on the cheek and ran back to the cable. "Now look," said the gripman, leaning on his lever, "that's no way to kiss a girl good night. Go back and do it right. We'll wait."

The young man kissed her until smoke curled out of her ears, returned ecstatically to his seat—and with a triumphant clang of its ageless bell, the cable swayed happily away into the little dream world that only a San Franciscan can know.

Kaleidoscope   The orange-tipped tower of the Bay Bridge, its fresh-painted head reaching through the fog's clutching fingers and smiling in the sun . . . The thick Sunday silence along Montgomery Street, where the skyscrapers sleep stonily and the only touches of brightness are the traffic lights, blinking red and green for the traffic that isn't there . . . Kearny Street's row upon drab row of empty shops, padlocked and forgotten—with the names of their owners fading in the grime; like headstones in a concrete cemetery of financial failures . . . The windswept cypresses along the Presidio wall, their tops cropped and chopped so that the economic royalty of Pacific Heights might have a clearer view of the Golden Gate Bridge; as good a view, almost, as that of the people they look down on, in the Marina.

On Powell, the dark and dismal Korean Church, its muddy bareness relieved only by a few skeletal shrubs that cling to its walls—as forlornly and desperately as Korea clings to life . . . A crowded California cable, silhouetted for a long moment at the top of a hill—looking like a fat old lady waddling home with too many bundles to carry . . . The ocean wind whistling hollowly through the clustered trees of Lafayette Square, that polite, mansion-ringed faubourg where, when the weather is fine, the nurses walk with the children and the well-dressed oldsters sit alone with their pearl-handled canes and their musty thoughts.

Laguna Honda Home, for the old and forgotten, and the Youth Guidance Center, for the young and sometimes misbegotten, sharing the airy eminence of Twin Peaks; impressive, depressive monuments to the woes of this world we call the city . . . Five P.M. along "Insurance Row" on the California slope of Nob Hill, when the great buildings open their doors and the workers tumble out in noisy knots, like kids going home from school—without homework to dampen their gaiety . . . On Grant Avenue, the natives staring at the tourists in their glass-enclosed sightseeing buses, and the tourists staring at the natives—each thinking the other quite strange and unusual and well worth staring at; it's all a matter of perspective.

The last cable car, rattling home emptily at midnight on Washington—and your eyes follow it down the hill until it disappears and you carefully file the sight away in your memory; for someday—who knows how soon?—the last cable car will indeed be The Last Cable Car . . . The faraway streets with strange-sounding names in the Marina, where a pioneering band of Italians imported a spurious Mediterranean atmosphere from North Beach—after they'd outgrown the uncomfortably real color of Columbus Avenue; to the flat Marina they went, to prove that they'd come up in the world . . . The traffic officers on their undignified tricycles, three-wheeling along the downtown streets and reaching out with their sticks to chalk the tires of parked cars; The Strong Arm of the Law, making its small, futile mark.

The busy bistros of Broadway, where the bartender is likely to burst into a passable operatic aria, the waiters speak at least two languages fluently, and only the customers seem dull . . . The weird, piping melodies, punctuated by off-rhythm clicks, that float up into the street from the Chinese "Musical Association" on Sacramento Street; the clicks are from the musicians who play ping-pong while their fellow artists are bing-bonging on their peculiar instruments . . . The blind Negro who sits on a camp stool and reads aloud from a Braille Bible on Geary, in front of the City of Paris; he draws no crowds around him, for as soon as the passers-by realize what he's reading, they hastily throw him a few coins and hurry off, a strangely uneasy look on their faces.

The brightly modern homes that have sprung up along the side streets of Russian Hill and Pacific Heights—hidden from casual view by the ageless, hunking mansions that, in almost human accord, turn their backs on these brash upstarts . . . The perfect dome of the City Hall, soaring in golden-lighted splendor over Van Ness Avenue during the nights of the opera—a reminder that sometimes the taxpayers' money is squandered on sheer beauty, and what is wrong with that? . . . The string orchestra that plays polite luncheon music in the St. Francis' Mural Room—the last reminder of a long-gone, non-union age when every restaurant worthy of the name had its orchestra, and the waltz was king, and the dollar went a long, long way before it went.

The doctors from the Fitzhugh and Union Square Buildings, who gather at noon on the Post Street fringe of Union Square to forget their patients' sickness in impatient discussions of the sickness of the world . . . The bright, scrubbed Italian children of North Beach, done up brown in their Kelly green uniforms, marching in helters and skelters to school at Saints Peter and Paul—whose spires etch the sky with sheer magnificence . . . The tenderloin's busy B-girls, their hard eyes masked with mascara, their thin lips softened under lipstick, hurrying down Taylor at 7 P.M. to their night's work of empty play—the hard work of playing hard-to-get with easy marks who can't see through the mascara, can't see under the lipstick.

The financial district's skyscrapers on the edge of Chinatown's tenements, the Fillmore's slums across the street from mansions, the Richmond's middle-class stability in the middle of decaying houses, the Sunset's tinny whiteness stretching to the edge of the solemn ocean, Skid Road's fetid odor reaching almost to the proud doors of the Palace Hotel, the solid Mission holding its good head high while the city grows away from it—this is the color, these are the contradictions that add up to the never-ending total we call Baghdad-by-the-Bay.

Barney & Tiny's Circus   Every city has characters to match its character, and San Francisco has had more than
its share.

You can see them parading in a grotesque file through the long
generations—Emperor Norton, the self-appointed overlord of everything, with his faithful dogs, Bummer and Lazarus; pitiful Oofty
Goofty, who'd invite anybody to wallop him with a baseball bat,
cackling inanely all the while; Slitzie the Pinhead, making one sound
over and over, a sound that can be approximated only as *"Apatha,
apatha, apatha."*

These, and a dozen other gentle, aberrated folk, chuckling, ges-
ticulating and even pontificating along the downtown streets, while
passers-by, typically San Franciscan, laughed with them, not at
them, and saw to it, through countless unheralded generosities,
that they never wanted for food, clothing and shelter.

Even today, when realities have all but crowded out the capacity
for whimsy, San Francisco takes its characters with commendable
seriousness—the same seriousness that perpetuates the anachronistic
cable car, the hillside hovel with the million-dollar view, an expansive Golden Gate Park covering a thousand acres in an overcrowded
city.

In the slightly second-rate, present-day array of San Francisco characters—a crazy sideshow of braggart shysters, bald-faced moochers, misfit millionaires, whining sycophants, and tin-plated underworld types featuring polished fingernails with dirt under the tips—two men stand out, head and shoulders above their measly fellow shirkers.

They are characters with character. In any phase of the San Francisco story, they would have qualified as bona fide members of their peculiar bon ton. They have the universal, timeless quality of the truly gifted metropolitan parasite: they can go on, day after day, year after year, without working—and not become objects of petty jealousy or outright hatred.

One is Tiny Armstrong, and the other is Barney Ferguson, and it is safe to say that every San Franciscan knows them and appreciates their efforts toward perpetuating the half-truth, half-myth that his city, among all others, is truly "different."

By virtue of a tacit agreement, Tiny and Barney keep to their own sides of the downtown sector. Powell Street, with its clanging cables and wide-eyed tourists, is Tiny's beat. The older, more pompous Barney—dean of San Francisco characters—confines his activities to the financial district.

Of the two, Tiny is the more ostentatious. He has not Barney's subtlety, his sly approach to the craft of living without a trade. Tiny is loudly and openly a guy who is looking for attention, and who appreciates all he can get.

Tiny, whose first name is actually Chester, first appeared on Powell Street a few years ago—a stout, waddling, blustery fellow blowing industriously on a particularly loud bird-whistle and greeting all the passing women with an airy "Hello, sweetheart, you look gorgeous today."

This, plus a fantastic silk hat festooned with gold stars, and a swallowtail coat over striped pants, was bound to cause some talk. The newspapers began referring to him as "the bird-whistle man." Soon he was being immortalized in the public print as "Tiny Birdwhistle" Armstrong, thereby becoming one of the few men in the world with consecutive nicknames.

Tiny flung himself at San Francisco's bosom, and the city received him with equal warmth. There is something about his wide smile and his breezy manner that keeps him far removed from the ranks of the offensive. Nobody ever gets angry with Tiny. Almost everybody laughs at him. And even his "touches" are comparatively painless, for when he asks for a quarter, he opens a toy cash register dangling from his capacious stomach—and when you comply, he slams the drawer shut with a loud clang, plus a shrill peep on his bird-whistle and assorted blasts from the several horns affixed to his person with safety pins.

Chester (Tiny) "Birdwhistle" Armstrong is rather mysterious about his background. Although actually he's an exclown, the legend has grown up that he was once a prominent businessman in an Eastern city, who suddenly tired of the hurly-burly of the commercial world and chose the vagabond life of the buffoon. The legend is bound to live, for whenever Tiny is questioned about it, he assumes a look of mock seriousness, slaps a hammy hand to his forehead and says with gargling emotion: "Son, I'd rather not talk about it."

Tiny lives in what he calls his "suite" at the smallish Jefferson Hotel on Eddy Street, where, thanks to an understanding landlord, his rent is appropriately low. However, his letters—and his correspondence is voluminous—are impressive. Every few days, Tiny wanders into the St. Francis Hotel and helps himself to a big sheaf of that hotel's stationery.

His closets contain a fabulous array of costumes (no one has ever seen him in an ordinary suit). One day, he will appear on Powell Street wearing a chef's cap and apron. The next, he will be dressed like a clown. Sometimes he wears a great, floppy beret, and other times a beanie with three propellers on it.

His favorite "charity"—he can now afford that luxury—is selling raffle tickets around town for various benefits. For this activity, the Golden Pheasant, a prominent restaurant at the busy corner of Powell and Geary, provides him with a sidewalk table, over which spreads an umbrella of brilliant colors with Tiny's name across it in big letters.

This is Chester "Tiny" Armstrong, the fifty-nine-year-old dispenser of daily joy along Powell Street. He can get a free drink or a free meal wherever he goes. When he blows his birdwhistle and rattles his bells—Tiny carries twenty pounds of junk around his shoulders and stomach—people smile at him with the kind of innocent good will they usually reserve for small children. He is a perpetual honorary guest of the Saints and Sinners, an exalted group of San Franciscans, and he is known by more people than the President of the Bank of America or the manager of the San Francisco Seals.

And yet people say he's crazy.

But "Old Tiny"—with true majesty, he refers to himself in the third person—"Old Tiny isn't crazy. But he sure works hard at the job of trying to look like he is."

A bit more complex is the story of Barney Ferguson.

In his youth—he is now seventy-nine—he was a top-ranking vaudeville performer, a nimble acrobat, and a tenor with a clear, piping Irish voice. He headlined many times at the Palace Theater in New York with the likes of George M. Cohan, and his salary was three hundred dollars a week at a time when such a sum was large potatoes indeed.

Then, one day, in a tragic instant, Barney Ferguson's life was changed. Down from the flies of a big Eastern theater hurtled a heavy sandbag. It struck the vaudeville star on the head. For weeks, he hovered between life and death. And when he was finally released from the hospital, he had "recovered"—but only physically.

In other ways, the once great headliner was never the same.

His stage career finished, he drifted to San Francisco and existed, barely, on the usual odd jobs—janitor, night watchman, dishwasher. But his old instincts—the touch of class—were still there. It didn't take Barney long to realize that the great and important men of San Francisco made their headquarters on Montgomery Street. And it must have dawned on him that if he could make himself known to them, life somehow would become just a little easier.

Soon, the poohbahs of the Big Street were noticing, with tolerant amusement, the strutting little gamecock of a man who had the wondrous temerity to stop A. P. Giannini on the street and pass a few words of advice to the chief of Bank of America, the world's largest. "Just do what I say, A.P.," Barney would say with sublime condescension, "and I'll make a big man out of you yet."

The Street was likewise impressed when Barney would stroll up to Millionaire Louis Lurie, presiding over his daily luncheon table at Jack's Restaurant, and address him with fitting humility: "Lou, my boy, is everything all right—or would you like me to have a few words with the Governor in your behalf?" And all eyes would be on Barney as he'd brush imperiously past receptionists and settle himself in the office of Parker Maddux, President of the rich San Francisco Bank, with this opening gambit: "Parker, I've been devoting a lot of thought to you, and the way you're running this bank. Now then——"

It is to the credit of these estimable gentlemen, and their confreres in the financial marts, that they have accepted Barney Ferguson on his own gilt-edged terms. They seek his counsel, addressing him obsequiously as "Governor" and "Senator"—two titles he uses quite frequently when signing his name to "business" correspondence. They see that he is fed, usually in the better places. And they see that he is well-clothed, in their only finest castoff clothing.

Governor/Senator Ferguson is only moderately impressed with this largesse.

Louis Lurie, one of his principal benefactors, was, in fact, a bit annoyed when Barney went into Richard Bennett's, one of the tycoon's several tailors, and announced to the manager, David Falk:

"Mr. Falk, I wish you would sell Louis a brown suit next time. I'm getting tired of his gray ones."

In his more unsophisticated days as a Ferguson sponsor, Lurie used to hand Barney his old suits without bothering to remove the tailor's label containing his name—a practice that he stopped abruptly one night a few years ago. Celebrating the acquisition of a new old suit, Barney journeyed down to San Mateo and eventually wound up in the drunk tank. Shortly after midnight, Mrs. Lurie received a phone call from an officer who, having "identified" Barney by his suit label, announced:

"Lady, we got your husband down here—drunk."

After a hasty glance at the other bed, Mrs. Lurie retorted stiffly: "Oh no you haven't. I've got him here—sober."

Barney's unnerving ability to make his benefactors feel unworthy is perhaps best illustrated by an incident that happened one noon in Carl Wilke's financial district restaurant.

Dressed impeccably in banker's gray, plus a harmonizing double-breasted vest in dovelike tones, Barney stepped up to Wilke and said loftily: "Carl, may I touch you for a one-dollar loan, please, so I can go somewhere and get a roast beef sandwich."

"Governor," replied the humble Wilke, "I would be deeply flattered if you would have one right here—and on me."

Barney looked a little put out. "Impossible, my boy," he snapped. "Your cook puts gravy on the roast beef sandwiches, and I don't want to get spots on my vest."

Suggested Wilke: "So take off the vest"—an innocent remark that proved highly offensive to Ferguson.

"Sir," he roared, "I will have you know that this vest was given to me by Louis Lurie, and I will never, no, never take it off. Now, sir, if you please."

Thoroughly cowed, Wilke handed over the dollar and watched Barney march off to spend it in somebody else's restaurant.

Barney Ferguson, with his vaudevillian's strut, his snapping blue eyes, and his pink, gnomelike face, has his sensitive side however. And on at least one occasion, his patrons along Montgomery Street proved themselves almost completely blind to the feelings of a little old man who—like all characters—is basically sad.

It was a vignette that Chaplin could have played.

"Barney," his powerful friends told him, "we're going to put on a testimonial vaudeville show for you—on a Saturday night at the

Presidio Theater. We've printed a lot of tickets, at a dollar apiece, and you get the money. Now let's all go to work and sell them."

For days, Barney lived high on a pink cloud. He rushed around the town, selling tickets. So did his banker friends. In a short time, some three hundred tickets were sold, and the money duly deposited to Barney's name at the San Francisco Bank.

Only one thing was wrong with this fine, selfless plan. The sponsors, who merely wanted to raise a little cash for Barney, had no intention of putting on a show. That part of it was, for want of a better name, a joke. And everybody was in on it except Barney.

During the week before the scheduled event, he worked feverishly. He wrote letters to Jack Benny, Bob Hope, Jimmy Durante, and others, asking them to appear on the stage with him. He bragged to Lurie and Maddux that Governor Earl Warren had accepted his invitation, "and Harry, too, of course—Harry Truman."

The excited little man even traveled out to the Presidio Theater, scene of the supposed testimonial, and asked Owner Carol Nathan how many patrons the place would hold. When Nathan answered "Oh, about eight hundred," Barney was properly miffed.

"Not enough," he scoffed. "Why, at my last testimonial, at the Geary Theater in 1936, eighteen thousand people showed up!"

At last, the big night arrived—the night of the midnight testimonial for Governor/Senator Barney Ferguson.

At 11 P.M., the man of the hour showed up, elegantly attired in top hat, cutaway coat and striped pants. The minutes ticked by, with Barney nervously pacing the lobby. At midnight, six people, as much in the dark as Barney, appeared at the door, took a tentative look around the quiet theater, and hurried away.

And then, finally, Barney Ferguson was in on the joke.

With his top hat in his hands, he stared for a long minute at the empty rows of seats in the dim theater. He fished his admission ticket out of his pocket and slowly tore it into tiny pieces. He put on his top hat and said to the uncomfortable ushers in a choked voice:

"O.K., boys, you can close up now. The show's over." Then he added with a touch of his old bravado: "If the Governor shows up, tell him he's too late. I'll phone him tomorrow."

As the lights went out, Barney walked slowly away into the night, the tears glistening like raindrops on his cheeks.

Sometimes it's awfully hard—the job of being a character.

Gloomy Sunday   The Magic City sleeps restlessly on a fog-filtered afternoon and time stands still in the unaccustomed hush.

It is as though everybody had pulled down the shades, locked the front door and gone out of town—leaving you in charge, free to wander where you please. Only the horns in the Bay, clearing the fog out of their throats, remind you that you aren't completely alone.

In the long valleys of Montgomery Street, the shadows rule the empty sidewalks, and the skyscrapers sit and stare at nothing through vacant windows. The armies of pigeons march alone through the stone paths of Union Square, their bobbing heads looking this way and that for the crumbs that aren't there. Even the mighty gray hulk of the St. Francis seems lost in its own dreams, its rooftop banners hanging listlessly on their staffs, its front doors mute and motionless.

On Powell, the cables wander up and down, their lopsidedness accentuated by their emptiness. The blind newsboy stands in a self-induced coma at the corner of Post, too dispirited to shout the headlines he can't read to the passers-by who don't pass by. And the

windows of the exclusive shops, filled with silks and fineries, look
bored and resentful at the lack of attention.

Sunday afternoon—when even the busy, clicking traffic signals
have closed their shutters and hung out the "Do Not Disturb" sign.

It's good to look at the relaxed city, freed for a few hours from its
constricting masses of people. Suddenly, it stands revealed in all its
magnificence and all its tawdriness.

Floating in the fog, the perfect dome of the City Hall rises in
sharp outline against the sunny Mission, its contours as noble as
St. Paul's in London or St. Peter's in Rome. On a quiet Sunday, you
can see the great building for what it is—cold and clean, far above
the little people who clutter its halls, gather in scheming knots on
its wide stairs, and plot their little plots in its shadows.

At the foot of Market, the Ferry Building squats defensively like
a broken relic of the past, while the sleazy waters of the Bay moan
a funeral dirge among the rotting piers. Near by, the liners, the
freighters and the rusting tramps pull sleepily at their lines, deserted as ghost ships. The waterfront wind plays free and alone
among the cobblestones, rustling through the discarded papers, dis-
turbing the old dust, sending the stray dogs whimpering toward the
alleys for protection.

In the produce district, the sprawling buildings drowse behind
their drawn shades, and here and there a bony cat prowls into
garbage cans and empty crates, in search of the scraps that might
have been left behind in the feverish frenzy that reigned here before
Sunday came.

You don't need a calendar to tell you that it's Sunday. The somno-
lent spell, as heavy as death, lies everywhere.

In Washington Square, where the old men in their black hats sit stonily on the benches and dream of their youth in Sicily. Along the Park-Presidio Boulevard, where the refugees, huddled in their thick, foreign overcoats, walk slowly along the shaded paths, thinking of other shaded paths they once trod in Berlin and Frankfurt and Munich. At the beach, where the cajolery of the barkers dies on their own foggy breath—and the tinny make-believe of the merry-go-round is lost in the pounding of the nearby surf.

On the wide drives of Golden Gate Park, the families move slowly along on their installment-plan wheels, and the children in the passing cars press their noses against the glass and regard each other with round-eyed detachment—so near, and yet so far away.

Encased in their own thick silences, the people wander through the corridors of the de Young Museum, looking and sometimes seeing, and in the heavy dampness of the Steinhart Aquarium, only the fish seem completely alive.

Near the ancient bandstand, the children tumble down the grassy slopes, but they do it quietly, without joy—as though they understand that children are supposed to tumble down grassy slopes on Sunday, even on a Sunday when there is grayness in the sky and in the faces of the people who watch them, intently, unsmilingly.

Sunday—and you can wander through the empty streets and see it all the way it is, the beauty and the ugliness, the old and the new, the creeping lines of age, and the sudden vistas that are always fresh, no matter how familiar.

The wooden monstrosities along Turk and Eddy and Ellis, their jigsaw gimcrackery falling to pieces, their naked old boards crying for paint, their foundations sagging like the shoulders of the people who have to look at these horrors and admit to themselves: "This is my home."

The bright, brave little houses of Anzavista, already fading and streaking under the ceaseless onslaughts of wind and fog, already taking on the patina of ageless age that gives San Francisco its obstinate charm—for in San Francisco, only that which has been grayed has charm.

The pretentious mansions of Sea Cliff, with their cold views of the cold sea and the bridge that is blotted from sight; the great houses of Pacific Heights, looking out over the bleak trees of the Presidio; the orderly, well-spaced villas of St. Francis Wood, shivering in lonely exclusiveness behind gates and hedges that keep out the unwanted—but not the unwanted fog.

Only in the Mission does the sun shine fitfully, lighting up the old houses with a touch of gold, and warming the trees and plazas of Dolores Street—the proof that Nature, in all her justice, doesn't give a fig for fashion.

Sunday and the city sleeps as a person sleeps—sprawled out, shifting occasionally, not always pretty, but always real and really itself. On other days, the city's face is lost in its own busy importance. On Sunday, it lies touchingly exposed for all to see and to understand and to marvel at afresh.

Our Own Zoological Garden   If you think I'm
brimming over with facts and figures about sea lions, you're wrong.

Like thousands of other San Franciscans, I'm content to go out
to the Cliff House on a fine Sunday, wrap myself around a Ramos
fizz, and peer through the windows at Seal Rocks. If particularly
moved by the sight—the rocks are rather symmetrical and good to
look at, especially when the waves are crashing high about them—
I'm likely to say something profound, like:

"Never could understand why they call 'em Seal Rocks when
there aren't any seals on 'em, just sea lions."

At this point, tourists usually crowd around, clapping their hands
childishly and imploring me to tell them all I know about the sea
lions on Seal Rocks. Aside from the fact that I happen to have
heard that they bear their young in June and July—and none of
your business why I remember THAT—my ignorance is limitless.

What little I do know I got from Paul Bonnot, who knows a lot
about sea lions. In fact, he knows so much about sea lions that he
thinks they should be called "sea bears," inasmuch as they resemble
a bear more than a lion. However, a male sea lion is called a bull,

and a female is a cow, and their offspring are pups, so maybe just plain "sea beast" would do as well.

How to tell a sea lion from a seal? Ah, that is a question that has been perplexing everybody except sea lions and seals for some time. However, the most obvious difference is that a sea lion has pronounced ears (pronounced "ears") and a seal sometimes doesn't. As you can see, this is an obvious difference in a rather obtuse way.

Speaking of ears, sea lions don't hear very well; they won't even turn around unless you shoot off a cannon alongside their heads. Furthermore, they don't seem to notice you at all. However, you'll notice them, all right, because they don't smell so good. They don't smell so well, either. They can identify each other only by rubbing noses.

The male sea lions, or bulls, collect their cows into a harem, but they don't get very bulligerent about their girls—and having seen a few sea cows at close quarters, I can't say I blame them. Each cow had only one pup, and the pups have to be taught to swim. What with the cows being pretty bad (or careless) teachers, about as many pups drown as live. If they survive, they live twelve to fourteen years.

All in all, I'd say a sea lion is dumb as hell, except for one little point: practically all the "trained seals" you see in circuses and other shows are sea lions.

And that's all I know about sea lions. I'm dumb as hell, too.

Mickey   Due to an experience which I shall describe in painful detail, I have become an expert on that peculiar San Francisco art form known as the Mickey Finn.

It is the only phenomenon of the city in which I have enjoyed personal participation, you should excuse the euphemism, and in a way, I am not sorry. Although I consider myself a true blue, dyed-in-the-fog San Franciscan, I have had only a vicarious connection with its other unique qualities. I have never handled the grip on a Powell Street cable car, I have never sung an aria from the stage of its golden opera house, I have never planted a tree in Golden Gate Park, nor swum to Alcatraz with a dagger between my teeth.

But I have had a Mickey Finn, and thus consider myself amply qualified to discuss it, both con and con.

My involuntary plunge into the sea of pure research began innocently enough. A recently arrived bumpkin from the wilds of Sacramento, I suddenly found myself the lofty proprietor of a daily newspaper column—and a few nights after I began spewing my limpid prose I decided to take a stroll into San Francisco's tenderloin district, to see what I could see.

Or rather, to let the awed natives see me. It is hard to conceive of any one more imbued with self-importance than a twenty-two-year-old columnist in the first flush of glory.

On Turk Street, I wandered into a long, narrow bar that looked exactly like all the other bars in the section. And it was, except that it had a "secret" gambling room that was the subject of much conversation.

Juvenile journalistic zeal welled up inside me, and for one warm, heady moment, I knew how Richard Harding Davis must have felt. I stood at the bar, bought myself a drink, and watched the flow of traffic through a door in the back of the saloon. I vowed, as Lincoln Steffens, Fremont Older, Joseph Pulitzer, and countless others had vowed before me, to Get The Story.

After a few minutes had passed, a small-time gambler I knew slightly walked into the place and headed for the back room. "Hiya, Swifty," I called out, to his utter embarrassment, and fell into step alongside him as we walked to the rear.

He stopped and squinted at me. "Hiya," he said briefly. Then he darted a quick glance around the bar and grinned humorlessly, "Look, I got business t'do. See you some other time."

He gave me a slight shove that was intended to be friendly, and half-ran to the back door. But I was not to be denied. Hard at his heels, I entered the room a split second after him. He looked at me blankly and headed for a corner, his slightly shrugged shoulders saying eloquently: "I never saw the jerk before in my life."

My wide Sacramento eyes took in the details of the famous back room in one foggy glance. Two dice tables, twenty players each. Two blackjack tables, four players each. In a corner, an eight-man poker table. Smoke. Sweat. The buzz and drone of cryptic comments. The rattle of chips and the rustle of paper money.

As I stood there, mouth attractively ajar, a man wearing a green eyeshade walked over to me, dug a finger decisively into my chest, and snapped: "This club is for members only. You ain't no member. That way out." And he indicated the door with his thumb.

But I had seen enough. I went to my office and wrote an indeed-colorful, indeed-righteous account of the illicit activities that were flourishing in the wicked tenderloin.

The results were immediate and startling. No sooner had the first edition hit the streets than sirens screamed, a police squad raided the room, and the paddy-wagon rolled away with a capacity crowd of customers, including Swifty and the man in the green eyeshade. They all got themselves bailed out in a hurry, but the "secret" back room was now publicly padlocked and the police department's icy "heat" swept over the tenderloin.

For this mighty blow in behalf of the public weal, I received no Pulitzer Prize. What I really needed, however, was a plug for the hole in my head. For, the very next night, I strolled again along Turk Street and walked into that same saloon.

My, the proprietor was glad to see me. "Well, kid," he greeted with a grin that would have melted in a cold frying pan. "Come in. Siddown—over here in this nice booth. Have a drink." He sat alongside me and signaled to the bartender. "Fix the kid a nice drink, best in the house," he ordered. My friend Swifty was in the place, too, and he sat on the other side of the booth, watching me with unwavering concentration. A couple of other people gathered around and shook my hand and said they were certainly glad to see me back so soon.

"No hard feelings, eh?" I said expansively, raising my drink. "Here's cheers. Better luck next time!"

They all laughed and said sure, it was just one of those things. And I had to admit privately that I was a little sorry I had caused them so much trouble, for they were such excellent sports about the whole thing, and even the salt of the earth after you got to know them.

After my third sip, I felt perspiration forming on my forehead. "Kinda warm in here, isn't it?" I said to the circle of faces whose eyes, no longer friendly, were watching me with cold intensity. Nobody said anything.

With a sudden stricken flash of understanding—Mickey!—I pushed the glass away. My mouth felt like it was stuffed with old copper pennies. The saliva began to flow, and the room wallowed like a ferryboat in a squall. Nausea hit me in the pit of the stomach with the impact of a sledgehammer. I rose unsteadily, pushed past Swifty and walked as straight as I could to the door. I vaguely remembered the figures around the booth, looking at me like a jury that had agreed on the death sentence.

Well, they almost had, at that.

I drove home, through red lights and stop signs, and got there just in time to live the nightmare in privacy. The apartment crawled and spun, and I crawled and spun with it, hour after hour. I threw up until there was nothing to throw up, and then I threw up some more. My heart pounded against my ribs as though it were looking for a way out. I lay on the floor in convulsions, wrung dry like an old rag, and stood up only long enough to decide to fall down again.

By dawn, six hours later, the invisible hand that was trying to pull my insides out in all directions relaxed its iron grip. I slept for an hour, drank a cup of black coffee, spat it out—and remembered, with the shock that only a deadline-conscious newspaperman can feel, that I hadn't written the column for the next evening's edition.

I knew the mob on Turk Street would be waiting for it and hoping the column wouldn't be there. But it was there. I forget what I wrote, or how, but it was there, with minutes to spare.

And then I parked my car on Turk, and walked past the saloon as jauntily as possible. The proprietor and Swifty and a couple hangers-on were standing on the sidewalk.

"Hi, fellas," I said with what I hoped was a reasonable smile, not too wide, not too narrow.

The proprietor took his cigar out of his mouth, but he could have jammed it right back without moving his lips. The mouth remained open. "Uh—how d'ya feel, all right?" he asked.

"Sure," I said, surprised-like. "Why?"

I pulled the first edition of the paper out of my pocket, and folded it so that my column was on the outside. "Here, have a paper," I said. "Hot off the press."

The proprietor, never taking his eyes off me, sailed it into the gutter, and I laughed and walked away. They didn't know whether their Mickey Finn had worked, and they would never find out.

The loathsome Mickey, in case you never heard of it, is an odorless, colorless, tasteless liquid that is dropped into a drink to "cure" an obstreperous drunk, gain cowardly revenge on an enemy, or make a particular point with an unreasonable columnist. Its effects are almost immediate, and so violent that they have caused countless fatalities. In the State of California, it is a felony to administer a Mickey. It is also a felony to commit murder, but people are still being murdered. And the Mickey is still being handed out by bartenders who would be surprised to learn that they are potential murderers. Or perhaps actual ones.

The archives contain remarkably little information on the history of the Mickey Finn, but historians generously concede it to be one of San Francisco's less notable contributions to the world of culture and gracious living. Besides, no other city has stepped forward to claim the honor. And so we are stuck with it.

Attorney Vincent J. Mullins, another serious student of the Mickey (but one without my first-hand experience), has unearthed the legend that the poison—for it is—was invented on the Barbary Coast, circa 1870, by a discredited Scotch chemist named Michael Finn. Finn, supposedly a fugitive from justice in Scotland, worked as a bartender on the Coast, and soon became known as a fine source of manpower for ship captains whose crews had deserted to the gold fields.

Under Mr. Finn's tender ministrations, sailors drinking in his bar became suddenly and surprisingly easy to handle, and could be Shanghaied aboard ship with no signs of protest. And, in most cases, very few signs of life.

And so Mickey Finn—"Miguelito" to the Mexican populace, "Mickola Finnola" to the wags, and just plain "Poison" to the toxicologists—became part of the San Francisco language.

If you are interested in recipes, there are several ways of concocting a Mickey. Sometimes it involves the use of Glauber's salts, a horse laxative. Sometimes it is made from chloral hydrate. But the true, historic Mickey is a preparation of antimony and potassium tartrate known as a "tartar emetic."

Fortunately for the recipients of a Mickey, the poison has an unique reverse quality. That is, the greater the dose, the greater the chances for recovery—for the victim throws off the poison so fast that it has no time to get in its deadliest work. However, it does accomplish its purpose: sapping its victim of all physical and mental powers of resistance in a matter of minutes.

Toxicologists are convinced that hundreds of deaths attributed to other ailments have been caused by Mickeys. Given the proper dosage, a person with tuberculosis of the lungs, for example, would hemorrhage massively and probably die. A pregnant woman would abort spontaneously. And a person with a weak heart would suffer an immediate attack due to the violent pressures. A ruptured artery would not be unlikely, even in a person in good physical condition.

And yet the Mickey lives on, administered with impunity by bartenders and others who avoid murder only because they unwittingly give too large a dose.

Prosecution is next to impossible because of the difficulty of proof. And yet it is common knowledge in San Francisco that an Army officer was killed in a widely-known restaurant after getting a Mickey. Third-rate saloons, where B-girls and owners rob helpless drunks, slip the sucker a Mickey after his pockets have been emptied, and throw him into an alley to die a thousand deaths.

Bartenders have been known to play their own version of the fantastic game known as "Russian Roulette," involving several drinks—one of which contains a Mickey. The glasses, one to a player, are revolved several times on the bar, and then, at a signal, each one grabs a glass and drinks. Good fun for all. Except one.

Despite the prevalence of the Mickey, there has been only one prosecution in the last thirty years for using the poison in San Francisco. The victims in this case were the members of an orches-

tra in a night club on Fisherman's Wharf. Apparently their music
had been a source of no pleasure to the staff of the club, for on
their closing night, the musicians were handed a large "Loving
Cup" of brandy and all were invited to take a sip.

They became violently ill. The bandleader, who, as befitted his
station, took the largest sip, was in bed for weeks. The aforementioned Vincent J. Mullins, then on the District Attorney's staff,
prosecuted four members of the night club staff, and convicted all
of them in what became celebrated in the headlines as "The Mickey
Finn Case."

But the notorious Mickey is still around. So are the bartenders who
serve it. And so are the people who drink one.

Most of them, anyway.

That Was San Francisco THE WONDERFUL
PEOPLE   As long as there's a San Francisco, they'll be troop-
ing gaily across the horizons of somebody's memory . . . Gertrude Atherton and George Sterling, the poet, on their daily strolls
along Post Street—Sterling half-running to keep up with Gertrude's
vigorous strides . . . Mimi Imperato, personally padlocking his
famed restaurant when Prohibition struck the city like blight-
ning; "No wine, no food," he shrugged simply, snapping the lock
and breaking a thousand hearts, including his own . . . The artists and writers who gathered in historic "Studio 7," that hotbed
of true bohemianism on an upstairs floor at California and Polk—
and the burning names scrawled on its walls by the free souls who
communed there: Theodore Dreiser, H. L. Mencken, Sterling, Hugh
Walpole, Blasco Ibanez . . . "Kid" Mohler, playing marvelous baseball for the old Seals even after his hair had turned snowy white
and his legs trembled as he stood at the plate—an old man in a
monkey suit, with greatness in his heart . . . Eddie Graney, the
self-styled "Champion Shoer of Fine Horse," making the sparks
fly in his smithy in an alley near Kearny and Bush . . . And the
nicest ladies in town, sneaking out to the Beach with gifts of calves

jelly for their idol, "Gentleman Jim" Corbett, as he trained for his fight with Ruby Bob Fitzsimmons . . . Golden people, these, in a golden age.

THE GRACIOUS DAYS   The cops broke into a North Beach saloon called "The Pup" one recent 3 A.M. and arrested its owner, Joe Parente, on a charge of selling booze after hours. Very routine stuff. Arrest. Boom. Jail. Boom. Bail. Boom. That's all . . . Things were done with more éclat during the Prohibition days here, when this same Joe Parente was the town's bootlegging king . . . One night, the Prohis crashed into Rex Glissman's speakeasy, the "Golden Fan," and carted off the Chinese bartender, Charlie Ting Gan . . . As the patrol wagon rattled through Chinatown, Charlie yelled to the driver from his seat of honor: "Hey, stop a minute. This is where I live. I wanna get something" . . . And so the wagon halted on Grant Avenue, and Charlie bounded upstairs and returned with an overcoat . . . "Might get cold in jail," he explained to the coppers . . . They nodded, and slowly the Black Maria rumbled off to the Hall of Justice . . . It just never occurred to Charlie to escape when he had the chance. And it never occurred to his captors that he would even try. They were gentlemen, in those days.

FAMOUS FIRSTS   The first secondhand store in town was opened by Abraham Cohen on Clay Street, in 1848—because laundry prices were so high; it was cheaper to sell your old clothes and buy new ones than to get 'em cleaned . . . The first newspaper peddled on the streets of San Francisco was the *New York Tribune;* an enterprising Yankee lugged 1500 copies around the Horn in '48 and sold them all in an hour at one buck a copy—even though they were months old . . . The first cigar factory was opened at 221 Sacramento by Isaac White, and his stogies must have been good; when the notorious murderers, Cora and Casey, were lynched by the Vigilantes in the windows of his plant, everybody was smoking White's cigars— the victims, the executioners, and the spectators . . . The first skyscraper, an eight-story job, was built in 1890 at Kearny and Market, and nobody in town liked it; "Eastern architecture," they complained . . . The first U. S. Mint was on Commercial Street, but in those days, gold dust was the popular medium of exchange here —and thus was born the term, "How much can you raise in a pinch?"

THE NIGHTS WERE GAY   They danced and drank and debauched till dawn along the Barbary Coast—and nobody lifted a finger to save the derelicts except a brave couple named Mr. and Mrs. J. C. Westenberg; on the fringe of the boiling Coast, they operated the "Whoever Will Rescue Mission," where there was comfort and coffee for all . . . You didn't know your way around Chinatown unless you were acquainted with "China Mary," the queen of the lotteries; the stuffed shirts railed at Mary, but she turned out to be a real queen during the firequake—when she gave away a fortune to help the helpless . . . A couple of fair dancers named Vernon and Irene Castle were headlined at Techau's—but the customers were more excited about an innovation: indoor ice skating on the first rink in the West . . . And everybody was talking about the huge new stage at Morosco's Grand Opera House— so vast that horses could rattle across it (and did), and even a fire engine in one steaming epic . . . They had medicine shows, too, in the vacant lot at Kearny and Bush, and the spellbinders were peddling "Snake Oil," guaranteed to cure everything from

heartburn to tapeworm . . . And if you didn't care for that, you
could hire a private trolley (two were available, "The Hermosa"
and "The Sierra") for a moonlight ride out to the Beach, with dancing at Sheehan's, or the Lark, or the Surf, or Jimmy Raggett's . . .
It was easy to have fun in those days—because everything was fun
in a world that was new.

ONLY YESTERDAY   Already there is a fresh crop of memories
to be filed away for future reference . . . It wasn't so long ago (and
yet it was) that there were mass brawls in the Black Cat saloon
over the burning question: "Who's the better artist, Luke Gibney
or Dong Kingman?" . . . There was a speakeasy on Telegraph Hill
where the big attraction was betting big bets on racing turtles, with
numbers painted on their shells . . . Dave Falk was a $20-a-week
necktie salesman at Berger's on Market, but he came to work in a
chauffeured limousine (who wasn't a millillionaire in those days?)
and the chauffeur opened the store door for him and bowed and
said with real concern: "Don't work too hard, Mr. Falk" . . . Everybody ate IXL Tamales at Old Recreation ball park and compared
Bert Ellison with Harry Wolverton; and Lefty O'Doul was just another sandlot kid in Butchertown . . . Harry Ryberg and his young
toadies snuck out and greased the cable car tracks on Hyde between
Clay and Broadway, and laughed fit to kill while the gripman tried
frantically to stop his car . . . A gray sea gull, white wings outstretched in flight, was the official San Francisco windshield sticker,
and everybody who loved San Francisco had one stuck on his Mar-
mon or Winton or Apperson Jackrabbit . . . And take it from me,
everybody loved San Francisco. Because San Francisco loved everybody.

You Can't Do That   For lack of something better to do, I've been breezing through the San Francisco Police Code—and pretty informative it is, too, in its own dull way. The Code, in case you never heard of it, tells you what is legal and illegal in our village, and naturally, it's right up to the minute. As part of our invaluable service, I have boiled it down to a pulp for you. Ready?

Take Article 1. This should be about something pretty important, but is it? I leave it to you: "It shall be unlawful to dump or discard any boat, vessel, barge or ark on the streets of San Francisco that are now submerged." That's not only unimportant, it's practically unintelligible. But illegal.

Article 1, section 12 makes it against the law "for any person to beat, sweep or clean any carpet or rug upon any sidewalk or street except between the hours of 12 midnight and 8 A.M." If you're wide awake and restless some 4 A.M., get up and beat heck out of the carpet. Perfectly O.K., no matter what the neighbors say.

Now, about kite-flying. This would seem to be a fairly innocent pastime, until you come to Article 1, section 28, which says you can't fly it "in that portion bounded by Divisadero, Castro and Army streets, thence easterly along Army Street to the waters of the bay, and thence northerly and westerly along the shore of the bay to the intersection of Divisadero Street with the waters of the bay."

My suggestion to anybody who feels like flying a kite is to go ahead and fly it. I don't know any cops who could figure out those directions, anyway.

Next time an unemployed gent hits you up for a quarter, just answer sweetly: "My good man, haven't you heard about Article 1, section 115?" Chances are he hasn't. And if you haven't, it states forthrightly: "It shall be unlawful for any person to beg or practice begging in or on any public street or in any public place." Even if he's only practicing, he's wrong.

Another thing our police are very stern about is vulgar language. In fact, anybody who has ever said "hell" or "damn" or even "fignewtons" in a crowded bar is a candidate for the pokey, unless Article 1, section 146 is only kidding: "No person shall utter within the hearing of two (2) or more persons, any bawdy, lewd, obscene or profane language, words, or epithets." After a check with Police Chief Mike Gaffey, I am able to report that "double darn" is acceptable in public, but just barely. Zounds.

There are, of course, a lot of regulations about gambling—it would seem to be against the law—but the most specific declaration is contained in Article 3, section 299. This says you may gambol, but not gamble, "on that part known as Ocean Beach between high and low water mark." They don't want you should get your cards wet, no doubt.

Two sections under Article 2 should bring back memories for the receding-hairline set (hiya yourself). Section 735 prohibits marathon dancing, even with persons of the opposite sex, and section 775 states that "all miniature golf courses within 100 feet of any occupied hotel, apartment house, rooming house, flat, residence, hospital or other dwelling"—all right, all RIGHT—"shall be closed between the hours of 12 midnight and 7 A.M." The fact that marathon dances and midget golf courses have disappeared along with Billie Dove and the Locomobile makes no difference. It's still against the law.

The Police Code continues to show a warm interest in the health and welfare of another anachronism—the common, or non-racing horse. Under Article 7 you'll find a section that makes you a lawbreaker if you ride a horse "while intoxicated"—you, not the horse, presumably—and another section says "two or more persons shall not ride any such horse simultaneously." That's what it says: "any such." Maybe they mean an intoxicated horse, at that.

Article 8, section 585, is maybe something you should know about too: "It shall be unlawful for any person to hitch any animal to any lamppost or hydrant, or any growing tree." I like that word *growing* in there. It's about the only human word in the whole code.

Our police are also appropriately concerned about the treatment of "The Star-Spangled Banner." Article 2, section 748, makes it highly illegal to play the National Anthem here "as part of a medley, or for dancing, or as an exit march." It has to be played "as an entire and separate composition or number." And as written. No jamming.

To change the mood for a moment, I recall that the last time Red Skelton was in town, he went to a Market Street theater to see a comedy, sat behind a woman wearing a tremendous hat—and finally asked her to remove it.

"I can't see the screen," he complained.

"Just laugh when I do," she snapped.

Now what Red should have done is slapped her over the hat with a copy of Article 2, section 764. In lordly legal phrases, it says in part: "No person shall wear any hat or bonnet or other head-covering within any licensed theater, nickelodeon (etc.) during any program or exhibition (etc.) but every such bonnet (etc.) shall be removed from the head of the person wearing same during the performance (etc.)." The (etc.)s are mine, and rather well done, if I do say so.

Anyway, the key phrase, as you see, is "every such bonnet shall be removed." It doesn't say by whom. So if you don't like that hat in front of you, reach over and knock it off. With a copy of the Police Code.

There are lots of other goodies about baddies in the Code—for example, you can't carry on the business of "crushing rock between 6 P.M. and 6 A.M. of the following day," and you can't "wear the clothes of the opposite sex with intent to deceive" (oh, you gay dawg!), and you can't "discharge a cannon in the city or county" without getting an O.K. from the chief—all adding up to the fact that our civil liberties are indeed in danger.

But only slightly. So lay that cannon down.

Gesundheit   Ah Chew is a middle-aged, slightly stooped Chinese. He has a perennial smile on his face, perhaps because so many Occidentals ask him his name (knowing it all the time) and then say "Gesundheit!" and laugh heartily, although to this day it is not certain that Ah Chew understands the joke.

And he is slightly stooped because, for years, he has carried a long pole over his shoulders, with wicker chairs dangling from each end. For Ah Chew repairs chairs for a living, just as most of the male members of his family have done for generations. In fact, the faded sign on his little shop on Stockton Street pointed out for years that Ah Chew is "Ah Fook's Nephew," Ah Fook being the most famous Chinese repair man in Chinatown's recent history. It's something like a violin teacher advertising himself as "Jascha Heifetz's Cousin."

When he has chairs to deliver or pick up, Ah Chew drapes the long, curved bamboo pole over his shoulders, with the chairs tied to the ends so they balance, and pads swiftly through the streets of Chinatown or the business district. And when people ask him why he doesn't use a wagon or a truck, Ah Chew answers simply: "Chinee boy always carry chairs on pole. No other way."

In San Francisco, where sentimentality is taken seriously, he became a beloved figure. And although nobody ever made a fortune repairing wicker chairs, Ah Chew did well at his trade. His dusty, dark shop on Stockton was always stacked high with unfinished work, and the wealthy people from Pacific Heights rolled up regularly in their big cars to bring him their broken chairs.

Some of them would look around his dank quarters, and peer into the back of the shop, where Ah Chew lived with his wife and four children in two rickety rooms, and when they'd leave, they'd talk to each other about that wonderful little guy, that Ah Chew. And they'd agree that he didn't live very well. And then they'd agree, more heartily, that the Chinese are like that and enjoy living in crowded quarters, and besides, he's a very happy little guy, isn't he?

But Ah Chew didn't know anything about talk like that. All he knew was that he had managed to save quite a bit of money. And he also knew, from what he had seen and heard, that something magical was happening.

For the first time in San Francisco's history, Chinatown was no longer an invisibly walled city within a city. The war had changed all that. In small, daring groups, the Chinese were moving outside of Chinatown, into nearby sections that were once closed to them by the Occidental land owners. Now, at their own price, they were willing to rent or sell to Chinese. Money talked louder than the thin, halting voice of tradition.

One morning, Ah Chew looked at his bank balance. Then he looked at his four children sleeping in their one old bed. And, without saying a word to his wife, he walked away through the bamboo curtain of Chinatown and into the white man's land.

On Greenwich Street, near Russian Hill, he found a vacant apartment in an old, cheaply remodeled home. Ah Chew looked around silently at the five rooms, and then at the basement garage where he could do his work. "I take," he said to the landlord.

And so Ah Chew and his family moved, carrying with them the faded sign that said "Ah Chew—Ah Fook's Nephew," and he put the sign over the garage door. His wife bought some used furniture, and pretty soon they were living in the kind of comfort they never dreamed possible.

At first, Ah Chew's regular customers tried to look pleased. They even tried to say the right things. This is wonderful, Ah Chew. This is the way to live. Comfortable. Like regular, ordinary people live.

And that was the whole trouble. They didn't want Ah Chew to be like regular, ordinary people—like themselves. They wanted him to be the colorful, quaint little man with the bamboo pole over his shoulder, living in a dank hole in Chinatown and bobbing his head obsequiously to the people who smiled at him on the street.

And so, although they never discussed the matter right out loud, the customers of Ah Chew began to take their business elsewhere— to an ordinary repair man in the neighborhood. It was no longer a pleasurable tradition to go to Ah Chew. Why, he lives on Greenwich Street now, not in the Chinatown that was good enough for his elders. And he's even taking about retiring his ancient bamboo pole and getting a little truck.

They didn't know why, exactly, but the whole idea made them uncomfortable. They might even have gone so far as to think, privately, that it was rather bad taste on Ah Chew's part.

Things are quiet around Ah Chew's shop these days. The work

is no longer piled high in the corners, waiting to be finished. And he doesn't know if he can go on paying the high Greenwich Street rent much longer.

But for all his simplicity, Ah Chew is perceptive.

"It's O.K., O.K.," he half-smiled one day. "I no lose much. Pretty soon, mebbe, we move back to old place on Stockton Street."

He looked into the distance, toward Chinatown, and ran his hard fingers over his old bamboo pole.

"I know what happen then," he nodded wisely. "Then all my old customers come back to Ah Chew and say 'Gesundheit!' "

These Foolish Things   Unkind rumors to the contrary, a columnist doesn't make a lot of money, but he has a lot of fun—and not the kind of fun you think. I don't mean the "fun" of meeting famous and/or glamorous people, of getting undeserved attention and service in fine restaurants and night clubs, of being recognized—as a town character—by cabdrivers, traffic cops, bookies and other exalted personages in the metropolitan scenery.

This is all pleasant enough, to be sure, but the extra, added inducement that keeps a columnist plugging along, year after year, is the real fun of stumbling across items that he finds amusing. And if he finds them amusing, he invariably prints them in the hope that the readers will find them amusing—and when THEY do, too, then, indeed, he runneth over in his cups and decides that a columnist's life is worth while beyond all measure.

Following are a few, assorted items that this not-so-particular paragrapher found amusing as he stumbled around San Francisco in search of those elusive nothings that fill a column. But then, as the patient readers soon learn, a columnist is easily amused.

For example, I was amused, a few hundred editions ago, to find something amusing in the funeral notices. A well-known firm of funeral directors, Dierks & Co., was advertising a "bargain" $68 funeral. A little later, they canceled that offer in favor of a "rock-bottom" $125 funeral.

News-nose aquiver, I wondered why, and found the explanation quite satisfying. Nobody wanted the $68 job. In the proud, insular words of a member of the Dierks firm: "San Franciscans like to go out the way they live—first-class."

At the Palace Corner bar one night, I found an intent little group being sworn into a new organization by its founder, Helen Hess, a travel agency executive. Miss Hess, it seems, was trying to break herself of the smoking habit by forming a clan called "Nicoholics Anonymous."

"The idea is simple," she explained. "Every time you pull out a cigarette, a member talks you into taking a drink, instead."

It was in this same Palace Hotel that I first heard about Mrs. Roy Buell's amusing jewelry. Around the time of the 1906 firequake, Mrs. Buell's father, Charles Wellshouse, was the chief engineer at the Palace, and as such, he carried a tremendous bunch of keys, to open and close all the important doors in the hotel. Mrs. Buell, wife of the telephone company's division manager, had those historic keys gold-plated, and she wears them as a necklace.

"As it is now," she smiles, "they're just a conversation piece. But my, how I wish those keys could talk!"

Then there are the quotes to be overheard, the signs to be seen as a columnist wanders around the ever-changing streets of his city . . .

The Municipal Railway being constitutionally in the red, a conductor on a K Line car amused his passengers as the trolley entered

Twin Peaks Tunnel: "Hold on, folks—here's where the Muni runs into the black!"

Ellis Tietze, a Yellow Cab driver, was slightly shocked one recent day to notice that one of his fellow cabbies had a big hole in the leg of his pants. "How can you go around looking so sloppy?" demanded Tietze. "Get those pants patched right away." To which the other driver replied: "Are you kidding? That hole is worth two bucks a day in extra tips!"

Shortly after the Korean war started, I overheard two attractive thirty-year-old stenographers discussing the situation aboard a Powell Street cable. "I hate to think of going through all that again," sighed one. "Yeah," snapped the other. "I can just hear 'em: 'Aw, c'mon, honey, this is my LAST night—we ship out tomorrow!'"

I was privileged to be standing nearby one night while Jack Dempsey, the great ex-heavyweight champioon, was trying to make a commercial television short for White Star Tuna in a San Francisco photographic studio. Everything went reasonably well, except for one line that Dempsey had to read over and over before he got it right. He was supposed to say: "It's the all-time tuna champ." But somehow, it kept coming out of Dempsey's mouth like this: "It's the all-time Tunney champ!"

There is always an item to be picked up in Golden Gate Park, and this one always amused me: As long as "Uncle John" McLaren was Superintendent of the Park, there was never a "Keep off the Grass" sign to be seen. But now that he's dead, there's one. It's on the plot of grass in front of the statue of "Uncle John" McLaren.

Dimitri Romanoff, a real-estate salesman on Geary Boulevard, advertises himself rather coyly as "The Only Romanoff Who Is Not A Prince." Which reminds me, inevitably, that a real Romanoff, a relative of the late Czar's, lives in San Francisco. His name is Prince Vasili Romanoff, and, whereas he makes a comfortable living as a wine salesman, he spends a good deal of time brooding darkly about the fame and success of the impostor, "Prince" Mike Romanoff (nee Harry Gerguson) of Hollywood restaurant fame. "Someday," the Prince is fond of vowing, "I shall open a restaurant in San Francisco —and call it 'The Original Gerguson's!'"

Following the outbreak of the war in Korea, housewives in nearby Redwood City began to collect fats and greases again, just as they did during World War II. Which accounts for this otherwise mystifying sign that was posted in a Redwood City butcher shop: "Ladies, Don't Bring Your Fat Cans in on Friday."

Yes, it can be fun just to walk along the streets with your eyes open reasonably wide. On Jackson Street, near Stockton, is a tiny store that peddles yo-yos, piggy banks, toy soldiers, cap pistols, girlie magazines, and so on; name of the store: "The Culture Shop." Near Columbus Avenue and Grant, an ex-Chicagoan named Stanley Becker opened a hamburger shop called "Krumbly Shop No. 5," and the curious ones soon discovered that there was no point in asking him where to find the other four, because there weren't any. "Psychology," he explained. And then there was the thriving little spot I wandered into one day on Mission Street. It turned out to be a combination coffee shop, cigar stand, and bookmaking establishment. "Whaddya want?" asked the proprietor pleasantly enough, "a bite, a light or a bet?" I bit on a bet and left considerably lighter.

There are the people a columnist meets, some of them famous, some of them obscure, but all of them with small talk to spare, tales to tell, incidents to relate . . .

One afternoon, in front of Hotel St. Francis, I noticed a red-faced couple, so obviously outraged that I couldn't help becoming inquisitive. They turned out to be Mr. and Mrs. Hank Dutcher of nearby Stockton—and they had just learned about San Francisco traffic, the very hard way.

All they wanted to do was to drive out of Union Square Garage and pick up a friend in front of the Powell Street entrance of the St. Francis—right across the street. But do you think that's easy? Ha. Follow the bouncing ball and the Dutchers:

They drove out the Geary Street exit of the garage, went up to Mason, turned right to Post and drove down Post to Powell. There they found a "No Right Turn" sign.

So they continued on to Stockton, turned left to Sutter, and then drove back to Powell. There they found a "No Left Turn" sign.

With a mixture of sighs and curses, they drove on to Mason, up to Bush, turned right to Powell, and, at last, drove triumphantly down Powell to the front of the St. Francis.

Your calculations are correct, friend. To drive from Union Square Garage to the hotel directly across the street—twelve blocks!

A stranger named A. C. Ight stopped me on the street one day to tell me about a recently arrived Israeli, now a San Franciscan, who had heard so much about ham-on-rye sandwiches that he decided to try one for himself. So he walked into a Chinese-American restaurant on Fillmore Street, where, after considerable difficulty, he managed to convey the idea to the Irish waitress, who shouted to the Negro cook: "Put a grunt between two dirty sheets!"

I happened to be lounging at the corner of Fourth and Mission streets one afternoon when a cab stopped within earshot, and out stepped a W. C. Fieldsian character.

"That'll be four dollars," said the driver.

"Oh no it won't," sniffed the customer, turning his pockets inside out. "I'm broke, and y'know what they say—you can't get blood out of a turnip!"

The driver jumped out of his cab and grabbed the penniless one. "Listen, Mister," he snapped, "you ain't no turnip, and your blood is worth four dollars a pint." With which he hustled him into the nearby Blood Donor Center, stood by while a pint was extracted, and collected his four dollars.

Strolling along Post Street, I ran into Lucius Beebe, the noted bon vivant, chronicler of dead eras and latter-day pioneer who has forsaken Manhattan for the comparative wilds of Virginia City, Nevada.

Beebe was about to step into Shreve's, the exclusive jewelers at Post and Grant Avenue, and the reason for his trip was rewarding. He had just acquired a St. Bernard pup, by the name of Mr. T-Bone. And, looking forward to the day when the dog would be bounding about the Sierra Nevada to rescue snowbound travelers, Beebe had ordered two silver casks from Shreve's, for the St. Bernard to wear under its chin.

One cask would contain the traditional brandy, and the other would carry creme de menthe. "In case the survivors would rather have stingers," Beebe explained reasonably enough.

Trivia, tidbits, memorabilia, sheer nonsense—all these are grist for the columnist whose mill must grind each day, whether he has anything to say or not . . .

On an otherwise quiet day, when the typewriter silently watched the approach of the deadline, I picked up one of my favorite stories

about Louis Lurie, the somewhat fabulous San Francisco millionaire. On his last trip to Washington, D.C., he had lunch with the
then Secretary of the Navy, Francis Matthews, and the Irish Ambassador to the United States, John J. Hearne.

Although they had never met before, Ambassador Hearne was so
warmly cordial to Lurie that the latter was overwhelmed. In fact,
he was even a little mystified by Hearne's constant attention, until
the lunch was over and they were parting.

"Well," beamed the Irish Ambassador, wringing Lurie's hand, "it
has certainly been a pleasure, meeting an Irish millionaire after so
many of the other kind. Good-by, Mr. Lowrey!"

This is the kind of silly little item that tickles most San Franciscans: In case you haven't heard, the Ford cars assembled in Texas
plants carry stickers on the back window, reading in typical Texas
fashion: "Built in Texas by Texans." Well, when one of these cars
shows up for repairs in Cecil Whitebone's Ford Garage on Van
Ness Avenue, a slight change is made. Whitebone's mechanics slap
THIS sign on the back window: "Rebuilt in San Francisco by
Americans!"

But let us change the locale and the mood. In England recently,
a publishing house put out a series of paintings titled "The Twelve
Wonders of the World," and inasmuch as the twelfth was advertised
as "The Golden Gate Bridge," several true-blue San Franciscans sent
for it.

Mrs. Frank Melka, president of the Association of Pioneer Women
of California, received her copy in due time, and she was a bit
dumfounded, to say the least. What she got was a picture of the
Bay Bridge, captioned "The Golden Gate Bridge, Connecting San
Francisco to California."

Getting back to Hotel St. Francis for a final item of foolishness, we will first have to explain that the hotel's general manager, Dan London, prides himself on an extensive collection of flags, which he flies whenever a distinguished visitor is in the hotel. For instance, when a three-star General is on hand, London flies a three-star flag from the Powell Street staff, and he has appropriate banners for everybody from a Cabinet member to a Minister Without Portfolio from South Rhodesia.

All this has added up to much publicity for the St. Francis, and only one untoward incident. Near the end of World War II, General of the Armies George C. Marshall stopped at the hotel, and London immediately ordered the five-starred flag flown.

The red-banner, with its five stars arranged in a circle, hadn't been up more than ten minutes when an irate lady stormed into London's office.

"You'd think," she ranted, "that a big hotel like this would have more than five men in the service!"

Mr. San Francisco   He'll park his car anywhere, drive where he knows he shouldn't, argue at intersections with everything but busses and trucks, curse at cabbies while driving like one, and agree fervently that traffic would be improved if fewer people drove their cars downtown—but darned if he'll be the first to give up the luxury . . . He knows all the short cuts to anything anywhere, and on rainy days he can walk from one block to another through adjoining buildings—but he still isn't sure which street leads directly to the Bay Bridge and complains loudly that "there oughta be more signs" . . . He professes great love for the fog—"so cool, so clean, so invigorating, mmmm"—but when he's shopping for a house, his first question is likely to be: "Say, this isn't in the fog belt, is it?" . . . More people should take an interest in politics, he'll tell you at the corner bar, but he can't name eleven members of the Board of Supervisors; or is it twelve? And of COURSE McSheehy, Uhl and Shannon are still on the Board—ya crazy or wot?

If he's a native San Franciscan he'll tell you the first time you meet him; if he isn't, he'll say that he was "practically" born here—because a real "Mr. San Francisco" never feels like a newcomer, even when he is . . . Although he hasn't been inside the place for years, he is secretly pleased that George Whitney rescued Sutro Baths from oblivion—for he hates to witness the death of a landmark; it reminds him too sharply that the city is changing, and change appalls him . . . And he'd never think of boarding a cable car while it's standing still; it's more typical to be the jerk that it starts with.

It's impossible to convince him, at this point, that Trader Vic is really from Oakland; the Trader is now "a San Francisco institution, with a branch across the Bay" . . . He is not as impressed with San Francisco's obviously best-dressed women—who can afford it—as he is with the Montgomery Street stenos and Post Street shopgirls who always look trim, neat, and attractive—even if they can't afford it . . . If you look into his wallet, you'll probably find the phone number of a bookie and the address of a jernt that sells liquor after 2 A.M.; not that he uses them very often, if at all—it merely gives him a feeling of being "in the know" in a city that isn't quite as wicked as he likes to think . . . He looks with slight suspicion on all commuters, scoffs when they say they get home in twenty minutes, snorts when they insist the sun is shining while the city is graybound, and is sure he'd get the bends if he ever moved outside the city limits.

He believes his own "aw, that's only a high fog" propaganda so implicitly that he seldom carries his raincoat on an overcast day— and couldn't be more surprised when he gets soaked . . . An especially warm, mellow mood sweeps over him when he lunches in the Palace Court—for he's certain that in the Good Old Days he's forever talking about, everybody lunched at the Palace every day, and probably with Emperor Norton and Senator Sharon . . . Although he likes our institutions pretty much left alone, he wouldn't mind one good hamburger stand or beer parlor in Golden Gate Park—and he's not altogether sure that an open-air restaurant in Union Square is such a bad idea.

He's no longer neurotic about the immensity of Los Angeles or the mushrooming growth of the East Bay; now, instead of fibbing slightly about San Francisco's population, he merely sighs openly that he wishes the city were smaller—more like its old, sane prewar self . . . He's a little surprised to see that Harry Bridges is getting older, that Bill Saroyan is losing his hair, that Jake Ehrlich is completely gray, and that Mayor Elmer Robinson doesn't get his pictures in the papers as often as he used to; and it'll take him awhile to get used to the new sign on the Flood Building, the handsome new marquee at the Fairmont, the new lobby in the old St. Francis and the new soda fountain in the Drake—for to Mr. San Francisco, his city stands still in perfect, unchanging splendor.

"When are they gonna get around to building that Broadway Tunnel?" he has demanded petulantly for years—and now that it's completed, he gets off cracks like "Aaah, it doesn't make much difference" . . . He has learned to exhale exclusively while walking behind a motor bus, inhale exclusively while strolling past a sidewalk flower stand, close his eyes to the ugly facts while driving through Skid Road, and plug his ears to the foghorn's distant warning while the sun is still shining through his windows.

He shrugs off Chinatown as "strictly for tourists," but is as eager as the next beaver when it comes to showing off the section to visitors: "Biggest Chinatown in the world, full of lotteries and gamblers and opium peddlers, be careful, follow me, I know my way around" . . . His sentimental heart is touched when he looks at the sagging mansions of the Western Addition, dying out their lives as boardinghouses—for he can still see them for what they were; the homes of the mighty, in the days when his city was young and brave . . . That, I suppose, is why he'd rather live in an overpriced house that "looks like San Francisco" than be comfortable in a new home that's like all the others on the block—and within his income.

He might change, himself, as the years roll along . . . But he'll never lose his feeling of pride when he views his city from a hilltop, never cease to be awed when he drives across the bridges, never stop missing the light-speckled sight of the ferries on the Bay, never feel anything but slight panic when crossing Market, never break the habit of cracking halfhearted jokes about Oakland, never stop correcting automatically: "Don't call it Frisco!"—and never stop congratulating himself on being "Mr. San Francisco," the man who knows what he wants in a city, and has found it all in Baghdad-by-the-Bay.

Index

Abbaticchio, Ray, 220
Abbott, Nancy Ann, 211, 221
Acapulco, 163–67
Aiken, Robert, 224
Alcatraz, 45, 50, 73, 85, 125, 155, 247
Allen, Larry, 220–21
Alper, Harrison, 97
Amelio's, 138
Amos, Minnie, 172–73
Amsterdam, Morey, 91
Anzavista, 49, 244
Arabian, George, 186
Armstrong, Tiny, 136, 192, 215, 233–35
Arthur, Chester A., 113–15
Atherton, Gertrude, 255

Baldwin Hotel, 193
Bal Tabarin, 40, 204
Bankhead, Tallulah, 146–47, 149
Barbary Coast, 11, 17, 147, 194, 195, 252, 257
Barrel House, the, 182
Barrett, Tony, 87–88
Bay Bridge, 16, 77, 78, 81, 84, 141, 184, 228, 273, 275

Bay Meadows, 69, 222
Bay Street, 40, 133
Beachcomber, Don, 169–71
Becker, Stanley, 270
Beebe, Lucius, 219, 272
Bennett, Richard, 237
Berger's, 258
Berk, Clarence and Edwin, 216–17
Berkeley, 38, 218
Bernstein, Joe, 65–72
Bernstein's, 54, 55, 186
Bette Lane Shop, 224
Bidwell, Harrison "Bid," 95
Black Cat Saloon, 258
Blake, Anson, 216
Blanding, Don, 171
Blue, Ira, 96
Blue Fox, the, 138
Blum's, 40, 62
Bohemian Club, 90
Bonnot, Paul, 245
Brady, Matt, 134
Bridges, Harry, 12, 38, 83, 209, 277
Brindley, Isabel, 95
Broadway, 74, 83, 141, 211, 216, 230, 258, 277

Brown, David, 76
Buddhist Mission, 82
Buell, Mrs. Roy, 268
Buell, Ross, 28
Buell, Roy, 28
Bundsen, Jerry, 208, 214, 222, 226
Bunny's, 186
Burke, "Palm Sunday," 112
Burlingame Club, 220
Burrows, Abe, 147–48
Bushkin, Joe, 147
Bush Street, 58, 63, 78, 187, 191, 255, 257, 271
Busse, Henry "Hot Lips," 204
Butchertown, 258
Byron, June, 201–2

Caen, Lucien, 102–5
California Street, 22, 47, 62, 136, 188, 191, 226, 228, 229, 255
Camille's, 84
Camp, "Turn Around Dan," 132
Canary Den, 39
Capital Theatre, 190
Casino, the, 132
Castle, Vernon and Irene, 257
Castro Street, 128, 189, 259
Central Avenue, 183, 192
Channing, Carol, 148
Chapeau Rouge, 132
Chase, John Paul, 124–25
Chatard, Russell, 79
Chew, Ah, 263–66
China Beach, 82
"China Mary," 257
Chinatown, 16, 19, 22, 62, 73, 75, 78, 83, 137, 153, 194, 195, 231, 256, 257, 263–66, 277
Chutes, the, 132, 134
City Hall, 11, 230, 242
City of Paris, 40, 91, 230
Civic Center, 118, 211
Clancy, Gene, 109

Clark, Dick, 83
Clark, Ida, 224
Clay Street, 192, 256, 258
Cleary, Elizabeth and Patrick, 53–54
Clegg, Charles, 219
Cliff House, 45, 50, 60, 134, 141, 205, 245
Clift Hotel, 92, 131
Clish, Herbert, 220
Cobb, Ty, 134, 220
Coffee Dan's, 192
Cohen, Abraham, 256
Coit Tower, 50, 71, 77, 137, 206
Columbia Square, 190
Columbus Avenue, 84, 99, 128, 139, 189, 229, 270
Commercial Street, 82, 257
Conrad, Barnaby, 216
Corbett, "Gentleman Jim," 256
Cort Theatre, 193
Coward, Noel, 29
Crawford, Bill, 217
Crocker Building, 84
Crosby, Bing, 190
Crosby, Bob, 40
Crosetti Bros., 87
Cross, Dr. Laurance, 218
Cuernavaca, Mexico, 158
Cullinan, Judge Eustace, 56, 109
Cunningham, Arthur, 132
Cunningham, Judge Leo, 110
Curran Theater, 87, 138

Dailey, Gardner, 211, 216
Dawson, H. Ward, Jr., 219
De Jesus, James and Providencia, 53
Dempsey, Jack, 269
Denver House, 107
Dewey Monument, 18, 49, 119, 211, 224
de Young Museum, 243

Diehl, Mrs. Ambrose, 215
Dierks & Co., 268
Dillinger, John, 88, 125
Dito, Marvin, 216
Divisadero Street, 133, 259–60
Doelger, Henry, 79, 210
Donahue, Peter, 61
Dooley, Mrs. Matt, 47
Drake Hotel, 40, 277
Dreiser, Theodore, 255
Dunne, Father William, 220
Dutcher, Mr. and Mrs. Hank, 271

East Bay, 13, 49, 76, 137, 277
Eddy Street, 115, 202, 234, 243
Ehrlich, J. W. "Jake," 39, 68, 209, 216, 219, 277
Eker, Captain Jack, 210
Elks Club, 118
Ellison, Bert, 132, 258
Ellis Street, 100, 115, 116, 134, 243
El Prado, 46, 136, 221
Embarcadero, the, 39, 63, 73, 82, 83, 136, 141
Emporium, the, 225
Ernie's, 222
Examiner, The, 25, 78, 95

Fagan, Paul, 210
Fairmont Hotel, 40, 124, 138, 188, 211, 213, 221, 277
Falk, Dave, 49–50, 116, 216, 237, 258
Falk, Marge, 49–50, 216
Family Club, 187
Fashion Stables, 134
Felton, F. L., 211
Ferd's News Stand, 78
Ferguson, Barney, 233, 235–40
Ferry Building, 39, 63, 73, 77, 82, 133, 137, 211, 242
Filbert Street, 132, 211

Fillmore District, 21, 231
Fillmore Street, 48, 63, 271
Finn, Michael, 252
Fisherman's Wharf, 16, 20, 77–78, 141, 181, 188, 223, 254
Fitzhugh Building, 231
Fitzpatrick, Eddie, 204
Fitzsimmons, Ruby Bob, 256
Fleishhacker, Herbert, 92–93, 225
Flood, James, 212
Flood, Mrs. James, 214, 225
Flood Building, 277
Fly Trap, the, 118
Fong, Esther, 96–97
Forbidden City, the, 138, 222
Ford, Bennie, 186
"Forty Strong, The," 63
Fourth Street, 111, 113, 114, 271
Friedman, Leo, 214
Friend, Ted, 218

Gaffey, Police Chief Michael, 220, 260
Gan, Charlie Ting, 256
Garcia, Luz, 216
Gardner, Ed "Archie," 147
Gardner, Otho, 87
Gargan, Bill, 148
Geary Street, 17, 38, 95, 131, 134, 186, 192, 195, 214, 230, 235, 271
Geary Theater, 138, 239
Geiger, Dr. J. C., 49, 210, 217
Geisendorfer, Mason, 217
Genthe, Arnold, 62
Gerum, Tom, 40, 204
Giannini, A. P., 61, 236
Gibney, Luke, 258
Gillespie, Bert, 221
Giroux, Lee, 222
Giuntoli, Bimbo, 40, 204
Glinsky, Walter, 221
Glissman, Rex, 256

Glover, John, 225
Golden Fan, the, 256
Golden Gate Bridge, 16, 46, 49, 75, 79, 82, 84, 120, 141, 184, 228, 273
Golden Gate Fields racetrack, 119
Golden Gate Park, 16, 35, 38, 45, 47, 56, 64, 74, 75, 104, 118, 120, 133, 136, 141, 143, 206, 225, 232, 243, 247, 269, 277
Golden Pheasant, the, 235
Goodell, Judge Julian, 90–91
Gordon, George, 61
Gotti, Vic, 222
Gough Street, 35, 36, 202
Graffe, Louis, 116–17
Graham, Bill, 221
Graney, Eddie, 255
Grant Avenue, 16, 83, 156, 217, 229, 256, 270, 272
Grauman, Sid, 182
Gray, N., 183
Greenwich Street, 211, 265, 266
Groody, Tom, 221
Gruenhagen's, 192
Gump, Richard, 217
Gump, Robert, 97–98
Gump's, 223
Gwin, Senator, 61

Hale Bros., 87
Hallinan, Vincent, 218
Hall of Justice, 202
Harris, Tommy, 182
Harte, Bret, 62
Hawaii, 167–71
Hearne, John J., 273
Heath, Tommy, 220
Heilmann, Harry, 134
Held, Anna, 193
Hellman, I. W., 215
"Hemstitch Nettie," 110
Herbert's, 104, 192

Herrscher, Edmond, 221
Hess, Helen, 268
Hildegarde, 122
Hillsborough, 211
Hilton, Conrad, 148
Hislop, Mrs. William, 93
Hobson, Greg, 54–55
Hof Brau Restaurant, 127, 191
Hoffman, Joe, 62
Hornsby, Rogers, 134
Howard Street, 47, 108, 109, 111, 165, 202, 212
Howe, Thomas Carr, 218
Hugh, Earl, 189
Humphrey, Bill, 210
Huntington, Mrs. C. P., 225
Huntington Park, 225
Hyde Street, 82, 131, 132, 136, 188, 191, 226, 258

Ibanez, Blasco, 255
Ight, A. C., 271
Imperato, Mimi, 255
India House, 76
Ingleside District, 136
Insurance Securities, Inc., 225
International Settlement, 77
Irwin, Will, 76
Italian Market, 83

Jack's Restaurant, 236
Jackson Street, 17, 188, 222, 227, 270
James, Bill, 132
Jamison, Glen, 210
Japanese Tea Garden, 128, 206
Jefferson Hotel, 234
Jefferson Park, 202
John's Grill, 88, 100
Johnson, Anna, 177–79
Johnson, Dr. Chester W., 221
Johnson, Stella K., 217

Jolson, Al, 122, 181–84
Jose, "Champagne Dick," 219

Kaiser, Henry, 209
Karesh, Joe, 92
Kasper's, 223
Kearny Street, 19, 39, 76, 109, 228, 255, 257
Kent, Skipper, 93
Kezar Stadium, 16
KFRC, Radio Station, 40
Killion, George, 222
King, Horace Brooks "Hitch," 117–18
King, Will, 132
Kingman, Dong, 96–97, 258
Kip, Bishop, 61
Klussmann, Frieda (Mrs. Hans), 189, 218, 226
KLX, Radio Station, 48
Koenigsberg, Alvin, 116
Korean Church, 228
Korper, "Jelly," 115–16
Koss, Paul, 79
"Krumbly Shop No. 5," 270
Kyne, Bill, 222

La Buvette, 84
Lacbay, "Original Andy," 216
La Favorite, 84
Lafayette Square, 229
Laguna Honda Home, 229
Lake, Frank, 116
Lake Merced, 137
Langenberger, Amadeus G., 56
Lapham, Roger, Jr., 213
Lark, the, 258
Larry's, 68
La Rue, Frank, 190
Lawrence, Gertrude, 29
Leavenworth Street, 117, 131, 136
Legion of Honor Museum, 211, 218

Lenoir, Henri, 225
Levi Strauss Building, 212
Lewis, Oscar, 215
Lewis, Ted, 192
Lieber, Myra, 224
Light, Garfield, 87
Lincoln Park, 16
Lincoln School, 224
Little Italy, 18, 83
Lombard Street, 56, 131, 136, 211
London, Dan, 274
London, Jack, 184
"Lonesome Swede, The," 110
Long, Baron, 186
Low, Charlie, 40, 222
Lowell High, 41
Lurie, Louis, 42–44, 215, 236–39, 273
Lurline Baths, 40

McAteer, Gene, 219
McAuliffe, Frank, 119, 224
McBride, Harry, 190
McCabe, Jimmy, 144
McDonough, Pete, 134
MacDuckston, "Scotty," 87
McEnerney, Garret II, 219–20
McInnis, Jim, 92
McLaren, John, 47, 144, 269
McLean, Dan, 79
Macloon, Louis, 42–44
McNab, Ethan, 89–90
Mac's Irish Grill, 84
Macy's, 91
Maddux, Parker, 215, 237, 239
Maiden Lane, 18, 132
Marin County, 13, 15, 55, 192
Marina, the, 48, 75, 150, 228, 229
Market Street, 15, 22, 39, 41, 57, 73, 78, 81, 82, 84, 87, 88, 106, 113, 114, 126, 128, 131, 133, 134, 141, 143, 189, 191, 192,

193, 201, 203, 204, 242, 257, 258, 261–62, 278
Mark Hopkins Hotel, 40, 96, 132, 138, 215
Marquard's, 131
Marshall, General George C., 274
Martin, Sir Humphrey, 172
Martinelli, Frank, 40, 204
Maskey's, 192
Mason Street, 27, 131, 134, 188, 189
Matthews, Francis, 273
Maxwell, Elsa, 29
"Maybe Hey Bernice," 110
Mein, Gardner, Jr., 216
Melka, Mrs. Frank, 273
Mencken, H. L., 255
Menuhin, Yehudi, 120
Merello, Joe, 40
Merry-Go-Round, the, 131
Metcalf, Larry, 215
Mexico City, 156–63
Miller, Edward "Bozo," 90
Miller, Joaquin, 134
Miller, Robert Watt, 214
Mint, U. S., 223, 257
Mission, the, 15, 21, 28, 53, 111, 114, 126, 128, 129, 134, 136, 138, 189, 231, 242, 244
Mission Street, 77, 78, 172, 173, 177, 182, 270, 271
Moar's, 186
Moderne, the, 40
Moffett, Mrs. Jackson, 217
Mohler, "Kid," 255
Monteux, Pierre, 120–25
Montgomery Street, 17, 20, 43, 49, 59, 60, 77, 80, 84, 89, 137, 143, 211, 215, 228, 236, 238, 241, 276
Moore, Colleen, 79
Moore's, 54
Morgan, Helen, 67

Morgan, Jane, 148
Moriarity, Red, 109–10
Morosco's Grand Opera House, 257
Morrisey, Will, 190
Mount Davidson, 79–80, 136
Mulford, Prentice, 63
Mullins, Vincent J., 252, 254
Mulloy, "Coattails," 117
Murfee, Emerson, 214
Murphy, Father Charles, 74
Murphy, Judge Edward P., 91
Murphy, Spud, 107
Music Box, the, 40, 204

"Nannygoat Hill," 133
Nathan, Carol, 239
National Theater, 182
Nelson, "Baby Face," 124
Newman's, 103
New Joe's, 83
New York City, 142–56
Niesen, Gertrude, 67
Nob Hill, 19, 77, 78, 121, 188, 190, 212, 214, 225, 229
Nolan, Shipwreck Van, 217–18
Noriega, Pedro, 74
Norman, Arvid, 79
Norman, Winston, 89
Normandie, the, 84
Norris, Frank, 62
Norris, Kathleen, 215
North, Henry, 220
North Beach, 16, 19, 22, 41, 45, 48, 58, 59, 63, 68, 74, 83, 84, 115, 118, 181, 188, 202, 229, 231, 256

Oakland, 13, 16, 90, 93, 94, 141, 211, 217, 223, 225, 276, 278
Ocean Beach, 16, 21, 35, 127, 260
O'Doul, Lefty, 186, 215, 258
O'Farrell Street, 131, 182, 204

O'Gara, Senator Gerald, 222
O'Kane, Father Thomas, 53–54
Oliva, Gus, 100, 101, 118–19
Olsen, George, 79
Olstad, Captain Ralph, 217
Olympic Club, 210
Omar Khayyam's, 186
Opera House, 17, 22, 123, 138, 151, 212
Orange Blossom, the, 192
Oriental Tea Garden, 128
Orpheum, 104, 192
Orr, Jimmy, 79
Our Lady of Guadelupe Church, 74

Pacific Avenue, 76, 83, 133
Pacific Heights, 21, 50, 189, 228, 230, 244, 264
Pacific National Bank Building, 211
Pacific-Union Club, 22, 78, 209, 212–14
Palace Hotel, 18, 39, 96, 104, 138, 190, 192, 204, 210, 221, 231, 268, 276
Papagayo, the, 138, 218
Parente, Joe, 256
Paris Louvre, the, 84
Pearl Harbor, 204–7
Pebble Beach, 217
Peninsula, the, 13, 30, 81, 97, 211, 215, 219
Pine Lake, 136
Pine Street, 136, 147, 187, 211, 212
Plaza Florists, 78
Politzer, James, 80
Polk, Willis, 212
Polk Street, 62, 255
Poodle Dog, the, 103, 190, 191
Portsmouth Square, 62, 202
Post Street, 16, 41, 46, 50, 51, 84, 134, 136, 138, 141, 143, 156, 182, 206, 224, 231, 241, 255, 271, 272, 276
Powell Street, 17, 50, 65–67, 71–73, 76, 84, 132, 136, 139, 182, 185, 186, 192, 207, 226–28, 233, 235, 241, 247, 269, 271, 274
Presidio Cemetery, 126, 129
Presidio Heights, 126, 128, 129, 228, 244
Presidio Theater, 239
"Princess Margaret," 191
Produce District, 82
Pup, the, 256
Purdy, Doris, 92
Purvis, Melvin, 88–89

Radich, Lydia, 174–76
Raggett, Jimmy, 258
Rand, Sally, 40
Redewill, Dr. F. H., 219
Reliable Pawnshop, 223–24
Remmer, Elmer "Bones," 210
Richardson, Nellie, 107
Richmond District, 126, 128, 129, 133, 138, 231
Rickey, Tom, 92
Rieder, Edmond, 210, 221
Riley, Harvey, 218
Rincon Hill, 61
Rishell, Mayor Clifford, 211
Robertson, Mrs. Cameron, 226–27
Robinson, Mayor Elmer E., 13, 209, 217, 277
Robinson, Mrs. Elmer, 215
Robinson, Noilden, 175–76
Rolph, Jimmy, 63, 131
Romanoff, Dimitri, 269
Romanoff, Prince Vasili, 270
Rome, Mrs. Harold, 226
Rooney, Tom, 218
Roos Bros., 117
Roosevelt, Franklin D., 80
Royal Camel, the, 132

Ruef, Abe, 61
Russ Building, 132
Russian Hill, 19, 22, 35, 131, 141, 230, 265
Ryberg, Harry, 258

Sacramento Street, 192, 227, 230, 257
Sacred Heart Convent, 214
St. Anthony's Kitchen, 214
St. Francis Hotel, 18, 76, 92, 100, 138, 183, 187, 191, 230, 235, 241, 271, 274, 277
St. Francis of Assisi, 11
St. Francis Wood, 18, 126, 128, 129, 221, 244
Saints and Sinners, 235
Saints Peter and Paul, 85, 231
St. Vincent de Paul, 53
Samish, Artie, 210
Sampsell, Lloyd, 89
Samson, Rudy, 55
"Sandwich Couple, The," 111
San Francisco Symphony Orchestra, 120
Sanguinetti's, 132
Saroyan, William, 38, 88, 140, 216, 277
Schonfeld, Judge George, 219
Sea Cliff, 221, 244
Seal Rocks, 45, 60, 245
Seals, the, 132, 141, 220, 255
Sears, 187
Sentinel Building, 61
Shadows, the, 76
"Shammy Kid, The," 110–11
Sharkey, Tom, 107
Shearer, Moira, 114
Sheehan's, 258
Shelley, Dan, 217
Shimmon, George, 97
Shor, Toots, 156
Shreve's, 119, 225, 272

Sinaloa, 138, 216
Sisler, George, 134
Skaff, George, 55
Skelton, Red, 261
Skid Road, 45, 106–12, 231, 277
Sloane, Tod, 193
Smith, George D., 215
Snook, Judge Charles, 55
Sodini, Al and Rose, 53
Solari, Fred, 39
Southern Pacific Depot, 116
South Park, 61, 77
Southwell, Billy, 90
Sox, Dr. Ellis, 221–22
Spreckels Lake, 16
Stackpole, Ralph, 76
Stanford, Sally, 98, 147
States Hof Brau Restaurant 127, 191
Steinhart Aquarium, 243
Steinhoff, Adolph, 204
Sterling, George, 133, 255
Stevenson, Robert Louis, 62
Stock Exchange, 76
Stockton Street, 16, 27, 76, 91, 264, 266, 270
Stockton Tunnel, 18, 81
Stoddard, Charles Warren, 62
Stonestown, 18
"Studio 7," 255
Sullivan, Jerd, 219–20
Sullivan, John J., 217
Sullivan, John L., 63
Sunset, the, 60, 131, 231
Surf, the, 258
Sutro, Mayor Adolph, 60
Sutro Baths, 276
Sutro Forest, 49
Sutter Street, 40, 78, 95, 221, 271
Swastika Club, 132
Sweeney, Dan, 181
Swenson, Earl, 227
Swig, Benjamin Harrison, 209, 221

Talmadge, Norma, 53
Tarantino's, 181, 219
Taylor, C. W., Jr., 57
Taylor Street, 20, 95, 134, 189, 231
Techau's, 103, 191, 257
Telegraph Hill, 17, 20, 21, 56, 73, 76, 77, 84, 89, 133, 141, 148, 258
Tetrazzini, Luisa, 184, 191
Third Street, 17, 19, 47, 61, 75, 77, 81, 89, 108, 111, 116, 196, 202, 219, 223
Thompson, Dorothy, 114
Thompson, Titanic, 68
365 Club, 87, 138, 204
Tibbett, Mrs. Lawrence, 30
Tico, Mrs. Mabel, 183
Tietze, Ellis, 269
Tiny Holmes's, 191
Top o' the Mark, 76, 135, 188, 206, 209
Torregano, Ernest J., 222
"Tough Tessie," 107-8
Town Club, 132
Townsend Street, 75, 116, 219
Trader Vic's, 124, 146, 158, 276
Turk Street, 71, 115, 243, 248, 249, 251
Twain, Mark, 46, 63, 171
Twin Peaks, 15, 49, 53, 135, 141, 229, 268

Union Square, 40, 46, 49, 84, 119, 137, 211, 224, 231, 241, 271, 277
University of California, 187, 211
University of San Francisco, 220

Vallejo Street, 188, 218
Vanessi's, 204
Van Ness Avenue, 48, 111, 219, 230, 273
Varda, Jean, 114

Veltri's, 138
"Velvet Fingers" Joe, 111
Vesuvio, the, 225
Veterans Building, 212
Vic's, 138
Vincent, Romo, 204

Waldorf, the, 192
Walpole, Hugh, 62, 255
Walsh, Harry, 186
Walton, Sydney, 212
Warren, Governor Earl, 220
Washington Square, 243
Washington Street, 82, 229
Weeks, Anson, 40, 132
Wells-Fargo Bank, 84
Wellshouse, Charles, 268
Wente, Carl, 209
Westenberg, Mr. and Mrs. J. C., 257
Western Addition, 277
White, Isaac, 257
White, Jerome, 221
Whitebone, Cecil, 219, 273
Whitney, George, 276
Wickman, Sally, 55
Wilke, Carl, 238
Williams, Al, 218
Williams, Tom, 133
Wilson, Eileen, 148
Winchell, Walter, 26
Wolverton, Harry, 258
Wong, Zeppelin Wai, 115
Woodward's What Cheer House, 63

Yacht Harbor, 75
Young, Frank, 146
Young, Howard, 48
Youth Guidance Center, 229

Zeitska Academy for Young Females, 61
Zombie Village, the, 93